DOWN MEMORY LANE

Peter Ellinger's Memoirs

DOWN MEMORY LANE

Peter Ellinger's Memoirs

by

Peter Ellinger

World Scientific

NEW JERSEY • LONDON • SINGAPORE • BEIJING • SHANGHAI • HONG KONG • TAIPEI • CHENNAI • TOKYO

Published by

World Scientific Publishing Co. Pte. Ltd.
5 Toh Tuck Link, Singapore 596224
USA office: 27 Warren Street, Suite 401-402, Hackensack, NJ 07601
UK office: 57 Shelton Street, Covent Garden, London WC2H 9HE

National Library Board, Singapore Cataloguing in Publication Data
Name(s): Ellinger, E. P. (Eliahu Peter), 1933–
Title: Down memory lane : Peter Ellinger's memoirs / by Peter Ellinger.
Description: Singapore : World Scientific Publishing Co. Pte. Ltd., [2023]
Identifier(s): ISBN 978-981-12-7102-1 (hardcover) | 978-981-12-7203-5 (paperback) |
978-981-12-7103-8 (ebook for institutions) | 978-981-12-7104-5 (ebook for individuals)
Subject(s): LCSH: Ellinger, E. P. (Eliahu Peter), 1933– | Law teachers--Singapore--Biography.
Classification: DDC 340.092--dc23

British Library Cataloguing-in-Publication Data
A catalogue record for this book is available from the British Library.

For any available supplementary material, please visit
https://www.worldscientific.com/worldscibooks/10.1142/13271#t=suppl

Desk Editor: Lai Ann

Typeset by Stallion Press
Email: enquiries@stallionpress.com

Man is born to trouble
as the sparks fly upward.
Job: 5:7

TO C.A.Z.
With sincere thanks.

About the Author

Peter Ellinger graduated from the Hebrew University, Israel with an MJur in 1959 and was called to the Israeli Bar. Following practice in Tel Aviv, he went to Oxford University, UK, obtaining his DPhil in 1964. He started his academic career at the University of Singapore (1961–1966). In 1963, he married Patricia Goh Peh Choo. He subsequently held Chairs of Law at the Victoria University of Wellington, New Zealand (1967–1976) and at Monash University, Australia (1977–1986). In 1986, he accepted the post of Professor of Law at the National University of Singapore. After his retirement from this position, he was appointed as a consultant at Rajah & Tann Singapore LLP and obtained a practice certificate. He also continued to teach as a Professorial Fellow at the National University of Singapore.

On 14 September 1998, Professor Ellinger was constituted an Emeritus Professor. During his academic career, he has published books, chapters in leading commercial law texts and numerous articles in regional law reviews as well as in the United Kingdom, Australasia, Canada, the United States and in Europe. *Modern Banking Law* (published by Oxford University Press) is a standard text on banking law and went into five editions.

Professor Ellinger has specialised in commercial law with particular emphasis on banking law. Over the years, he has acquired an experience in opinion work and drafting of documents. He has also appeared as an expert witness in local and foreign courts. In 2008, Professor Ellinger retired from his position as a consultant of Rajah and Tann but continued to teach as a Professorial Fellow at the University. His wife passed away in 2011 after a lengthy battle with cancer. He retired from teaching in July 2013 and has remained in Singapore since.

About the Cover Illustrator

Marcus Lim is Asia's first and only historian painter, devoted to preserving various aspects of Singapore history through his paintings. Whether it is a portrait or a painting, every artwork he creates is a story behind the legacy worth preserving for posterity. One such story is the portrait painting of Venerable Ho Yuen Hoe, founder of Man Fut Tong Nursing Home, and unveiled under the grace of President S R Nathan in 2007.

Among many other accolades, Marcus' life and work was made into a full-feature TV documentary titled "City Footprints" (城市生命线) in 2008. His painting of a samsui woman, titled "One Bowl of Water", made the cover of the *Asian Geographic* magazine, with the cover subsequently named as 'Cover Art of the Decade' in 2009. In the years that followed, Marcus' work continued to be of interest, receiving interviews from various radio and TV media.

He also became the first Singaporean artist to represent his country at the International Portrait Artists' Conference in Washington DC, and was also named the Heritage Ambassador of the Asian Geographic Society, both in 2010. The Society is the non-profit organization society of the *Asian Geographic* Magazine.

In May 2013, Marcus Lim became the first appointed court artist for the controversial "Shane Todd Coroner's Inquiry" judicial proceedings. In October the same year, his series of court paintings was featured in CBS News' documentary titled "48 Hours: Spies, Lies and Secrets".

In 2020, Marcus was commissioned by the Singapore Puxian (Hinghwa) Network (新加坡莆仙同乡联合会) to create a 1.5m-long triptych painting, honoring the contributions of HingHwa people in Singapore. This artwork was published in the book titled *Notable Hinghwa People in Singapore: Connecting Hinghwa People* (《南洋莆仙人物志 新加坡卷 心系兴化人》) the following year.

Contents

Foreword

I thank my good and old friend, Professor Peter Ellinger, for giving me the privilege of writing the foreword of his absorbing memoirs. I have known him since 1961, when he first arrived in Singapore.

Peter was born in Vienna, Austria, to Jewish parents. As the threat of Nazi Germany looked imminent, the Ellinger family managed to escape and sought refuge in Palestine. Palestine was then ruled by the British under a mandate from the League of Nations.

Peter saw the birth of the new nation, Israel, a homeland for the Jews. He grew up in Tel Aviv and studied law at the Hebrew University of Jerusalem.

At the suggestion of a friend, he went to Oxford to study for the doctorate degree. Oxford changed him, intellectually and in other ways. He became proficient in English, his third language.

With the blessings of his parents, he decided to embark on a career as a law teacher. His first job was in Singapore. He arrived in 1961 and left in 1966 for a professorship at the University of Wellington, New Zealand. From Wellington, he went to teach at the Monash University, in Melbourne, Australia.

Peter eventually returned to Singapore, where he began his journey as a legal scholar. Peter was married to a lovely Singaporean, Patricia, who has passed away. I was his Best Man at the wedding. They have no children. Patricia was Chinese educated. Because of the cultural gap between Peter and Patricia, the marriage was not successful.

Peter Ellinger is one of world's leading authorities on banking law and the law of letters of credit. He is a great asset to the NUS Law School and to Singapore.

I recently asked Peter whether he saw himself as an Austrian, an Israeli or a Singaporean. He replied that he is a Singaporean. We are happy to welcome him to the Singapore family. Peter will be 90 years old on the 25th of April 2023. I wish him happy birthday in advance and many more years of good health and happiness.

Prof Tommy Koh
Ambassador-At-Large
Ministry of Foreign Affairs, Singapore

Preface

A private edition of this book was self published in 2018 and circulated to a few close friends. At that time, I assumed that I had arrived in Ithaca. Three major developments induced me to come up with a new, revised version. First and foremost was my realisation that the era best described as *Pax Americana* was drawing to its end. I should have sensed this when President Trump was elected in 2016. His isolationist agenda indicated that the accepted world order was in jeopardy. The bitter 2020 American election and the ensuing debacle removed any doubts that might have been induced by wishful thinking. Secondly, the Covid-19 pandemic led to mayhem in both the East and the West. Even here, in Singapore, we have experienced lockdowns and other restrictions. Thirdly, the electronic revolution and online trade have gained momentum. Ordinary shopping and the use of hard copies in business transactions continue to decline. Far from enjoying peace and quiet, the world has been experiencing shock waves. Currently, in 2022, we are facing further commotion and an uncertain future.

It took me years to find the resolve to write my memoirs. Before embarking on the original exercise in 2008, I was inclined to write an autobiography and actually made some headway. However, when I showed the completed parts to my God-Daughter, she observed that an individual's odyssey was usually of interest only to his closest friends. In contrast, his memoirs might be of interest to a wider circle of readers, provided he has highlighted events of common interest. I accepted her advice. The reason was simple: my odyssey has stretched over many years and many political upheavals of the 20th and the early 21st centuries. I survived the Holocaust, found refuge in Palestine (when it was still a British Mandate), saw the foundation of the State of Israel, practised law in Tel Aviv, went for further studies at Oxford and taught law in Singapore, in New Zealand and in Australia.

I opted for retirement in Singapore. Notably, when I had first arrived in the City of the Lion in 1961, it was still a Crown Colony. I witnessed its becoming part of Malaysia and how it metamorphosed into a sovereign state.

To ensure that my memoirs convey an accurate — and hence objective — picture, it is essential that I narrate the events as they transpired. A knowledgeable reader is bound to sense whether the story is objective or marred by fantasies and myths. Putting it plainly, in memoirs — unlike in novels — the narrator should not seek poetic licence.

Naturally, objectivity has always been in the eye of the reader. A writer ought to be aware that the truthfulness of his narrative might be doubted by some and accepted by others. Even today (in 2022), when I have embarked on the revision of the original text, I have remained convinced that, in this regard, I should not be an exception.

I pause to add that some of my own autobiographical novellas are memoirs of certain episodes, or periods, in my life or in those of my close friends. In most of them, I hid myself behind a smoke screen. In these memoirs, I shall strive to disperse the fog. That, actually, was my main reason for embarking on the task of telling my tale. Notably, some memories trickled back to me during the last few years.

If I succeed to capture my entire trip, I shall be facing the mirror as nude as Hans Christian Andersen's emperor, when an objective onlooker — an innocent boy — proclaimed that the emperor was naked. I am not certain that such an experience would be gratifying, even if the author were prepared to assume the roles of both the emperor and the objective bystander. But, be this as it may, I have the wish to relate the true story of my life and the epoch covered. Readers will have to decide whether or not the story is of interest to them.

One of my remaining quandaries concerned the literary form to be used. I have opted for a series of letters — an epistolary — addressed to close friends, because I knew full well that they would be able to tell fact from fiction. An attempt to tell them a coloured version was bound to fail: They know me too well.

My assertion is true in respect of every close friend I have or had. One was familiar with my life as a young man; we grew up together. Regrettably, he passed away. Another knows me from my days in Oxford and is familiar with my professional achievements. Yet another — my God-Daughter — comes from a comparable, mixed, background. She has listened to my memoirs again and again and would know whether I have told the truth or strayed into fiction. Another friend I met in Singapore has a knack for pulling me back to earth when she detects flights of imagination. Finally, I have a friend who, like myself, is of mid-European origin and has a similar assessment of our brave new world. He would be frank if asked to be.

I pause to add that, originally, my intention was to address these letters to my closest friend from my days as a professor at Monash University. He knows all about my mid-life years. Further, we have remained in close touch even after I left Australia. But, he knows little about my early days. True, he is not one-eyed. He would not allow his reserve and his spirit of friendship to dim his wide-open eyes if I were to wander away from the facts. But the internal conflict of a multicultural person is not within his life experience. So, occasionally, he may fail to detect an inaccuracy. The same is true about my other close friends as, of course, none of them was witness to my entire odyssey. So, in the end, I have decided to address the letters to my 'friends'. I shall strive to maintain the respect that every one of them has (or had) for my candour.

Most of these letters were written quite a few years ago. I have revised all of them in the course of the last few months. This final polishing did not lead to major changes. For this reason, I kept the original dates on which I composed each of them. In some cases, though, I had to revise the texts substantially. In such cases, I added the date of the final fine-tuning.

As I kept revising the text, I realised that my odyssey was by no means of a unique character. It is the story of a mid-European boy who has proved himself as a survivor. My winding way starts in Vienna and is likely to come to its end in the City of the Lion. A friend of mine — of a similar background — has migrated to the United States and lives in New York. Yet another has ended up in Michigan. Every one of us had to build up his career. And the road has been long and turbulent. However, I have one extra qualification: I witnessed the establishment and growth of two states. To this extent, my experience is special.

Some of my friends have already experienced the end of their odyssey. I hope I shall not run out of time before the publication of this edition.

Peter Ellinger
Singapore
15 October 2022

Part I

QUO VADIS (GROWING UP)

9 September 2017
Singapore

Dear Friends,

Letter 1: The Holocaust

Why are these letters addressed to you? The reason is spelt out in the Preface. So, please do let me know whenever you think that I am moving from fact to fiction. Actually, I suspect the two are not worlds apart. In more than one way, they complement each other. By way of illustration, when is a battle lost? Very few soldiers declare defeat. In the ultimate, the outcome is assessed by military historians, each of whom tends to highlight facts supporting his theory. For instance, did Napoleon meet defeat or victory in Borodino? Who knows?

Before turning to my childhood recollections, I want to narrate the little I know about my family's background. This can be understood only in the light of the Jewish 'Diaspora', a word meaning 'dispersement'.

The Jewish Diaspora is believed to have commenced with the destruction of the Northern Kingdom of the Israelites and its capital of Samaria in 722 BCE by the Assyrian King Sargon II. It is generally accepted that many of the people exiled in the process were sold as slaves throughout the Levant, but in due course established settlements of their own.

This first exile was followed by the destruction of Jerusalem in 586 BCE by Nebuchadnezzar II, who deported a substantial population of the Jews to Babylon. Some returned to Juda under an edict issued by Cyrus the Great of Persia and built the Second Temple. This, however, was destroyed by Vespasian Caesar and his son Titus in 70 CE.

Even prior to this time, many Jews moved to different cities in the Levant, such as Antioch and Damascus. The largest congregation lived in Alexandria, where Jews formed a considerable segment of the population. There was also a community in Rome. Notably, the second Roman Emperor, Tiberius Caesar, exiled the Jews from Rome in 19 CE. Whilst his successor (Caligula) issued no edicts against them, Claudius Caesar — one of Vespasian's predecessors — exiled them from Rome again in 41 CE.

It is important to add that not all Jews left Juda (or Judea, as it was named when it became a Roman province) as exiles. As early as the 5th century BCE, Judean mercenaries settled in Elephantine, Upper Egypt, and erected a temple. Further, there is evidence of Jewish mercenaries employed by the Ptolemaic Kingdom in its wars with the Seleucids.

Over the centuries, the Jewish Diaspora spread to many countries in Europe and Asia. By and large, the Jews who lived in the European continent, especially in Central and Eastern Europe, became known as the Ashkenazim. Jews congregating in Asian countries, such as the Levant and Persia, became known as Sephardim. Initially, these could be divided into two groups: the Oriental Jews and the Jews living in Spain. After the exile of the Jews from Spain and Portugal (in 1492 CE), most deportees fled to countries in the Muslim world. In due course, they lived and inter-married with the Oriental Jews and, for all practical purposes, became recognised as a single — Sephardic — group.

With this background in mind, I return to my family's history. My paternal grandfather ran a grocery shop in Ottakring — at that time a working-class district of Vienna. I believe he opened the shop around 1890, when the Habsburg Empire was still intact and encompassed what has become the Czech Republic. I believe my paternal great grandfather migrated to Vienna from there. My paternal grandmother probably came from the Spanish Diaspora via France. Her maiden name was Berger.

My maternal grandfather came from a Jewish Eastern European background. I was told that he had to flee from what is currently Ukraine (the Russian part). He must have spent a few years in Kolomea (then Poland). I do not know when he married Julia Tyndel. I came to know her well later on, after we had fled to Palestine.

My late mother was born in Kolomea in 1907, and so was my Uncle Henry in 1912. From there, my grandfather left for Vienna, where his youngest son, my late Uncle Karl, was born in 1917. Grandfather Feuer built up a successful general export and import business. Before long, he became wealthy. Years later, when he was an ageing widower, he told me that his was a 'business empire'. Did he exaggerate?

My mother went to primary school in Vienna. She retained a smattering of Polish but was not conversant. Her natural language became German. She and Karl helped Grandfather Feuer in his business. In contrast, Henry — a rebel by nature — attended a gymnasium and then enrolled in the University of Vienna, majoring in Chemistry. Uncle Henry had a crooked arm from birth. To 'compensate' for the disability, he became a mountain climber. He was also a keen football player but (according to his own words) did not shine.

My late father graduated from a business school (*Handelsschule*) and became an import agent, representing Spanish and Italian owners of citrus fruit groves. Grandfather Feuer was one of his clients. I believe Father met Mother in Grandfather Feuer's premises.

Father told me that Mother had not been the first woman in his life. In general, Viennese girls were liberal with their favours. I believe Father was captivated by Mother's solemnity and strictness. He courted her and, in due course, they fell in love and were married in 1926. They rented premises in the 2nd District — Leopoldstadt — which was populated mainly by prosperous Jewish families. Grandfather Ellinger continued to dwell in Ottakring.

Before I discuss the Jews of Vienna in general, I consider it important to add a few words about my mother. If she had been interested, she could have easily passed some preliminary examinations and then enrolled in the University of Vienna. I believe she had the attributes of an accomplished family physician. However, like many Jewish girls of her generation, her main ambition was to have a happy family home and bring up a number of children. Regrettably, her modest dreams — and up to 1933 they were realistic — were shattered with the advent of World War II (WWII). So were the dreams of the entire Jewish population of Vienna.

In point of fact, the Jewish population in Vienna was effectively split into two worlds. Regrettably, Arthur Schnitzler did not cover this point in his memoirs, *My Youth in Vienna*. One comprised the orthodox, highly observant and traditional Jewish families. Their centre was the synagogue and the Kosher restaurant attached to it. The other group comprised the assimilated Jews, who retained a certain ethnic flavour but tended to describe themselves as 'Austrians of the Jewish faith'. All the same, many of them supported the Zionist dream (which I propose to discuss later). Further, they were clannish and tended to inter-marry.

Theodor Herzl — the father of Zionism — was a typical member of this group. So were my parents.

For a number of years following her marriage, Mother remained childless. I understand that she had a number of miscarriages. I was born in 1933 — the fateful year in which Adolf Hitler won the elections in Germany.

Naturally, my childhood recollections are blurred. I believe that they highlight the twilight zone between fact and fiction. For instance, Mother told me that little Peter'le showed his appreciation of a visit paid to him by one of Mother's fair friends in a manner not uncommon to little boys. But is the vague recollection in my memory banks genuine, or the product of Mother's incessant repetition of an anecdote that might or might not have taken place? Did I really pull the key out of the car's ignition screaming that "a mother is not a driver"? Hm. Truth be told: I cannot recall this amusing incident.

My first genuine recollection is of a show, probably in the Prater (Vienna's amusement park) in 1936 or 1937, depicting the major stages in a human's life: birth, spring, summer, autumn, winter and death. I recall vividly the shock of the realisation that life has a beginning and an end. In all probability, I was unaware of the process before then. Another recollection of about the same period is of a group of children in a park near our house. One boy, whom I liked, proudly gave me a Swastika pin. My nanny threw it into the gutter on the way home.

My next recollection is of what I believe was my fourth birthday party. I recall the nice cakes, the lovely gifts and the festive ambience that prevailed throughout it. Auntie Ida's eldest — Ted — was riding an exercise bike and another boy — Erich Tyndel — was clapping enthusiastically. At the time of writing — 2022 — Ted had to be moved to a retirement home in

Sydney. He was a successful solicitor, who formed a finance company of his own and lived comfortably in a pleasant family house. I am told that, on one occasion, he was nominated as candidate in the New South Wales election but was not elected. Thanks to Cathy's (my God-Daughter's) initiative, I came to know him and his family very well. I have remained in touch with them to date.

I do not know what had happened to Erich. I suspect his parents procrastinated and missed the chance to escape from Vienna. I know that Erich's first cousin fled with some members of his family to Palestine and later migrated to New Zealand. I met him during my years in this country.

One of the presents given to me just before (or during) that birthday party was a small riding elephant. It had a cord located near its head. If you pulled it, the elephant emitted a pleasant sound. I was fond of it and recall 'riding' it in Palestine. I still possess a photograph of 'Peter'le and his elephant'.

Another memory of that period is of a trip to Bad-Vöslau (near Vienna), where Father took me to the renowned swimming pool. I recall the cool touch of the water and how I clung to Father's arm.

The next two memories are less pleasant. To explain them, I must refer to the political climate of the period. As I have already mentioned, I was born in the fateful year, 1933, when democratic Germany voted Adolf Hitler into power. Naturally, I have no recollection of his ascent and never suffered physically during the Holocaust. It is, however, common knowledge that Adolf Hitler's design was not confined to exiling the Jews from Germany. His objective was to exterminate all Jews in Europe, which was to become part of his Third Reich. The only option left to the Jews was to flee to any place that would admit them. Effectively, Adolf Hitler initiated a new Diaspora.

Mother told me that when Chancellor Schuschnigg, who wanted Austria to remain outside the Third Reich, was forced to resign, the writing was on the wall. German Jews knew that all hope was gone even earlier than that; once the Enabling Act of March 1933 (passed in the wake of the burning of the Parliament [Reichstag]) gave Hitler, effectively, the power to do as he wished. But despite all these catastrophic omens, some people lacked the resolve to uproot themselves and flee. They were culturally attached to a home that no longer wanted them. Further, many of them had nowhere to go because many countries, including the United States, introduced restrictions on immigration.

Some members of my own family remained behind. Most of them were never heard of again. Fortunately, Father's two sisters — Alicia and Ida — fled, respectively, to Argentina and to Australia. Many years later, I had a warm reunion with Ida's sons — Ted (whom I have already mentioned) and Henry. Both live in Sydney. Mother's two brothers — Henry and Karl — fled to the United States. I remain in touch with Karl's offspring. Henry, who passed away after his 97th birthday, remained childless. Following Mother's demise, I rang Henry every week until his natural end.

With this background in mind, I return to my unpleasant early memories. One is of Mother returning to our flat after she was forced, together with some other Jewish women, to mop the pavement. This was a typical anti-Semitic episode, albeit non-violent, which suited the Viennese temperament and outlook. I recall Father's contorted face as Mother returned to us and how she muttered some words of consolation. I believe her spirit was not shattered by this outburst of long-suppressed hatred.

The other memory concerns a mini easy chair, which was one of my choice toys. One day, Mother asked me to give it to a man I did not know. He had — so she said — a small boy who needed this type of toy more than me. I complied but felt deprived. I feel certain that Mother was made to give it. Did the man really have a small boy, or did he intend to sell it for whatever he might get?

My next recollection is of saying goodbye to Father, who had to flee from Vienna a few weeks before my mother and I followed him. To date, I recall the warmth of his hands. Occasionally, I wondered why we did not leave together. It is possible that Mother wanted to remain behind so as to secure the release of Grandfather Feuer from the detention centre. I know that she managed to bribe him out. Had she failed, he would have remained a detainee until the Nazi takeover. He would then have been sent to a concentration camp.

One task left to Mother was the packing of our choice possession, including her Steinway grand piano and her porcelain. She must have also packed my toy elephant. All effects were crated. The papers respecting the lift-van were left with non-Jewish friends, who later on shipped it to us.

Having covered the background, I return to my odyssey. I recall our reunion with Father (probably in the autumn of 1938). Mother claims it took place in Trieste, but my memory is of the Piazza San Marco in Venice. I believe my recollection is correct because the pigeons were so big. Be this as it may, I recall hugging Father and fearing he might leave again.

We travelled via Naples to Sicily, where some of Father's clients resided. I do recall the months we spent in Palermo. In the morning, the peddlers appeared on the street. The housewives did not deign to walk down from their multi-storied apartment buildings. Instead, each would lower a basket with money and a shopping list. I recall the vociferous haggling. Another recollection is of a picnic, in which I strayed away and fell into a lime pit. Fortunately, I got out in time. I further recall how Mother left the parcel with her meagre purchases for our evening meal back in a shop. Fortunately, the sales assistant came running after us with the parcel. It was a lucky break. Unlike other victims, I never felt pangs of hunger during our year and a half as refugees.

My most vivid recollection though is of a session in a church in Palermo. A family friend wanted me to immerse my hands in the holy water and cross myself. But something — probably the expression on Mother's face — stopped me. Years later, I found out that we had the option of converting to Catholicism and being given the protection of the local mafia. Father was prepared to go ahead. Mother, who had always been a woman of character, would not hear of it. I have also been told that our loyal friends accompanied us to the railway station, to the train to Paris. I have no memory of the trip, except my having misplaced my pink teddy bear. Father looked for it and found it.

We stayed for a few days in Paris but then moved on to nearby Chantilly, one of the refugees' havens in France. I am told that kindly jockeys used to advise Mother about the placing of bets on horses competing on the famed racing course. My main recollection, though, is of the fine pâté in the modest hotel in which we and other refugees found shelter. Years later in my mid-life years, when I revisited Chantilly, I realised that the hotel was an old and ramshackle building. This was not how I recalled it. Another recollection of our stay in Chantilly is the generosity of another little boy, who gave me all his toys when his family was granted visas to the United States.

During our months in Chantilly, I contracted my first attack of bronchitis. I must have run a high fever because the physician instructed Mother to wrap me in wet towels. I recall the sufferings; the treatment must have been worse than the illness. Still, those tense months were not void of pleasant moments. I recall that during my sickness, Mother read to me *Dr. Dolittle* (in German translation, of course, with the name pronounced as Doelittle) and how we went, after my recovery, to gather mushrooms and wild strawberries.

Another memory, still fresh in my mind, is the tension which built up whenever Father returned late from his illegal working engagements, probably in Paris. Mother, who feared the long arm of the police, showed her relief whenever he arrived with his modest pickings of the day. Father, I am proud to say, remained positive and optimistic throughout our days as refugees. The only sad moment I recall was when he wept after reading the letter advising that his own father (who had remained in Vienna) had died from a heart attack, following his being assaulted at high noon.

Chantilly also led to my first reflections about justice. Father used to play a game involving his pulling my chair away before I sat down. To please him, I always 'fell', shrieking in terror as I 'landed'. Then, one sad evening, it occurred to me that it would be nice to pull the chair away when Mrs. N (whom I disliked immensely) was about to sit down. The poor matron fell but, luckily, did not hurt herself. Enraged, Father thrashed me. In effect, he gave me a demonstration as to when wrong was right and vice versa. This lesson was useful years later in developing my courtroom strategy.

I have often reflected on the people in the hotel. I do not think the word 'refugees' was ever used. Actually, the atmosphere was not depressed. People joked, had fun and expressed their view about the cuisine. Although everyone was out for himself, there was a certain *esprit de corps*. Those who managed to get visas to safe havens — such as the United States or Australia — were warmly congratulated by those left behind. Everybody was hoping for a lucky break or, perhaps, a miracle.

In our case, the miracle took place after a spell of time in the hotel. Initially, we were granted visas to Palestine. I recall Father's happy smile when he showed us the official letter. A few days later, Father told us we could also obtain visas to Australia. He thought we should accept them. Mother, though, insisted that we proceed to the fabled land of milk and honey. I often wonder what it would have been like to grow up in Sydney or in some other town in Australia. But these, of course, are idle speculations. As always, Mother made the family's final decision.

All the refugees I recall deserved respect. Most of them were middle-aged people whose livelihoods and very existence and safety were in jeopardy. But they did not lose heart and, as far as I can recall, remained positive. Perhaps all of them knew that, when it suits her, Fortuna would smile.

Chantilly had yet a further effect on my boyhood. I had, of course, realised by then that men and women were different. I was also aware of the special bond that bound my parents to one another and knew that they were my protectors. Still, during my days in Chantilly, I became infatuated with the hotel owners' little daughter, Collette. I recall her light-haired pigtails, her blue eyes and her smile. Naturally, the facts of life — as we call them — were still a closed book. But the attraction to the little girl was there. I liked to play with her, often listened to stories she told me and, occasionally, savoured a banana or a cake she brought me. What I appreciated was not the tasty morsel but the happy smile that descended on her face as she watched me. Was it a case of puppy love? I don't know what happened to her.

My parents' decision to migrate to Palestine required our moving from Chantilly to Marseille: the Mediterranean port from which ships sailed to Palestine. We hoped to find a berth in a suitable vessel.

Our short spell in this ancient port town yields just two recollections. One is of the excellent cuisine. The other is of the police station. Father and I were rounded up by the police and, as we had no papers with us, were taken into detention. The gendarmes considered pressing Father into the Foreign Legion. Mother was asked to come over and take me home. She told me many times that the fuss she made on her arrival at the station ended with Father's temporary release coupled with the stern warning that he would be taken in unless we left France within ten days. Candidly, I have no recollection of Mother's appearance but remember that one of the kindly policemen got me something to eat and a cup of tea.

Before the end of the week, Father managed to secure a place in a ship sailing to Haifa. I remember that we travelled on deck and that, to spare me from the chill of the night, a sailor agreed to take me to his berth. Still, I cried bitterly and insisted on being handed back to my parents. The deck, I recall, was crowded with refugees escaping from occupied Europe. The trip took about three days.

I am told we secured a cabin after the stopover in Alexandria. But my only memory is of the Egyptian peddlers and their exotic wares. We, of course, had no money to spend on such trifles.

In my next letter, I propose to cover our first few years in Palestine. But today I intend to discuss what induced so many Jewish refugees to seek shelter in Palestine. Both demographically and geographically, the country was unsuitable. True, Palestine was governed by Great Britain under a mandate of the League of Nations. It was, all the same, a small stretch of land amidst the Muslim world. Until the end of World War I ("WWI"), it had been part of the Ottoman Empire. Its atmosphere, climate and economy were alien to European Jews. The United States, Australia, Canada and South American countries such as Argentina appeared as more suitable destinations for European migrants and refugees.

Notwithstanding these negative factors, the 19th century saw the emergence of the Zionist movement. Its premise was the promise made by God to Abraham, to the effect that Palestine as a whole was to be the domain of his offspring (Gen.15:12–21; Deut.1:7:8; Sam.II.7:9–11). As is well known, modern bible critique has thrown doubts on the very existence of the patriarchs and their period. To some Jews of the 19th and 20th century Diaspora, however, the promise was real and historically binding.

It is a historical fact that a Judean state existed in Palestine until its destruction by Flavius Vespasian and his son Titus at around 70 CE. An additional destruction took place after the second Jewish Revolt during Hadrian's reign (135 CE). Thereafter, there were some isolated Jewish settlements in Palestine (especially near Jerusalem). The Jewish people survived mainly in other countries — that is, as a Diaspora.

Notably, though, the nexus with Palestine remained part and parcel of the Jewish folklore. For instance, at the end of each Passover feast (the Seder [סדר]), the congregation said, "Next year in Jerusalem." Further, the teaching in the Jewish primary school, the Heder (חדר), emphasised the historic nexus of the Jews with Palestine.

The Zionist dream gained momentum from the pogroms in Czarist Russia. It developed into a movement and led to some migration of Jews to the region. I believe that had it not been for these pogroms and the 'ethnical cleansing' of the Third Reich, very few Jews would have migrated to the Middle East. True, some, like Mother and Uncle Henry, professed Zionism and even joined movements like the Hashomer Hatzair (השומר הצעיר). But they would have never left their home in Europe and their comfortable middle-class existence, had they not been driven out by the Nazis. In a strange way, the persecution of Adolf led to the materialisation of the old Jewish dream of a return to Jerusalem: a city known to most Jews from reading the Bible but, in all other regards, remained terra incognita.

I also believe that the notion of an independent, self-governing Jewish state was not on the cards at that time. The plan was to acquire land by means of purchase. Eventually, an ordinance enacted by the British Government in 1941 put a stop to such acquisitions. The British authorities noted the inequality of the parties' bargaining power. The efforts leading to the foundation of Israel gained momentum only after the end of WWII.

Will the newborn state retain its existence as an independent and sovereign state? The textbook answer is that only time will tell. Doubtless, for the last sixty years, Israel has overcome all military and political challenges and has stood its ground. All the same, in my eyes, a Jewish state amidst a vast Muslim world resembles the Crusaders' Kingdom of Jerusalem. A united Muslim world could deal Israel a fatal blow similar to that inflicted by Saladin's counter-crusade. Accordingly, my prognosis for Israel was — and has remained — one of unease. Israel's successful economic rise has not changed it.

Time will tell whether or not I am unduly apprehensive. The measure of tolerance in matters of culture and religion is best demonstrated by the clashes between Catholics and Protestants. In my eyes, an undisputed majority is, occasionally, sufficiently secure to tolerate a minority which does not seek political control. But this tolerance fades into thin air when two ethnic groups, with different cultures and religions, strike out for themselves.

Naturally, these ruminations are not of an autobiographical nature. Still, they affirm that, even at this late stage of my life, I have remained a pessimist. Is this state of mind traceable to the Holocaust? Some psychiatrists may provide an answer or come up with a theory. For a narrator, the best approach is to adhere to the facts and leave explanations to the specialists.

With all best wishes and kindest regards.

Yours as ever,
Peter

19 September 2017
Singapore

Dear Friends,

Letter 2: Childhood in Palestine

We arrived in Palestine on 19 September 1939 and, to my recollection, proceeded directly to Tel Aviv, a settlement populated by Jews and bordering on the ancient town of Jaffa. At that time, in 1939, Palestine was still a British Mandate. Jews had already migrated to Palestine whilst the country was part of the Ottoman Empire but, after the end of WWI, the League of Nations granted Britain a mandate to administer the territory.

As might have been expected, the Arab world opposed this "ascent" (Aliyah) of Jews to what they believed was their country. Indeed, there were Arab pogroms against the Jewish population (the 'Yishuv' [ישוב]) in 1929 and later on in 1939. To pacify the Arab population, the British introduced quotas limiting Jewish migration to the country. The Jews who escaped to Palestine from Germany as early as 1933 usually got papers that entitled them to take up residence. Most Austrian Jews — and some latecomers from Germany — arrived illegally. I recall that the ships of some of our family friends were diverted to Mauritius before they were finally allowed to proceed to Palestine.

The Jews who arrived before WWII built townships in the country. One of them was Tel Aviv, which was distinguished by its Germanic architecture. Years later, when I travelled through Europe, I noted the similarity between the architecture of some German towns and that of Tel Aviv.

We were amongst the lucky ones who were granted papers or, in other words, the right to migrate. My maternal grandparents arrived (with papers) a few weeks later, and we rented an apartment in Dizengoff Street in Tel Aviv. It was a winding street with scattered houses, separated by vacant blocks of land and sand dunes. The new building of Israel's renowned Habimah Theatre and the Frederic Mann Auditorium had yet to be constructed.

I was now over six years old and so, quite naturally, my recollections become clearer: the fog of early childhood had been blown away. My principal recollection is of Grandmother's fine cuisine: she was, and has remained, the best chef I have come across. She knew how to turn poor ingredients into splendid dishes. I recall her *Kishke* (stuffed intestines) and the *Halzel* (stuffed chicken necks).

Another recollection is my first acquaintance with the 'enemy'. An Arab peddler gave me some mushrooms he had picked up on his way from Jaffa to Tel Aviv. His little boy dismounted gracefully from the small donkey that carried their wares in the large pockets of a saddle and invited me to have a ride. They were friendly.

Both Grandfather and Grandmother were good to me. Grandfather, though, did not get on with my father. In Vienna, both Grandfather and Father were prosperous businessmen. In their new home, they were poor. Both were argumentative and hot-tempered — they often quarreled. After some months, Father and Grandfather were *broiges* (ברוגז) or, in plain English, not on speaking terms.

In consequence, my parents had to look for new quarters. Eventually, we shared a four-bedroom apartment in Melchett Street with Julius and Mimi Lenk, family friends from Vienna who had also fled to Palestine. We stayed there for many years. Under the Rent Protection Ordinance, enacted in 1941, the rent could not be raised; and the tenants could not be evicted as long as they paid their rent punctually.

For years, the Lenks were childless. They treated me as if I were their own son. In due course, Julius Lenk prospered and built a house in Herzlia. The flat in Melchett Street was retained by us. Sometime around 1949, Mother bought the flat from the owners.

Our flat was on the first storey of the building. The frontage of the land had been excavated and the house was built on stilts. The first storey, facing the street, was actually at the ordinary level of a second storey of a normal house. Beneath our flat was a laundry, which was also the quarters of its owner and a store-house. A flight of stairs led to our main entrance door. At the back, our flat rested on the ground. Occasionally, I climbed into our flat from the back balcony. The kitchen had no electric or gas stove and (like most dwellings of that period) had an ice-box instead of a refrigerator.

There was no sitting room. Two rooms were occupied by the Lenks and two by us. Later on, when the Lenks moved to Herzlia, Mother converted their rooms into a study and a sitting-cum-dining-room. A sizeable bookshelf was placed in what became my bedroom. Notably, the flat had two front balconies, one in the original Lenks' area and one in ours. Both faced the street. Later in life, I read good reviews about the fine architecture of Tel Aviv in the forties. I enjoyed reading them.

Melchett Street was closer to the centre of Tel Aviv than our earlier quarters. A five-minute walk got you to Allenby Street — Tel Aviv's Regent Street. I have a clear recollection of our neighbourhood. Both sides of the street were lined with three-storied blocks of walk-up apartments. Lifts were uncommon. The sun was kept out by blinds, which were a regular feature. The compact front gardens were, usually, maintained by the house owner. There were no off-street parking lots. The odd car owners had to park their vehicles on the street in front of their houses.

Melchett Street was residential. The only shops I recall were a greengrocer and small grocery in a nearby lane. Sheynkin Street, which crossed Melchett, had more shops, such as stationers, hairdressers and, surprisingly, an antique store. All shops were at street level. Supermarkets and department stores had yet to arrive. Restaurants were usually located on main streets or near the centre of the town. None was to be found in Melchett Street, but I recall one in Sheynkin Street.

Very few people living in Tel Aviv were wealthy. To understand the Jewish community — the Yishuv — it has to be recalled that it was made up of different groups of migrants. The first wave — the Aliyah Rishona (first ascent) — departed from East Europe before the turn of the 20th century. Most came from Russia and were induced to migrate by the anti-Semitic policies of the Romanovs. Many of these migrants were also inspired by idealism and by the historical dream of a return to a lost fatherland. Later ascents usually followed the growing anti-Semitic trends and pogroms in Eastern Europe and, to a certain extent, the hostility of the Arab world.

Most of the early migrants ascended to Palestine by choice. They could have readily migrated to Western Europe or to North America. Further, many of them were prepared to give up their professional careers in order to build up a new Jewish home. Idealism required sacrifice and hardship, such as doing manual work, including the planting of eucalyptus trees in the marshes so as to gain fertile land.

The refugees fleeing Europe with the rise of Nazism were different. Many went to Palestine because they could not find home in other countries. The United States, for instance, had a quota system. So did Australia. The WWII refugees tended to miss their fleshpots and complained of lack of employment. Their plight was understandable. Father, for instance, could not continue his business in Palestine. Italian merchants did not export their goods to our region. Desperately, and unsuccessfully, he tried to find a new vocation.

As already mentioned, Julius Lenk — Uncle Julius — was lucky. Back in Vienna he had run a modest textile manufactory. In Palestine, he became a supplier of cloth to the British Army.

Indirectly, his success provided employment for Mother. Initially, my mother and Mimi Lenk — Auntie Mimi — ran a *table d'hôte*. It was a successful enterprise, and, for a while, the cars of entrepreneurs and businessmen parked in front of our house every day during lunch time. However, the constantly rising price of food and competition from other enterprising housewives caused Mother and Auntie Mimi to close down their venture.

Shortly thereafter, Mother became a freelance employee of Uncle Julius. The cloth produced by his manual looms had many faults and imperfections. Mother's work was to repair and make them good. I recall, sadly, the many hours spent by her viewing one table-lengths of the cloth after another to detect and eradicate weaving faults. Nowadays, her work brings to my mind Thomas Hood's *The Song of the Shirt*. Still, Mother worked at home and, to her credit, I never heard her complain. Her meagre takings helped us through those hard times. So did the modest amount of money raised from the sale of her Steinway grand piano. I recall the day I came home to find it was gone.

My parents were typical mid-European migrants in two other ways. The refugees who had migrated from Russia and other Eastern European countries in the early decades of the 20th century were intent on making a fresh start and, in the process, discarded many of their cultural ties. Yiddish — the spoken jargon of East European Jews — was frowned upon. The ancient biblical language — Hebrew — was revived (in 1922) and became the lingua franca of the emerging new nation. In contrast, mid-European refugees, like my parents, sought to preserve the cultural milieu in which they had grown up.

There was, however, a marked difference between German and Austrian Jews. The former realised that their departure from their original *Vaterland* was on a one-way ticket. They did their best to master Hebrew and to become part and parcel of the Yishuv. I recall with amusement how a German émigré, who had opened a grocery store, had a heated argument with a customer as to whether a shop like his was to be described in Hebrew as *makolet* or *markolet*. When I sided with the shop owner, he rewarded me with a delicious sweet drink!

The Austrian Jews had, by and large, a different approach. My parents, for instance, never mastered Hebrew. At home, we continued to converse in German. Further, German literature and music were put on a pedestal. I recall with affection the old gramophone, on which we played music of Schubert, Beethoven and, of course, Strauss. In the confines of my home, I grew up as a Viennese boy of Jewish descent. In school — and I intend to narrate a great deal about my school days — I turned myself into a young, Hebrew-speaking member of the Yishuv.

The second demarcation between mid-European migrants (including both Austrian and German Jews) and other members of the Yishuv was of an ideological nature. Earlier migrants leaned towards socialism. They believed in equality, in the virtue of manual work, in honest remuneration policies and in the social contract. Communes, that is, the Kibbutzim, were held in high esteem. Merchants were frowned upon. I recall how a leader of the Boy Scouts told me, with an aura of confidence and condescension, that every merchant was a cheat.

Like many mid-European migrants, my parents, however, had always been and remained merchants. They had grown up in a capitalist society and had no affinity or sympathy for socialism. From their point of view, socialism was just as undesirable as communism. Stubbornly, they clung to the 19th century values and outlook of the very society that cast them out of Europe.

Today, I realise that my parents' views were out of place and were inconsistent with the lessons taught to them by experience. All the same, I can sympathise. Discarding a life philosophy is a difficult task, except where it is dictated by a new dogma or by an idealistic breakthrough. These are uncommon. Suffice it to say that Israel of the 21st century is as materialistic as contemporary Europe or North America.

Naturally, these views were formed by me long after our early days in Palestine. But I consider it important to reiterate that my parents' outlook was common at that time. Family friends — who had migrated to Palestine during the Third Reich period — had a cultural hangover similar to my parents'. Back in Vienna, in Danzig and in many German towns, they had founded small Zionist clubs. Their objective had been to encourage Aliyah (ascent) to Israel. In Tel Aviv, some of these clubs united under the banner of the Ha'Boneh Ha'zioni (הבונה הציוני: Builder of Zion). Needless to say, they were now preaching to the converted. In due course, Ha'Boneh grew into a social club of German-speaking Jewish migrants. Even the newsletters they published from time to time were written in German. The truth is that mid-European migrants (though in reality a minority of the Yishuv) felt culturally superior to the other members of the Jewish population of Palestine: Jews of Eastern European and Middle Eastern origin.

I should like to think that I lived comfortably as a Viennese boy at home and as a young Israeli outside it. The truth is far more complex. I tried hard to keep my two worlds apart. For instance, I never told my friends in school how conversant I was in German literature. And I usually refrained from discussing at home the religious and political beliefs and views of our teachers.

How did this complex state of affairs affect me? I must confess that, all in all, I was never at ease with my social environment. It were as if I was living in two worlds at the same time. My home was alien to my outside existence. And the precepts of my schoolmates and teachers militated against those of my home milieu. A daily transformation early in life is hard to cope with.

Two further factors — one personal and the other general — marred my childhood. Sad to relate, I suffered from asthma. The initial onset took place after my bronchitis in Chantilly. In Tel Aviv, the disease plagued me. The specialists and charlatans to whom Mother kept dragging me were of no help. Steroids and antibiotics — the medicines of the future — had not arrived. Nowadays, I have no doubt that, if Mother had given up her smoking habit, my condition would have improved. But in those days, and up until the sixties, smoking was not considered harmful.

My personality was also affected by the treatment of the disease. In those days, patients were kept in bed. In consequence of the lengthy spells in my sick bed and of the restrictions commanded by the physicians, I was unable to keep up with the activities of normal children of my age. All in all, I had to be a loner: an introverted human being with hypochondriac tendencies. Still, this state of affairs had one favourable side effect. It caused me to develop a reading habit. My multilingualism was an additional stimulus. I was conversant with the works of German authors such as Remarque, Werfel and Zweig. Often, I read books borrowed by Mother from a local library. Many of them were, of course, well above my head. But some struck a chord. I recall vividly how I read German translations of *David Copperfield* and *Bel Ami*.

My reading habit was, further, nurtured by an external set of circumstances. The Yishuv comprised Jewish migrants from many different countries: France, Germany, Austria, Poland and Russia. Most migrants were bilingual and, quite naturally, liked to translate masterpieces written in their respective lands of origin. I feel grateful to all of them. By the time I finished primary school, I had read English, American, French, German and Russian literature in Hebrew (and occasionally in German) translation.

The other external factor which marred my childhood was the knowledge that the entire Yishuv was in great danger during WWII. Adults frequently make the mistake of underestimating a child's capacity to observe and to comprehend. I was aware of the fear that descended on the Yishuv when Tobruk capitulated to Rommel's army. Mother and Father tried to spare me: they spoke in Italian whenever they discussed the situation. True, I had by then lost my smattering knowledge of the language. But I read my parents' frightened expressions.

Further, schoolmates told me of the state of mind that prevailed in their own homes. It was common knowledge that if Rommel took El Alamein, his forces were bound to penetrate into Palestine. Modern historians, writing decades after that fateful period, have sought to convince the world that Rommel was opposed to the genocide policy of the Third Reich. But during the raging campaign in North Africa, Rommel was considered nothing but another Nazi soldier. Everybody realised that a conquest of Palestine would lead to the deportation of Jews to concentration camps. We heaved a sigh of relief whenever Montgomery and his legendary troops put a spanner in the wheels of the German war machine and put it to a halt. In my eyes, 'Monty' was, and has remained, a great hero.

This atmosphere of fear was augmented by the awareness that the Yishuv was not in the good books of the rulers of Palestine — the British. We also knew that the Arabs were opposed to us and knew all about the race riots that had prevailed during earlier decades. The future did not look rosy.

Nonetheless, my childhood had its own happy spells. Every summer, my parents would send me to a holiday resort or home. One year, I spent an entire month in a home in Motza (מוצא), near Jerusalem, and in another year, with family friends near Haifa. Generally, I mixed reasonably well with the other children in the resort or holiday home. I recall how we went out to catch colourful butterflies, how we went on sojourns to harvest bamboo and sugar cane and also our many visits to the sunny beaches of Herzlia. One summer, I mastered swimming and, actually, excelled in this healthy sport. In another year, our group went out for lengthy hikes in the forested areas in the Galilee and, in yet another year, we went to visit historical sights.

Rowing, too, was fun. The Yarkon — the river of Tel Aviv — was flowing slowly. My bosom pal, Zvi (alias Paul), whose family had migrated from Danzig, and I used to ride our bikes to a boating station on the upper part of the river. We then hired a boat and rowed upstream, returning the boat early in the afternoon. I also enrolled in a club, which encouraged its members to row out into the sea.

Candidly, I preferred the peaceful trips upriver. In particular, I liked to play with the water buffaloes (colloquially called *Jamoossim*) which often raised their heads as our boat passed beside them. Usually, they were just curious and easily satisfied with a piece of bread. Still, I noticed that one water buffalo swam over to us as soon as our boat appeared on the horizon. Before long, I concluded that our regular visitor was a she-buffalo (dubbed *Jammoosa*), who decided to be friendly with us.

My dream came to an abrupt end when, on one occasion, we were joined on our river excursion by Ze'evik, a young upstart from Haifa, who gave vent to his contempt for the poor rowing skills of unsporting Tel Avivis. As he mounted the stern and called on heaven to be his witness of our incompetence, Zvi and I rocked the boat hard and looked on with mock horror as our guest fell into the Yarkon with all his clothes on. Instantly, *Jammoosa* detached herself from her flock and started to swim slowly and protectively around the dunked Haifa braggart. As we dragged Ze'evik out of the river, Jammoosa, too, emerged from the water, and I was dismayed to note 'she' was a huge bull-buffalo. Whilst our wet friend dried himself on the bank, Zvi and I rowed upstream, purchased a loaf of bread at a kiosk and returned to base. Jammoosa (now dubbed Buffalo Bill) munched happily, looked at the three of us lovingly and rejoined his mates.

Naturally, Ze'evik returned to Haifa with his tail between his legs. He never joined us again on the Yarkon. Buffalo Bill, in contrast, remained our good friend. Occasionally, we rowed upstream to bring him cheesecakes and scones.

So, despite my severe asthma, the memories of my activities during my primary school days are quite happy. So are my memories of our warm and comforting home. My parents gave me their full support. So did the Lenks. For years, I loved my Auntie Mimi just as much as my own mother. So, all in all, I enjoyed a good childhood. True, the tension prevailing during WWII affected all of us in Palestine. It hung like the sword of Damocles over the Yishuv. I recall with affection how the faces of my father and of Uncle Julius radiated happiness when the radio announced the capitulation of Germany in 1945. At that time, I was 12 years old.

Hoping that my friends do not find this letter too gloomy.

As ever,
Peter

26 September 2017
Singapore

Dear Friends,

Letter 3: Primary School

Having described my years as a refugee and our home in Tel Aviv, it is time to turn to my school days. By the time we arrived in Palestine, Hebrew had become the tongue spoken in daily life of the Yishuv.

Naturally, the Arab community retained its own tongue. The language used in the High Court was English. Hebrew, though, had permeated into the courts of law in towns of the Yishuv, such as Tel Aviv. It was also the language used in our schools. Unfortunately, the government allowed the schools to promote segregation. The schooling of Jewish children had been entrusted by the British authorities to the Jewish Histadrut (הסתדרות), which, of course, insisted on the use of Hebrew. The Arab community had its own schools, although the rate of illiteracy amongst Arabs was high. The children of the British administrators were usually sent to boarding schools in England.

It was natural that I was enrolled in one of our schools. This meant that I had to become proficient in Hebrew. During our years as refugees, I had picked up a smattering of Italian and some French by osmosis. My parents felt that Hebrew would be better mastered by tuition. Thus, Mother engaged a tutor who really put his heart into teaching me. My command of the Hebrew alphabet and of the *Nikud* (punctuation) was the fruit of his instruction. All the same, I am convinced that I picked up a great deal of vocabulary from mixing with other children and adults. I recall vividly that one day I mastered the word 'olives' simply recalling the word used by the grocer. Similarly, I picked up words such as 'orange' and 'lemon' from the greengrocer.

After a few months of private tuition, it was time to enrol me in a school. Father wanted to enrol me in the Alliance Française of Tel Aviv. Mother thought it better to enrol me in a traditional local school. I believe she was wrong. The conversational French I had mastered would have been a good bridgehead for further tuition in the tongue. Indeed, children who went to the Alliance became fluent in French. My attempts to study it later in life bore no fruit. I had forgotten what I had picked up as a child and hence had to start at the beginning; and I was (and have remained) a poor linguist.

For a few months I went to a private school — the Balfour Gymnasium (named after Lord Balfour, who issued the 'Balfour Declaration' to be discussed later on). However, a year later, when sending me to a private school became too costly, I was transferred to a public school named after the Hebrew writer Ahad Ha'am (אחד העם). Whilst Balfour was a co-educational school, Ahad Ha'am was a boys' school with a traditional, although not an overtly orthodox, bent.

My memories of the year in Balfour are more favourable than the tedious years in Ahad Ha'am. In Balfour, we were taught folk dances and some games. Every Friday, one pupil would bring a cake baked by his mother, which the class devoured during the break. The atmosphere was light-hearted and pleasant. In Ahad Ha'am, the teachers considered it their mission to turn their pupils into good Zionists with a traditional outlook. Many of their precepts clashed with those of an assimilated home, like my parents'.

Still, even in Balfour I did, occasionally, feel the odd man out. For instance, most pupils acquired the *Tales of the Bible* with the highly stylised etchings of Gustave Doré. I alone got a book with Rembrandt's far more refined prints. Mother was proud of the acquisition. I felt the social divide, especially when our teacher came to browse through the book after the class was over. I was also irritated when Mother came to take me back from school. Other children walked unaccompanied: I felt small.

In Balfour, most children came from well-off homes. Ahad Ha'am had pupils from all segments of the Yishuv. Only one boy, Bertie, came from a background similar to mine. Quite a few schoolchildren came from Middle Eastern homes. The classes were less homogeneous than in well-to-do Balfour.

My clashes with tradition started during my first year at Ahad Ha'am. Unwisely, Mother made me sandwiches with non-Kosher food — for instance, ham — for lunch. Children from Orthodox homes resented such transgression and, I am sad to tell, many a teacher sided with them. In addition, one of my classmates discovered that Mother purchased meat at a non-Kosher butchery. Is it surprising that I was lampooned? On many occasions, Bertie stepped in and sided with me. The sneers, though, remain fresh in my mind.

I was about nine years old when my scepticism matured into sheer agnosticism and disbelief. Initially, scepticism set in when I was told of all the miracles the Good Lord could (and would) do for his 'chosen' people. My small boy's eyes saw no evidence of them. Then, my Hebrew tutor (who had migrated from Prague) explained to me that, if you knew how to pronounce the Good Lord's name correctly or in full, you were entitled to a miracle. In reply to my question, he claimed that he himself was, of course, able to pronounce the real name of the Good Lord. Naturally, I wanted to know whether he would do so and ask that I be cured of asthma. He promised to try but quickly left my room. Well, his promise did not lead to any improvement in my condition. Further, I took in his shabby appearance. Is it surprising that this childish episode nurtured my doubts?

Our biblical studies classes added fuel to the fire of my disbelief. Was the crossing of the Red Sea and the fall of the Walls of Jericho more believable than many of the fables of Greek mythology? Weren't the sagas of Homer as real as many of the miracles described in the Bible? Was the prowess of Samson all that different from the feats of Hercules? I used to discuss these questions with Bertie and with Zvi. They were just as dubious as me.

The home environments of the three of us exacerbated our difficulties in accepting fictions or dramas as facts. Zvi's father, another member of the Ha'Boneh club, was as untraditional as my parents. I believe so were Bertie's parents. The three of us grew up in secular homes and simply followed the trend of doubting dogmas. We sensed that many did not make sense. Were we, then, heretics?

Insofar as biblical studies were concerned, my memories of our school have remained negative. One event is of specific importance. It concerned the story of Moses being taken out of the reed boat by Pharaoh's daughter. Exodus relates how she named the child 'Moses' because she soliloquized that she had pulled him out of the water (Ex. 2:10). The play on words works out in Hebrew, where Moshe (Moses) stems from the same root as Mashoh (משה, 'to pull out'). However, this play on words does not work out in German, which had remained my second or perhaps main language. Bewildered, I asked our teacher whether Pharaoh's daughter talked to herself in Hebrew. The ringing of the bell saved him from the need to reply.

Back at home, I raised this query with Father, Mother and Auntie Mimi. They backed out by pleading that they did not have a command of Hebrew. In consequence, I turned to Uncle Julius, who was less of a sceptic than them. His answer has remained fresh in my mind:

"Look here, Peter'le. Our Bible gives rise to many queries of this type. You may choose to doubt it or resolve to accept the Bible as the word of God. The decision has to be your own."

This clear reply firmed my agnostic approach to our faith. Moreover, I became sceptical of many other dogmas preached to us. Nonetheless, I recall my school days with warmth when I think of the useful subjects covered. To start with, my basic knowledge of mathematics goes back to my schooldays. I recall with amusement the impatience often displayed by Mother and Auntie Mimi when they realised that I found it difficult to memorise the multiplication table. Unfortunately, they were unable to help me study the basic arts of reading and writing. As already mentioned, the language of instruction was Hebrew which neither spoke or read. They were equally ignorant of Hebrew literature. Still, Mother taught me the Latin alphabet and also to read German. Regrettably, I never mastered the art of writing German and its grammar has remained incomprehensible.

My command of German poetry stood me in good stead when we covered the Hebrew verse written by poets who had grown up in the Diaspora. The problem arose because Hebrew was pronounced in a different manner by Occidental and by Oriental Jews. The former group intoned the penultimate syllable of a word (מלעל); the latter usually intoned the last syllable (מלרע). When Hebrew was revived in Palestine, the choice fell on the Oriental mode of speaking. The result was that many poems, composed by Jews of Russian origin, did not read well when recited in Modern Hebrew. Their blank verse compared poorly with the neat metre of German poetry. I recall being the first boy in our form to note the defect. Our teachers did their best to explain the problem. In the event, it did not take long for nonconformists, like Bertie and me, to wonder about the pronunciation of Hebrew during the biblical period. To date, the answer has remained shrouded in doubt.

Another issue arose from the fact that the Hebrew alphabet comprised only consonants. To get a clear picture, assume 'his', 'has' and 'house' are all spelt as 'hs'. To mitigate the difficulties arising from such a script, some consonants were used instead of vowels. For instance, the Yod would be used after the 'h' in 'his'; the aleph would be inserted as indicating how to read 'has'. This development can already be seen in old documents, such as the *Dead Sea Scrolls* (ca. 250 BCE to 70 CE). Later still, probably in the 8th century CE, the scribes of the Yeshiva (an Orthodox institute of leaning) in Tiberias developed a set of vowels (comprising mainly dots and hence known as *Nikud)* written either beneath or above the consonants.

In our first two forms, our study books were written in this easy-to-read manner. In our third year in school, we were given books written without *Nikud*. We were told that all newspapers and books published in Modern Hebrew (except poetry) were printed in that way. I recall the shock all of us felt when we had to face these 'difficult' texts. Still, within a year, we mastered the system. Contextually, it is, of course, easy to grasp whether the word ought to be read as 'his', 'has' or 'house'. Nevertheless, the use of consonants in lieu of *Nikud* facilitated reading.

Father, Mother and Auntie Mimi never appreciated the problem involved.

All of us at school felt a similar shock when, one day (again in Form 3), we were asked to discard our pencils and to use pens with nibs that had to be dipped in an ink-well placed in the centre of each bench. Fountain pens were proscribed till the end of the year. I still wonder how medieval scribes mastered the art of sharpening a feather and using it to write their beautiful calligraphy.

The only foreign language taught at primary school was English. I think we had our first classes in Form 4, when I was about nine years old. We had an excellent teacher, but I recall with horror our study book. One chapter included a dull discussion of the hair. Our teacher decided to skip it because he thought it was not topical. But he had no option but to guide us through a play called *Cox and Box.* One day, I may comprehend why it was considered suitable for boys in Palestine and further might appreciate its humour. Fortunately, our teacher provided materials not included in the syllabus. I remember the passage from *Samson Agonistes* in which Milton bemoaned his blindness. I also recall, with affection, how we read *The Happy Prince* (Oscar Wilde), *The Country of the Blind* (H.G. Wells) and a short passage from D.H. Lawrence's *Sons and Lovers*, entitled 'Paul's First Day at Work'.

English grammar was a different matter. The 'sequence of tenses' is just as absurd as some of the declinations in Hebrew and in German. And, of course, prepositions never made any sense. You just had to memorise them! Is it surprising that Bertie and I concluded that the only object of the rules of grammar was to torture the innocent learner?

Still, the study of English underscored my reading habit. I recall reading Dickens' *The Pickwick Papers* in the English original together with a Hebrew translation, which helped me to comprehend difficult passages. Another book I worked my way through was James Joyce's *Dubliners*. As a boy, I admired the stories (although some passages were well beyond my comprehension). In 2022, as an aged person, the tales are readily comprehensible but, I fear, less impressive. Unfortunately, I also read the works of lesser writers, such as Edgar Wallace and Agatha Christie.

The pedagogical outlook of Ahad Ha'am underwent a subtle change in the Fifth Form. Our teacher explained to us that, under the educational systems of Western Europe, we were now ready for secondary school — the gymnasium. Undoubtedly, our courses broadened in the remaining four years. In particular, we had some basic courses on history and geography. All in all, though, the school retained its narrow, traditional outlook accompanied by constant preaching of Zionism and Jewish consciousness.

This is all I have to say about my schooldays. However, I consider it important to add a few words about my experience as a Boy Scout. I joined the organisation because many of my playmates were members and I had no wish to be left behind. Bertie, too, enrolled.

Notably, though, the instructors at the Boy Scouts preached Zionism. They understood the organisation's motto — 'Be Prepared' (based on the name of Baden-Powell, the movement's father) — as an edict directing them to prepare us for the struggle leading to the Yishuv's independence. In my opinion, the Boy Scouts cell in Tel Aviv was a political instrument, far removed from the founder's true object. The emphasis was not on scouting (as such) but on the Yishuv's ideological orientation.

It must be clear by now that my childhood was problematic. Still, it prepared me for the next leap forward. But before I turn to this, I have to relate my awakening.

I shall do so in my next letter.

Yours as ever,
Peter

5 October 2017
Singapore

Dear Friends,

Letter 4: Awakening

Every school year was followed by the 'long vacation', commencing in June and ending in August. As already related, my parents usually sent me to a resort or holiday home. I recall a resort in Jerusalem, to which I went after I completed Form 2. The premises were in one of the outskirts of the town. The people who ran the resort were German Jewish migrants, who needed to supplement their income.

Jerusalem, Haifa and Tiberias were amongst the towns with a mixed population. Our vacation quarters in Jerusalem — housed in the second storey of a big bungalow — were typical. The family of an Arab policeman lived in the annex. Before long, I became very friendly with his son Sa'id, who was a few months older than me. Sa'id taught me how to construct and fly a kite. You had to run against the wind so as to raise it and then let it skirt in the wind whilst you navigated it by pulling a line to which it was attached.

A point that is blurred concerns our means of communication. I believe Sa'id had a smattering of Hebrew and I had acquired a few Arabic words. By and large, though, I believe we used sign language. It was adequate.

I was dismayed when, about one month after my arrival, Sa'id told me that they had decided to move to other premises. A family of recent migrants, who lived on the first floor of the bungalow, made their life intolerable. The migrants were noisy and inconsiderate, expecting others to conform to their ways. Sa'id's father — I cannot recall his name — thought it would be best to find other quarters.

I never met Sa'id again. The experience, though, has remained fresh in my mind. I realised that the ways of our own people were often intolerant. Further, they could be off-putting and lacking in the appreciation of the sensitivities of others. Yet another point — that I later realised — was the fact that the friendship could indeed be formed. I fear that nowadays young Arab boys are unlikely to befriend Jewish boys. Is it possible that Sa'id's offspring live in squalid quarters in the Gaza strip or are Jihadists?

In the following year, I was sent to a holiday home in Motza, near Jerusalem. During the two months I stayed there, I discovered the meaning of what we call 'the facts of life'.

I must have been nine years old (or perhaps ten). The home was run by an unmarried woman who had migrated to Palestine from Germany. Ms Lisa Ginsberg treated the boys and girls entrusted to her care as a flock of protégés. Today, I realise she was a lonely female, who tried to solace herself by showering attention on, and by constantly interfering in the privacy of, her charges.

Most boys and girl stood in awe of her. Those who did not demonstrate affection or respect became targets of her resentment and, occasionally, her wrath. Right from the start, she took exception to my lonesomeness and my tendency to brood. In her eyes, children ought to mix and play together. Notwithstanding her enormous bulk and weak legs, she taught us folk dances and exercises and also encouraged us to sing.

She even insisted that boys and girls shower together. The only exception was Miri, who had had to repeat a year in school and, in consequence, was about one year older than most of us. Unlike other girls in the home, she was becoming an attractive young woman. Ms Greenberg ruled that Miri should bathe on her own and encouraged her to wear a suitable swimsuit whenever we went to the pool.

Miri was an excellent swimming instructor. She taught me backstroke, butterfly stroke and diving. Before long, I became fond of her, especially as she looked a bit like my Auntie Mimi. Another girl I liked, Ziva, was just a few months younger than Miri but continued to look like a child. She still had a flat chest, used to run like a boy and enjoyed collecting butterflies and hunting for colourful bugs, caterpillars and lizards. Most boys and girls feared her sharp tongue and the stern looks she bestowed when others irked her. I was one of the few who liked to play with her. All in all, she appeared harmless, and I felt confident she had a good heart.

One day, after we had returned from the swimming pool to the house, I ran into the two girls who, I could see, were arguing heatedly.

"What's the matter?" I asked with trepidation.

"Miri insulted me!"

Miri was a soft-spoken girl. She would not set out to insult Ziva, with whom she was friendly and who, like Miri herself, was one of Ms Greenberg's pets. I was still searching for appeasing words when Ziva explained that Miri had not made any remark. Miri had simply refused to have a shower together with Ziva.

"But why is this an insult? Ms Greenberg said Miri should shower on her own because she is growing up," I reasoned.

"But I am almost the same age as Miri. And I'm sure Lisa did not think of me when she made her decision."

I was nonplussed. "I really didn't understand what Ms Greenberg meant. Honestly, why is Miri so different?"

"Miri is growing up, Eli. Doesn't she look different from other girls?"

"She looks a bit like my Auntie Mimi or my mother."

"And do you take your shower together with them?"

"I did, when I was a little boy. But not now."

"Don't you know the reason?"

"I am not sure. I didn't ask."

"Don't you know how children are born, Eli?" interceded Miri, dumbfounded.

"Oh, Mother told me."

"But do you know how a woman gets pregnant with a child?"

"Some women pray to God and so he gives them a pregnancy. Like Hanna."

"I suspect Eli does not know all the details. Why don't you tell him, Ziva?" Miri spoke kindly.

"All right. And you go and have your shower — on your own!"

Patiently, Ziva explained to me the nature of procreation, the attraction of grown-up men for women and vice versa and the implications of marriage. She emphasised that every normal human being went through the process of puberty, in the course of which he (or she) grew from a child into an adult. Generally, girls matured at a younger age than boys.

"So it is a natural process, Ziva? Everyone goes through it?"

"Of course. Our bodies are planned this way. It's not voluntary!"

She then added that her mother, a medical specialist practising Skin, Hair and Venereal Diseases, regarded the process as demonstrating the role of evolution. Her father, a well-known Ear, Nose and Throat Specialist, thought it proved the perfection of God's planning. Occasionally, her parents would lose their tempers when they discussed the issues and, to restore peace, Ziva and her siblings rushed out of the room.

"But what are you brooding about, Eli? You are lost in thought. You don't think I am making all this up?"

"Of course not. But you say that whether you like it or not, you turn from a child into an adult? So our teacher, Mr Livni, is wrong when he says we have free choice?"

"I'll have to ask my parents. Honestly, I am not sure what people mean when they speak of 'free choice'. But you know, I don't think Lisa remained single out of 'free choice'."

"Why then? Ms Greenberg is a lonely woman."

"Perhaps she is not so good-looking. And she is bossy. Mummy says some men hate this. So perhaps nobody wanted to marry her."

The chat with Ziva did not change my relationship with the two girls. I continued to swim with Miri and to hunt for butterflies, caterpillars, bugs and lizards with Ziva. I remained fond of both of them.

Then, one day, I had a fall when I climbed a tree. Luckily, I did not break any bones. But I pulled a muscle and my bruises healed slowly. For a while, I had to stay put in the house and could not play or swim. I then recalled that my teacher, Mr Livni, had asked me to write to him during the break. He was aware of my misgivings on matters of faith and was keen to hear whether his persuasive words had struck a chord. In my letter, which I marked 'confidential', I told him about my chat with Ziva and asked him to explain why growing up did not remain a matter of 'free choice'. Regrettably, I described my fall and referred to the bruises as 'internal bleedings'.

Two days later, Ms Greenberg told me that my description of the bruises as 'internal bleedings' was an overstatement. She sent the letter on to the recipient with her explanation. When my father came to visit me during the weekend, she complained to him and described me as a sickly child and a hypochondriac. Father did not hide his disappointment and, to my surprise, took no exception to my letters being opened and read without my consent.

The matter was set right by my mother when she came over during the next weekend. I am not certain what transpired during her one-hour session with Ms Greenberg. Still, that very same evening, Ms Greenberg called all of us up and announced she had opened and read our letters with the best intention. However, Eli's mother had complained about the practice. Accordingly, she would no longer censor letters of anybody who did not want her to read them.

Most boys and girls looked perplexed. Then, Ziva insisted that everybody had a right to privacy and that a personal letter should not be opened by anybody except the addressee. Ms Greenberg fidgeted and then asked all those who would prefer her not to open their letters to raise their hands. Reactions were mixed. She then turned to me and asked for my preference. Bluntly, I told her I had decided to post all my future letters personally at the post office.

Ms Greenberg flushed. Miri looked at me disapprovingly. Obviously, she took Ms Greenberg's side. From that day onwards, she ceased to swim with me. Is it possible that, when Miri's parents came over, Ms Greenberg 'had a word' with them?

Ziva, in contrast, continued to play with me. Further, when my mother came over two weeks later to take me back home, Ziva asked me to call on her in Tel Aviv. For a few months, I continued to visit her. I remember how she took me to the zoo and to Galley Gil, a swimming pool opened on the outskirts of Tel Aviv. Then came Ziva's turn to mature. Before long, she was going steady with a nice soldier. When I tried to greet her when I ran across them, she did not 'notice' me. I took offence and never visited her again.

All in all, the sojourn in Motza and its aftermath left their impact on me. To start with, I had become aware of the basic facts of life. In other words, I understood the physical process of procreation. The more subtle elements of a lasting union remained unclear. I am not certain that most humans appreciate them. I also comprehended that some people (like Miri) might take offence when you disapproved of their idols and that even a closer association (as with Ziva) may come to its end when situations changed.

However, the main conclusion related to my inner convictions about the order of things. Mankind had been carefully planned. To my mind, there could be no doubt on this point. But my misgivings about the existence of a supreme being remained intact. Who was right: Ziva's father or mother? It did occur to me that, in all probability, the matter was unsettled. My sympathy, I must say, was with the views of Ziva's mother. If 'evolution' provided a convenient or easy answer, why should one bother about faith?

I believe that during these few weeks, my innocent childhood came to its end. From then on, my perceptions were those of a youth or, perhaps, of a young adult. So were my views of life. I shall have more to say about them when I describe my youth.

In the meantime, all the best to you.

As ever,
Peter

15 October 2017
Singapore

Dear Friends,

Letter 5: The Independence Move

It is common to regard childhood as being followed by boyhood; but I find the two overlapping. The distinction is, I believe, arbitrary. My own progress was from childhood to youth. It took place during my holidays in Motza: From then on, I developed my skill of politely doubting everything. Acceptance of matters preached in sermons, be they anchored in faith or in dogma, became subject to my own analysis. So was the daily metamorphosis from my home image to my primary school or world image. Still, during my last two years in Ahad Ha'am, I moved closer to the idols of the school — the idols of the Yishuv — and, in many ways, distanced myself from the milieu of my Viennese home. It amuses me to recall that, even at home, I tended to solicit a modicum of orthodoxy and, of course, Zionism.

The explanation of the change in my outlook was plain. The Yishuv was facing tribulations from the Arabs. During WWII, the British protected us against annihilation by the Third Reich. Their victories were ours. When the war was over in 1945, the Yishuv started its struggle for independence. The British — whom everybody started to demonise — were caught in the crossfire between the Yishuv and the Arab community. The former postulated free Aliyah (ascent) of Jews to Palestine and insisted on the foundation of a Jewish state. The Arabs were opposed to both.

The Yishuv relied heavily on the historical right of the Jews to their original home country. The Arab world — primarily countries bordering Palestine, such as Transjordan, Syria and Egypt — maintained that the country was part and parcel of the Muslim world. The Arab community in Palestine claimed that the land was theirs.

A political analysis of the competing claims is best left to scholars working in the field. They have spent many hours on interpreting the promise given to the Zionist Movement in the Balfour Declaration of 1917 (made whilst WWI was in progress and Palestine was still part of the Ottoman Empire).

There can be no doubt that the Declaration was made after careful consideration of its wording and that it assumed the form of a letter, addressed by Lord Balfour (the then Foreign Secretary) to Lord Rothschild (a prominent figure of the Zionist Movement). Objectively read, it was a declaration by the British Government of its intention to facilitate the establishment in Palestine of a "national home" for the Jewish people "provided that nothing shall be done which may prejudice the civil and religious rights of existing non-Jewish communities in Palestine". The Yishuv relied on the promise made in the Declaration. The Arab community emphasised the proviso.

The British Government tried to pacify both communities by setting limits on the ascent of Jews to Palestine. The Yishuv combated them by sponsoring the Ma'apilim (מעפילים) — migrants seeking to enter Palestine without visas.

What led to my support of the struggle of the Yishuv? Why did I, like many of my contemporaries, believe that every Jew had the right to migrate to Palestine? Naturally, I had my doubts about the alleged promises made by God Almighty (of whose existence I was uncertain) to mystical figures like Abraham or King David (on whose existence I kept an open mind). I could readily think of too many purported divine promises or dogmas which encouraged certain nations to perform horrid acts of cruelty and oppression. The exploits of the conquistadors were a constant reminder.

I believe that, like many other youngsters, I was simply swayed by the propaganda machine. It was active in the Hebrew press, in school, amongst the Boy Scouts and even in the streets and the theatres. Further, the emerging folklore became the subject of songs, of tales of heroism and of sagas. It became impossible to be a member of the Yishuv and withstand its pull.

One further point was apparent to me. In 1945, the Yishuv had become a large settlement of a migrant population. It was a substantial minority (of about 33.3% of the population of Palestine). Still, it developed an identity of its own, introduced a new language, had its own new literature and, in more ways than one, established distinct cultural trends. Further, many of its members — the men and women born in Palestine (the Sabres) — were practically monolingual, felt no affinity to any place other than Palestine and, of course, regarded it their home. Nobody could see any good reason for their being governed by any outside power. They had turned marshes and wasteland into fertile farmland, had built towns and villages and had created an environment of their own. If they were prepared to share what they created with survivors of the Holocaust, did anybody have the right to stop them?

Today, at my very advanced age, I can see the flaws in the arguments. The last Jewish state was destroyed and laid bare by the Romans in 135 CE. For about two thousand years — until the last decades of the 19th century — the Jewish Diaspora made no determined effort to regain, or to return to, Palestine. Could any rights which had been in abeyance for so long a period be reasserted? Did the Jews have any political right to rely on divine promises made to the patriarchs, if indeed such promises had ever been made? By the end of the 19th century, Palestine had been populated for eons (albeit sparsely) by Arabs. True, the country had been deforested by the Turks. Much of the land had turned into marshes and sand dunes. But did this deterioration confer any rights on people living in other parts of the world?

The issue has of course been discussed in treatises written by political scientists. I have no wish — and suspect that I am not in a position — to enter their arena. All the same, I have seen flaws in the arguments respecting the Balfour Declaration. First, it was made by the British Government long before it had obtained the mandate over Palestine. Unless it could be construed as encompassing a promise, why was it binding when the political situation changed; that is, if it was binding at all? Secondly, the Declaration referred to a "national home". I am not satisfied that this expression refers to a self-governed state. Thirdly, who was entitled to rely on such a declaration? The Zionist Movement was initiated by Jews in the Diaspora. Could they possibly be regarded as an entity with a political bargaining power? Further, could the Yishuv be regarded as an ex post facto body that was in a position to invoke a declaration made in a completely different political situation?

I am of course aware that, under Public International Law, a unilateral declaration made by a sovereign state has a special standing.

It differs from the common law, which (subject to narrow exceptions) holds that the only person entitled to enforce an agreement is the promisee. Candidly speaking, I continue to prefer the strict common law approach — geared in common sense — under which an agreement is a bargain made between parties with legal capacity to negotiate.

These considerations continue to trouble me today (in 2022). As a youth, or teenager, I felt the pull of the propaganda and the right to self-determination of the Yishuv. Like virtually all my contemporaries, including Zvi, I felt that the establishment of a Jewish state in Palestine had to become a reality.

Still, in one regard, I distanced myself from the emerging conventional wisdom. While most members of the Yishuv regarded the British forces as the new oppressors, I was unable to forget that Monty and his men had been our heroes during WWII. How then could they, suddenly, become enemies?

My doubts were reinforced by an incident that occurred during the Jewish carnival, Purim, probably in 1946. We had four days of school holidays and, like most primary school pupils, walked along the streets in masquerade. My friend Hezi dressed up as Blackbeard the Pirate, wearing a long beard borrowed from a theatre group and mock pistols. Omri dressed up as Captain Hook and I wore the uniform of a partisan. We paraded with dignity down Rothschild Boulevard, which had a nice pedestrian avenue laced with shrubs and benches in its centre and traffic arteries on both sides. As we proceeded, Hezi fired his noisy and harmless toy guns into the air, Omri made swipes with his hook and raised his Jolly Roger high above his head and I brandished a mock sword and carried a long knife between my teeth.

The three of us relished the applause of the onlookers, who loafed on benches, and enjoyed the admiring glances of pretty girls, most of whom were dressed as Queen Esther, although one tall and attractive lass assumed the guise of Delilah. She was scantily dressed and carried scissors and a sheaf of hair (of one Samson) she was supposed to have cut with it.

It all seemed friendly and happy. Then, unexpectedly, a real disturbance took place. A group of terrorists — presumably the notorious Stern Gang — attacked the nearby premises of Barclays Bank. Real rifles were fired, and we heard the clap of machine guns. Instantly, everybody in the pedestrian avenue rushed for shelter in the doorways of houses along the street. As the three of us got ready to jump across the fence of one house, an English armoured vehicle sped down the street. At the sight of three boys clad as brigands, one of the soldiers grabbed his gun. Then, as I raised my hands, he broke into a smirk and, I believe, winked. I feel confident that, had he been an excitable French or Italian soldier, he would have shot us with a view to answering questions later. Fortunately, the British soldier retained his cool.

Regrettably, our escape into the basement of a house did not bring the episode to its end. As we mopped the sweat off our brows, we saw a middle-aged man, with a number tattooed on his arm, who had suffered a shock. He was as pale as the wall he crouched against, shivered all over and seemed to have lost his voice. Before long, the three colourful brigands became, once again, dutiful Boy Scouts (or Good Samaritans). With the assistance of Delilah and two Queens Esther, we led the shattered man to a nearby clinic of the Red Star of David (Magen David Adom), where he was given treatment. Soon thereafter, Hezi undertook to see Delilah home, claiming she lived not far from his parents' flat. Omri and I, who lived in the same house in Melchett Street, went back somewhat deflated.

The encounter in Rothschild Boulevard made me realise the danger of extreme reactions and approaches to violent situations and the importance of a cool head. It reinforced my tendency to consider everything before subscribing to a dogma or an orientation.

Shortly thereafter, a chat with my teacher, Mr Livni, made me think about matters religious. When our school reopened, he talked to me about the letter I had sent him from Motza. He felt disappointed by the opening of my letter by Ms Greenberg. His main concern, though, was my observation about free choice. He agreed that the stages in the life of a human being were preordained. But he failed to see what this had to do with the notion of free choice.

"But, Sir, why must a person grow up if he does not want to become an adult?"

"Well?"

"Where is his 'free choice'?"

"I see what you mean. But, Eli, free choice refers only to the option between good and evil."

"But why?"

"You must learn to opt for good in all the stages of your life: childhood, youth, mid-life and old age. The stages in a human's life are preordained."

"But, then, how do we distinguish between good and evil?"

"You can always find the answer in the Bible and in our traditions. Good is what God wants; evil is opposed to his teachings."

For a while, the answer satisfied me. It then occurred to me that both 'good' and 'evil' were hard to define and identify. Was it really 'evil' to switch the light on after dusk on Friday evening — Sabbath eve? Could we dub everything forbidden under any faith as being evil per se? It took me years to try to work out the answer. Doubts, though, set in from the very start. Odd to say, they have remained intact to this very day when I am close to 90 years old.

The last event worth mentioning from my primary school days is my Bar-Mitzvah, which took place on 25 April 1946. Under Rabbinical Law, a Jewish boy must observe all commands and traditions from his thirteenth birthday. On that day, by about mid-morning, he is called to the Torah — kept at the central platform of the synagogue — and has to read out, with the proper intonation, the Haftara (הפטרה): a passage from one of the books of the prophets. Usually, the Bar-Mitzvah boy has to study intonations under the guidance of a Rabbi during the months preceding his being called to the Torah.

I remember with affection my calling — the excitement of being the centrepiece of the congregation in the large synagogue. A prayer book presented to me by the congregation remained on my bookshelves for years. In the afternoon, my mother gave the customary reception. The tables were covered with plates of delicatessen and the wine was flowing. Our flat had never been as crowded as that before. Every friend and acquaintance and, of course, all members of the Ha'Boneh were present. I received many gifts, including a sparkling new bicycle. Two gifts — a silver-plated *Kiddush* [blessing] goblet and two volumes with writings of a famous 18th century Jewish playwright — still grace my collection.

In the evening, I went with some friends to the theatre. It was an excellent show of *Othello* (in Hebrew translation), which I found easy to comprehend. As I walked back to Melchett Street, I basked in the honour of having passed my religious maturation. But, needless to say, I never observed the religious duties conferred on me on this special day.

Initially, I considered these duties too cumbersome and unreasonable. Later in life and up until the present day, I have taken exception to many of the rituals. It seemed to me that observing rituals did not pave the way to an act of faith. Years later, following my wife's illness, I returned to the Jewish community of Singapore. The motive, though, was to declare my ethnic association with it. On issues of dogma and faith, I have remained the eternal doubter: an agnostic.

Still, in more ways than one, I am jumping the gun. The next chapter in my young life — to which I wish to return — took place in Tichon Ironi A, my gymnasium. I am looking forward to narrating all about these wonderful years.

With best regards.

As ever,
Peter

25 October 2017
Singapore

Dear Friends,

Letter 6: Secondary School — Tichon Ironi A

Some three months after my Bar-Mitzvah, Mother took me on a tour of Italy. We spent most of the time in Canazei, Val di Fassa, a fashionable holiday resort in the Dolomites. I believe my parents must have saved hard to finance the tour. They hoped that a change of climate would break the hold of my asthma and I believe my welfare was their first priority. Regrettably, the local pollens triggered off one of the worst attacks I had in my life. After it was over, Mother and I had splendid excursions, including a day in Cortina d'Ampezzo, the best-known resort in the area and a car-racing centre. Father came over to visit us during weekends. He had by then started to recover his old business connections in Italy.

From Canazei, we went to Bologna and stayed in a hotel. I got to know Bologna quite well and roamed about freely. It soon dawned on me that the values imbued in young people in Palestine were alien to the people of Italy. Very few knew anything about Palestine and the

Levant in general. Before long, I realised that Palestine was not the centre of the earth.

Shortly after we returned to Tel Aviv, I started my first year at the gymnasium or, in plain language, my secondary school. In one sense, it was a revisit to old grounds. Tichon Ironi A — fondly called Tichon (or TA.1 to indicate we were No. 1) — took over the very building of Balfour, where I had been enrolled in primary before my transfer to Ahad Ha'am. Moreover, the pupils of Balfour continued to attend it as their secondary school. Their class — the original Form I had attended in 1940 — became Form 4 of the first intake of Tichon. Form 1 was a boys' class. Bertie, whom I knew from Ahad Ha'am, was enrolled in it. Form 2 was a girls' class and Form 3, which I was enrolled in, was co-educational.

Tichon was an elitist school. With the exception of Form 4, the pupils were selected from amongst the top leavers of primary. We came from different districts of Tel Aviv — its North, South and Centre. The objective of Tichon was to prepare its pupils for a suitable white-collar career. Most of us ended up as doctors, lawyers, accountants, civil servants and academics.

As could be anticipated, the teaching regime was rigorous. Those who were unable to cope moved to less demanding schools or simply dropped out and found jobs. A special problem arose at the end of our third year of studies. The Teachers' Training College accepted any boy or girl who completed three years at a secondary school. Quite a number of my original classmates set their hearts on teaching careers. Indeed, departures were so numerous that, eventually, Form 4 (Balfour) and ours were merged.

The four years in Tichon were amongst the happiest in my life. I recall with affection the four-storey building, situated near the corner of Balfour Street and Melchett Street. The school stood on an elevated block of land, facing the narrow street. On one side of it was a water tower. During intervals between classes, we used to play in the school's spacious yard and on the first platform of the tower. Occasionally, we climbed up to the roof of our building, with a view to throwing water bombs (paper cans filled with water) at colleagues and teachers we disliked. Our school principal, dubbed Sheen, was a popular target. Anyone who 'scored' was treated to a pita falafel. I was a lousy marksman and always had to buy my own pita falafels.

Tichon had excellent teachers. My favourite was the History Master, Mr Ben Zvi, who was also in charge of our form. His heart was in the ancient world, and, to date, I owe him my love for the forgotten empires of the Levant and of Asia Minor, for Greece and for the Roman Republic and Early Empire. On his promptings, most of us read translations of Herodotus, Thucydides and Euripides. I recall with affection how a number of us accompanied him to a performance of *Oedipus* at the Habimah Theatre. Mr Ben Zvi tried also to interest us in Plato, but I am ashamed to confess that, in my case at least, he drew a blank. I found the epigrams of Diogenes far more satisfying.

Modern European history was another interesting subject. His masterful analysis of the rise of Protestant Germany, of the Thirty Years' War and of the French Revolution has remained fresh in my mind. Regrettably, the history syllabus also included a substantial section on the Jewish Diaspora. I liked this part of our syllabus just as much as Mr Ben Zvi enjoyed teaching it.

Mr Ben Zvi also taught us geography which I found boring. Hopefully, internet tours can now augment the dull analysis of places, such as Poland or Russia, which we had never seen. Regrettably, our course did not cover Asian History and Geography. My knowledge of these topics — including the Mongol Empire — is based on autodidactic coverage when I joined Singapore's law school.

Another teacher I appreciated was Mr Simon, the English Language Master. He encouraged us to read English literature in its original language. He looked rather bewildered when two of our girls presented book reviews of D.H. Lawrence's *Sons and Lovers* and *The Fox* and reminded all of us, shamefacedly, that *Lady Chatterley's Lover* was proscribed by the censor. But he was enthusiastic when my friend, the future plastic surgeon Dan Mahler, presented a review of H.G. Wells' *The Invisible Man*, and when I came to ask him questions about some words used by William Faulkner in *Intruder in the Dust* and in *Light in August*.

My only objection to Mr Simon was his selection from amongst the texts included in our schoolbook — *Adventures in English Literature*. I fail to understand why he gave a wide berth to the excerpts of *Paradise Lost* and to *The Song of the Shirt*. I found — still find — Milton's epic and Thomas Hood's poetry more instructive and eye-opening than endless poems about skylarks and women walking in beauty. Further, I thought — still think — that the English language would have lost nothing if Browning had never written *The Pied Piper of Hamelin*. As I used to argue these points vociferously, Mr Simon concluded I was a philistine. Another unfavourable recollection concerns his pedantic approach to understanding *Macbeth*. To date, I dislike Shakespeare.

Intellectually, all of us benefitted from our endless Biblical Studies classes. In our first year, one tiresome teacher managed, at the very least, to convince us that the Old Testament (as it has come down to us) is a collection of texts selected by the compilers. From then onwards, I knew that interpolations and patent errors were to be expected in the manuscript. I also realised that the legends told in the scriptures had to be taken with a pinch of salt.

The true influence as regards the Old Testament came during our last two years in Tichon, when Mr Frank was put in charge of our bible studies. By the time we had gone with him through *Job* and *Ecclesiastes*, we started to appreciate the magnificence of our cultural heritage. Old Frank was an agnostic. His influence on me has lasted the rest of my life. I also realised that good and evil were often nothing but two sides of the same coin. Be this as it may, whenever I reread *Job*, I think of Frank's masterful analysis of the book's philosophy and of the brilliant blank verse. No wonder our orthodox classmates and teachers looked at Old Frank askance. So, alas, did the principal — a highly orthodox believer.

Another subject I loved was zoology. Whilst I had no particular interest in the classification of plants and animals, I was impressed by the lectures of our teacher, Ms Garten. Quite apart from covering what could have been a mundane and tiresome subject, she made a point of explaining natural phenomena on the basis of the theory of evolution.

Naturally, Ms Garten was viewed unfavourably and with suspicion by the orthodox component of our form. To them, 'creation' provided an adequate answer. Moreover, it was common knowledge that Ms Garten had led a tempestuous life, having been twice divorced and had an affair with one of our teachers. I recall how she once took over the Biblical Studies class of a colleague who had fallen ill. Two of the girls in our form asked Ms Garten to explain some point in the prophecy of Hoshea, to whom the Good Lord had told: "Go take to thee for wife a woman of harlotry" (Hoshea 1:2). Feigning ignorance, they asked our teacher to explain what 'a woman of harlotry' meant. Ms Garten was not abashed. "You better ask your Rabbi," she retorted.

Ms Garten was aware that some of us were keen to learn more about evolution. On one occasion, she invited 'all interested' to attend a lecture to be delivered by a doctoral fellow of the Hebrew University. It was an eye-opening session, especially as some of us prepared ourselves by reading Thomas Huxley's *Darwinism*.

A few days later, I went to see Ms Garten after a zoology class and asked her to clear one point. We had been told that linear evolution was subject to sudden mutations. Was it possible that these mutations, as well as plain evolution, were a component of a plan, yet to be discovered? Further, was it possible that evolution and sudden mutations had all been planned at the beginning by a prime mover or creator?

"This is a difficult question, Eli," she told me. "It is hotly debated in theological, philosophical and scientific circles. How did you come to think of it?"

"The difference between the views expressed in the lecture and those held by my teacher in primary school."

"You will have to make up your own mind on this issue," she replied. "I doubt if anybody can guide you."

One widely disliked subject was Hebrew Literature. We had to study the writings of Diaspora Jews. They had dealt with the problems of their own day: the pogroms in Eastern Europe, the emergence in the Diaspora of the notion of Zionism, the struggle of the pioneers and so on. In our days, these topics were passé. There was at the same time fine, contemporary, modern Hebrew literature and poetry. We had to read those works on our own. Yonatan Ratosh, in particular, was admired by many of us. I still have a volume of his poetry, including

Black Canopy (in which he assails the Jewish marriage system). It is to be hoped that today, in the 21st century, the modern authors have attained the place they deserve and that the 'oldies' have by now been kicked out of the curriculum.

An even more detestable subject was Hebrew grammar. To this very day, I believe it was developed by scholars with a strong sadistic bias. I am one of the few who managed to master it. But I shudder when I think of the effort involved. In any event, it was a sheer waste of time. Hebrew and its grammar have metamorphosed over the years. Currently, even grammar begins to make sense.

Up to now, I have concentrated on our classes in Tichon. Our form, though, socialised even after school hours. Mr Ben Zvi ensured that, at least twice a term, we had a *Kumzits* (a Hebrew slang for 'picnic' derived from the Yiddish term 'come and join'). *Kumzitses* were common in the Yishuv as from the early ascents. By the time we joined Tichon, they had become fashionable.

We used to bake potatoes, brew strong coffee and every one of us brought some finger food for the party. Normally we had our *Kumzitses* on the banks of the Yarkon. The people who lived in multi-storey apartment blocks nearby used to yell at us. In a sense, this became part of the proceedings. I recall one woman in the neighbourhood who possessed a singularly rich invective vocabulary. My friend Pilkin and I used to provoke her by cursing in Arabic. All in all, she had the upper hand. I suspect she enjoyed herself!

Naturally, we had to quench the fires we had lit during the *Kumzits*. On some occasions, we carried water from the Yarkon. Eventually, we used the 'Gulliver method'. On such occasions, the girls withdrew.

Apart from the *Kumzitses,* we also went to theatre shows and occasionally to ballets. Television had not yet arrived in Palestine and so many of us went to the cinema about twice a week. Quite often, a few of my classmates joined me; we watched excellent American, British and French films. *City Lights* and *Kind Hearts and Coronets* were amongst our favourites.

By the end of our second year in Tichon, my parents' spacious flat became a meeting place of many members of our form. We read books together, played games such as bridge, dominoes and *mahjong* and often listened to classical music. During the examination period, we used to cram together.

At about the same time, many of us joined my parents' club — Ha'Boneh. We managed to pass a resolution changing its name to Yahad (יחד) [meaning: 'Being Together']. Membership was not limited to members of our form. At one stage, we had about fifty members. The advantage of joining the club was in our having premises for meetings, discussion groups and other social activities.

My four years in Tichon laid the foundation of my future. I recall them with pleasure and feel ashamed of only one event that took place during our second year. Our Physics teacher was universally disliked. Although he was a kind-hearted man, he antagonised us by his attempts to get everybody interested in a subject many found dull. In addition, he developed a habit of ejecting from the classroom any pupil who was unable to answer a question. We avenged ourselves by making his life miserable, including playing childish tricks such as ringing the bell of his dwelling and running away as he came to open the door. On one occasion, we posted a notice advising that he had a room to let. As accommodation was scarce in those days, the poor chap had callers for well over two days. In the following year, he found occupation elsewhere. I hope it was suitable for him.

When I was admitted to Tichon, Palestine was still governed by Britain. The Yishuv was a minority (about one-third of the population). Despite the restrictions imposed by the government in 1939, many migrants ascended illegally. The struggle to attain independence had gained momentum.

I intend to tell you about it in my next letter.

In the meantime, all the best.

As ever,
Peter

3 November 2017
Singapore

Dear Friends,

Letter 7: Foundation of Israel

As promised in my last letter, I now turn to the developments in Palestine leading to the foundation of Israel. It will be recalled that during my first two years in Tichon, Palestine was governed by Britain under a mandate conferred by the League of Nations and affirmed by the United Nations. Unsurprisingly, the official language was English. The population, though, was not English-speaking. It could be neatly divided into two worlds: the Jewish Yishuv (about one-third of the population) and the Palestinian Arabs (a two-third majority).

Segregation had by then taken place. Most towns (such as Jaffa, Nazareth and Ramallah) were peopled by Arabs. Others (such as Tel Aviv, Netanya and Rischon LeZion) were populated by the Yishuv. Very few towns (e.g., Jerusalem, Haifa and Tiberias) boasted populations of both groups.

Whilst the Yishuv's language was Hebrew, the Arabs spoke a special Arabic dialect used in Palestine and Syria. In addition, most residents had a reading knowledge of English but were not conversant in it. Notably, some Arabs spoke Hebrew and — I am proud to say — our form opted for instruction in Arabic rather than French. I was becoming conversant but, alas, have forgotten what I had managed to acquire.

Before I recount the events of the period, it is important to emphasise that I am writing only of what I have seen or experienced. I am aware that the period ending with the departure of the British and the founding of Israel has been the subject of learned books and articles. I have read many of them but feel that my best course is to relate what I know. In a way, my personal impressions are more objective and reliable than the accounts of researchers who frequently sought to validate conclusions they had reached long before they embarked on their project. Mine is, actually, an eyewitness account. In the common law tradition, I prefer it to hearsay.

As already mentioned, during WWII the Yishuv considered the British our protectors. So did our main military organisation, the Haganah (meaning 'Defence'). Regrettably, the extreme right — the Irgun and the Stern Gang (also known as Lehi) — took a different view. As from 1944, they considered the British our enemies and were actually prepared to negotiate even with the Nazis to ensure the ascent of Jews to Israel. In due course, they shifted their allegiance to Soviet Russia.

The Stern Gang and the Irgun carried out terrorist attacks. I have already mentioned the attack on Barclays Bank. They also bombed King David Hotel in Jerusalem, where many visitors stayed, and in 1948, carried out the treacherous Der Yassin Massacre, practically wiping out an entire village of Arabs supportive of the Yishuv's cause. As anticipated, many dwellers of neighbouring villages fled to Transjordan. Another unforgivable act was the kidnapping and execution of two British soldiers.

The man behind these events was Menachem Begin, who would become the sixth Prime Minister of Israel. The majority of the Yishuv distanced itself from this type of brutality. In the eyes of people of my generation, terror acts were counterproductive. I recall how my late father and Uncle Julius contemplated writing a letter on behalf of Ha'Boneh, condemning the Stern Gang. It then turned out that some of our own club members sympathised with the Irgun.

When I reconsider the facts today and try hard to see them objectively, I believe that the Zionist desire to settle Jews in Palestine overlooked one important point. Undoubtedly, settlement and colonisation occurred regularly in mankind's long and winding history. For instance, the Han people wiped out the earlier occupants of China and European migrants settled in North America, destroying the culture of the indigenous population. In those cases, though, no power rose to protest. The position in Palestine differed. The Arab League as a whole stood up to resist any interference with the Palestinian Arabs. True, the Palestinians populated the land sparsely. Vast stretches were not used. This, however, did not give anybody the right to take the land away from them.

I am not overlooking the dilemma faced by European countries. Their options were to resettle and compensate the victims of WWII, or to help them to 'move away'. The leaders of Europe knew that anti-Semitism was dormant at home. They had no wish to see new outbursts of it. Is it, then, surprising that they opted to get the victims out of their own domain?

Another important factor respecting the period was the difficult position in which the British found themselves. When the United States joined WWII, President Roosevelt made it clear that his people were not going to assist Britain to retain her empire. By the time the British decided to withdraw from India — the Crown Jewel — there was no point in retaining a few pink dots on the world map. Britain lacked the economic and military resources to continue governing her former domains of influence and felt the need to rebuild and resuscitate the homeland.

Furthermore, the Mandate for Palestine was unprofitable. Having won the post-WWII elections, the Labour Government was far more concerned with the problems at home than with overseas territories. In addition, the recollection of the disruptions that followed Britain's withdrawal from the Indian subcontinent remained fresh in the minds of all contemporary politicians. Nobody wanted an encore. In 1947, Britain notified the United Nations officially of its intention to withdraw from Palestine in 1948.

In my opinion, the British withdrawal from the Middle East is to be seen as part and parcel of the wider process involving the dissolution of the British Empire. The notion that the British sought to return to Palestine as saviours once the Yishuv was attacked by the Arab world is incorrect. It is a fabrication of the propaganda machine.

The United Nations tried hard to find a solution. In the event, it recommended the establishment of two sovereign states: the Jewish and the Arab. The two states were expected to cooperate on economic matters. In view of its special meaning to Christianity, Islam and Judaism, Jerusalem was to be constituted an independent state to be administered by an international regime. Notably, the Jewish Agency was prepared to accept the partition proposal; the Arab League rejected it.

Nowadays, when I review the matter dispassionately, I am satisfied that the plan for two states could not have been put into effect. Any diplomatic solution to a conflict requires cooperation of all the parties involved. In this instance, the conflict was too deeply rooted to be handled amicably. Further, I have studied in detail the boundaries proposed in the plan. They were unappealing to both sides because, in reality, the segregation between the Yishuv and the Palestinian Arabs ran on indefinite lines. The partition plan did not appreciate the complexity of the situation.

One further point is of major importance. A substantial part of Iraqi oil was pumped through a pipeline ending in the port of Haifa. Any plan which failed to take this important economic lifeline into account was bound to fail. Regrettably, the United Nations did not come forward with any specific proposals respecting it.

It will be recalled that during the period involved — 1946 to 1948 — I was still a teenager attending a secondary school — my beloved Tichon. The majority of our teachers adhered to the curricula of their respective subjects. Mr Ben Zvi, for instance, covered the religious wars of Europe without ever straying into local politics. Ms Garten was bent on imparting to us the details of the theory of evolution and did not wish to digress into contemporary events.

Two teachers, though, were too emotively involved in the political developments of the period to refrain from speaking about them. I recall in particular how one of them told us that the Yishuv enjoyed the support of the Zionist organisations in the United States, which were in a position to influence President Truman and his administration.

The Foundation of Israel took place on 14 May 1948. I believe that, initially, the leadership of the Yishuv was divided. Some wanted to procrastinate. David Ben-Gurion, an outstanding orator, convinced them of the need to act promptly. Their decision was broadcast on Radio Israel in the evening hours.

Instantly, crowds built up in the strand to celebrate. I joined some of my friends and marched with them. The celebration was gathering momentum, comprising men and women of all ages. No automobiles were to be seen and the crowd proceeded against the traffic, chanting the slogans of the day.

One single car, a convertible, tried to proceed against the horde's direction. I was shocked to see how the mob set on the driver, stopped his car by force and beat him up. He was bold and I recall how a few young men clubbed his bare head. Fortunately, one woman, in her early thirties, intervened to stop this shameful behaviour. She managed to pull the hapless fellow out of his car and, with the assistance of a few of us, carried him to a side road. Before long, we found a Good Samaritan, who drove the highly distressed man to a nearby first aid station. I was about to take my leave with a view to rejoining the procession when the woman noted my disarrayed and worn-out appearance. Observing that I was bathed in sweat, she told me she was living in the neighbourhood and offered to give me a cup of coffee.

The Israeli–Arab War gained momentum on the very next day, but, before I turn to this, I pause to revert to Tichon. After just two days of school holidays, we resumed work. Our first class — with Mr Ben Zvi — dealt with the American Independence War. Resisting the temptation to comment about current events, we were steered conscientiously through George Washington's liberation battles. When one of my friends asked Mr Ben Zvi for a comparison of that war with our own struggle, he declined to give an answer. However, Mr Ben Zvi offered to have a discussion after school hours. It turned out that he had actually been an active member of the Haganah for years. I recall how he told us — with patent relief — that the Irgun and the Stern Gang had agreed to join fronts with the Haganah in the interest of the forthcoming struggle.

Initially, the Arab forces outnumbered the Israelis. Furthermore, the Haganah was not properly armed. Despite these disadvantages, the

Haganah fought heroically and, in due course, defeated the combined Arab forces. A major reason for the Haganah's success was the lack of unity in the Arab world. King Abdullah of Transjordan was keen to keep his hegemony but did not seek to interfere in the struggle in the Negev (the South). Egypt, which had been expected to fight in this area, did not send adequate troops to the region. In addition, Israel obtained substantial supplies of arms during two spells of a short-lived truce. By the end of June 1948, the Israeli Defence Force ("IDF") was adequately equipped and became a formidable force.

During the entire conflict, I lived in Tel Aviv. I am, therefore, unable to describe the battles that took place. There are, however, two episodes of which I have a clear recollection: the *Altalena* debacle and the murder of Count Bernadotte.

The *Altalena* was a ship acquired by the Irgun prior to its merger with the Haganah. It carried a load of arms donated, apparently, by the French Government. The ship arrived in Israel at the very beginning of a ceasefire that came into force on 11 June 1948 and which proscribed the acquisition of weaponry while it lasted. The arrival of the *Altalena* was an embarrassment to the leaders of the IDF, of which the Irgun had, by then, become an integral part.

It is, of course, possible that that the arms were loaded on board the ship before the truce started. In any event, the ship was abandoned upon arrival in Israel, remaining an eyesore for years to come. My main recollection is of Begin's impassioned speech — broadcast on Radio Israel. Begin complained that his Irgun had been betrayed and that the IDF leaders sacrificed the ship due to their conflict with the Irgun. It is difficult for me to express a definite conclusion about the event. There is no doubt that both Arabs and Jews used the ceasefire period so as to rearm and regroup. I suspect that, without building up its arsenal, the Yishuv's chances were poor. The *Altalena* affair, though, was a blatant breach of the vital ceasefire. It is not surprising that the military leaders of the Yishuv washed their hands of it. The tone of Begin's hate speech has remained fresh in my mind.

An even more disturbing event was the assassination of Count Folke Bernadotte on 17 September 1948 by the Irgun. Bernadotte was commissioned by the United Nations Security Council to mediate between the two sides to the Palestinian conflict. He did come up with a partition plan closer to the stalemate than the original plan sponsored by the Security Council. In the event, the plan was rejected by both Israel and the Arab League. However, to ensure that his plan would not come to fruition, Begin's Irgun ambushed Bernadotte's car and shot him dead.

The moderate faction of the Yishuv condemned this wanton act of terror. Sighs of relief were heaved when the 1948 conflict came to an end at around October 1948.

Whilst the State of Israel has been recognised by the large majority of the international community, new outbreaks of warfare remained on the cards. Regrettably, Israel and its allies objected to the foundation of a Palestinian State. To date, the vacuum left by the British withdrawal has not been properly filled. Although Egypt and Transjordan have signed peace treaties with Israel, Syria and other political entities such as Hezbollah and Hamas are still waging war against Israel.

It is important to consider the consequences of the 1948 conflict. To start with, the departure of the British led to unemployment. In reality, the Navy, Army and Air Force Institutes ("NAAFI") was an excellent employer and counterparty. My Uncle Julius, for instance, lost his major client. In due course, his business had to close down.

In addition, all trade with neighbouring countries ceased. Merchants like my maternal grandfather and my father lost many clients and had, once again, to face the struggle of eking out a living. In the event, my father had to migrate.

Another consequence concerned the Palestinian Arabs. Many fled their homes during the 1948 conflict. The news media sought to convince the Yishuv that the Arabs left by choice. Smilansky Yizhar exposed the fallacy in *Khirbet Khizeh*. I am able to verify his conclusions. Prior to the Independence War, Jaffa was an Arab town. Today, it is a Jewish town as the Arabs had to flee in 1948. Similarly, near Herzlia Pituach was the Arab Village of Sydney Ali (viz. Ali's Fountain). Its inhabitants had to flee in 1948 and their village became a ruin.

All in all, many Arabs fled from their homes to neighbouring countries, ending up in refugee camps. Notwithstanding all its effort, the United Nations has been unable to solve this human problem. Notably, the neighbouring countries, such as Transjordan and Egypt, were unwilling to take the refugees in.

Israel, too, faced serious economic and financial problems. Its currency had to be devalued, and before long, the Yishuv experienced food shortages. The government was forced to introduce a rationing system — the Tzena (צנע). At one stage, even toilet rolls were rationed! As could have been expected, a black market emerged and thrived.

Another problem arose from the mass migration to Israel from Europe and the Orient. To teach the migrants Hebrew, the government founded the *Ulpanim*: adult schools which conducted crash courses in Hebrew. It is believed that the success rate was only approximately 50%. In consequence, the standard of spoken Hebrew deteriorated as did Hebrew grammar and style.

The compensation for these setbacks was that after two thousand years as a Diaspora nation, the Jews acquired a home governed by themselves. Only time will tell whether this home is transient or permanent.

In my next letter, I propose to tell you more about the early years of Israel. They coincided with my last two years in Tichon.

In the meantime, all the best.

As ever,
Peter

10 November 2017
Singapore

Dear Friends,

Letter 8: Israel — The Early Years

It is now time to turn to my experiences during Israel's early years. By and large, my own life proceeded on an even keel. I continued to study at Tichon. In the third year, the form split into two streams: the scientific and the humanist. I opted for the latter as it coincided with my intellectual outlook, temperament and interests. Philosophy was one of the optional subjects in which I enrolled. It was a good choice, although I benefitted far more from reading prescribed texts than from the teacher's lectures. Another course I opted for was *Talmud*. We dealt mainly with the *Mishna* (משנה) which is the first part of the *Talmud* and written in Hebrew. We also covered isolated sections from the *Gemara* (גמרא) — the later part of the *Talmud*, written in Aramaic. Notably, the *Mishna* was written in Javneh, in Judea; the *Gemara* was composed principally in the Persian Diaspora.

The main geopolitical event that happened during the period was the mass ascent (עליה) to the newly founded Israel. Many migrated from post-WWII Europe. In addition, Operation Magic Carpet enabled Jews from Iraq (with the support of the then Iraqi Prime Minister,

Nuri al-Said), Yemen and Morocco to come over to Israel. Initially, many were housed in *Ma'abarot* (temporary dwellings or huts [מעברות]). The ascent from the Muslim world was timely because anti-Semitism grew in the wake of the Independence War. For instance, pogroms broke out in Yemen in 1948.

One undesirable effect of the mass migration was that the Yishuv became divided on an ethnic basis. The migrants from European countries felt superior to the migrating Oriental Jews. It was not a division I had sensed before the foundation of Israel. To my way of thinking, it came close to a separation or segregation based on racial grounds. It was, therefore, undesirable.

The majority of the Occidental (Ashkenazi) Jews had their origin in Eastern Europe (mainly Poland and Russia). Within this group, Central European Jews — originating in Germany and Austria and dubbed Yekes (יקה: יהודי קשה הבנה — Jew of Poor Understanding) remained a small minority. Still, in my opinion, their presence was of major importance. They adhered to the humanist values of the Enlightenment.

By 1950, the mass ascent had reached its peak. I have no doubts that new *Olims* (ascenders: עולים) had to face a grim economic reality. I recall the flea markets, in which many European *Olims* sold items brought by them from home. Some of the antiques acquired by me in these markets still grace my collection.

Many young migrants were conscripted to the Israeli Army. Actually, the law compelling army service applied across the board. As from the end of 1948, every male secondary school leaver had to serve a period as a conscript. I was one of the few who were exempt for reasons of health. In general, until they reached a certain personal age, all males became part of a national militia, ready to defend the state in the event of new outbreaks of hostilities. Whilst initially conscription applied only to males, it was in due course extended to females.

Orthodox Jews were, however, exempt from army service. The excuse given for this exemption was based on their being conscientious objectors. The real reason was political. Although Mapai (Israel's Labor Party) was the biggest political party, it failed to attain an absolute majority in parliament. The Orthodox parties were needed as partners to the coalition and hence could dictate many terms.

I doubt if army service changed the personal orientation of individuals. The life philosophy of most of my friends remained intact. Like me, they were secular. Undoubtedly, they were being subjected to a strict military discipline. They were taught to obey orders. But they did not lose their original inclinations, involving the doubting of conventional wisdom.

Regrettably, the advent of the military service had an undesirable effect on the Yishuv in general. Traditionally, the Jews were regarded as the 'nation of the book'. They enjoyed a higher rate of literacy than the majority of the population in the countries in which they had settled. Jewish children were brought up according to the established traditions and, in addition, had a sound grasp of basic mathematics and of spelling and grammar of their native tongue. With the victory in 1948, the traditional values of learning and meditation were replaced by a cult of militarism. In a sense, prowess was put on a pedestal. Learning and the development of the intellect were placed on the back burner.

I sensed this change during my last two years in Tichon. Boys and girls who used to boast about fine performances in school or at recitals were now singing the praise of military attainments. Publishers, who used to thrive on translations of French and English classics, were publishing translations of second-rate Russian wartime books. In an attempt to revert to our traditional values of intellectual excellence, I published in our form's biannual periodical a book review of Remarque's *All Quiet on the Western Front*, decrying the oppression and perversion of wars and military service. A few weeks after publication, Mr Ben Zvi had a chat with me:

"So you go against the tide, Alyosha," he observed, using a pet name he had bestowed on me.

"In what way, Sir?"

"Here we have founded a new state. We need our army and have to praise its valour. And here are you: preaching pacifism!"

"But surely, war and military attainment are means. My fear is that they are becoming the end."

"For the time being," he replied, "this may be a necessity. We cannot afford to dilute our people's courage and willingness to sacrifice their lives for a cause."

He believed in what he had said. All the same, his words fell on deaf ears. The memory of WWII, and the horrors of the warfare involved, had remained fresh in my mind. The idea of new forms of militarism appeared to me objectionable.

At about the same time, my life philosophy firmed, for the time being, on matters religious. Here the catalyst was Jean-Paul Sartre's *Existentialism and Humanism* (1946), which convinced me that 'existence' need not be investigated. It was a state in which we found ourselves, and, hence, there was no need to explain it. The attempt by religions to substantiate it on the basis of creation by a God was, accordingly, misguided.

As I write down these memoirs, I feel the need to concede that, over the years, my life philosophy has undergone a subtle change. Reading Sartre directed me towards pure atheism. Over the years, agnosticism became more comfortable. It enabled me to keep a foot in the Jewish door but did not turn me into a traditionalist.

My negative perception of the emerging policies of Israel and of religion in general gained momentum when I joined a small party, which called itself the Canaanites (כנענים). Founded by Yonatan Ratosh, the ideology of the party was to encourage the Yishuv and the Israelis to adapt themselves to the Muslim world surrounding us after the foundation of the state. Our main objective was to distance ourselves from the 19th century ideology of the Zionist world and to come closer to our Palestinian neighbours: the heirs to the ancient Canaanite cultures of the Levant. We also emphasised that during the period covered in the Old Testament, the people of both the Northern Kingdom and of Juda were polytheistic and religiously tolerant. According to the prophets, many worshipped the Canaanite Ba'al.

As from 1948, the Canaanites published a quarterly called *Alef*: the first letter of the Hebrew alphabet. Quite a few of us contributed articles to it. Regrettably, the ideas of a group of intellectuals were dismissed as irrelevant. To date, though, I believe that our approach was sound. Regrettably, our proposals were preached too late, that is, after the policy and outlook of Israel had been determined.

By the time I rose to my third, penultimate, year in Tichon, I had become an active member of the Canaanites. My home became the meeting place of a small section of the party. I also expounded our doctrines in school and in Yahad (the new name of Ha'Boneh). However, I made very few converts. The Canaanites remained an elitist organisation, which failed to strike a chord in the hearts of traditionally inclined people.

I had greater (unintended) success in encouraging a number of my colleagues to opt for a legal career. My first encounter with the law took place at the end of my second year in Tichon. All of us had to sit for examinations in algebra and geometry, conducted by the Council for Education. The hall in which these exams were conducted was near the building of the Courts of Law. During the lunch break, I sneaked into one of the courtrooms and watched a criminal trial.

The accused were prosecuted for the illegal import of refrigerators to Israel. I was impressed with the manner in which the defence counsel, Israel Bar-Shira, conducted the case. His searching cross-examination of the prosecution's witnesses established that the accused were not hardened criminals but respectable businessmen, whose offence involved a technical breach of recent legislation which they had not fully understood. They were convicted but the judge imposed a nominal penalty.

I started to frequent the courts. In particular, I went to watch Israel Bar-Shira's appearances. Frequently, Bar-Shira appeared for the defendants in industrial accidents and motor car accidents. Later on, when employed by him, I discovered that he was regularly commissioned to appear in cases in which a well-established insurance company had a commercial interest.

My visits intensified during my third year in Tichon. Frequently, the humanist stream finished its classes by about 11.00 o'clock. I used to sneak out before the class ended and rush over to the Courts of Law. Two of my friends accompanied me. They too found the law intriguing. After a while, both the judges and Bar-Shira came to regard us as part of the furniture.

After one of my visits, when I went for lunch at the Court's cafeteria, Bar-Shira came over to my table and asked what interested me about the cases I came to see. He nodded when I told him I found his technique of breaking a witness intriguing. Occasionally, I thought he anticipated the answer he forced out of the witness in cross-examination. He explained that he never asked a question unless he had ascertained the facts ahead of time. His impressive performance was the result of detailed and meticulous research by his team. Often, the preparatory work was mundane as, indeed, was a great deal of a lawyer's work. The drafting of companies' resolutions, of standard contracts and of preparing mortgages involving title tracing were lucrative work, or, he grinned, the lawyers' bread and butter. What I saw in the courts was the glamorous side of the law. He concluded by saying that, if I ever decided to opt for a career in the law, I should feel free to go and see him.

I knew that my mother wanted me to become a physician. However, I sensed that my hypochondria and the fear of disease and of blood rendered me unsuitable for such a career. My real dream was to major in archaeology but, again, I sensed that my constitution was too weak for the arduous work often involved. In the event, I discussed my plans with my two companions. They urged me to enroll in a law course and, to my surprise, opted for it themselves.

None of us had any reason to regret his choice. One of us developed a thriving practice dealing with claims involving insurance companies. His twin brother joined the government's legal department and, in due course, became the Attorney General of the District of Tel Aviv. I ended up as a law teacher, specialising in international trade transactions. Today, when recounting my memories, I am surprised by the extent that fate often drove me in a given direction. Had the examinations been conducted in another place, I might not have strayed to the courts; and I might have ended up as an unsatisfactory and unfulfilled medical practitioner in Tel Aviv.

My last two years in Tichon were in effect the days of personal orientation. My political views had by then crystallised. I was and have remained a Canaanite with strong pacifist tendencies. In addition, I had identified my vocation. Mother was, of course, disappointed but did not try to influence me. Father approved. He knew I did not have the making of a physician.

The early years of Israel did also affect the professional lives of my father and maternal grandfather. Jacob Feuer had built up a modest but reasonably successful import business, dealing mainly in exotic goods. Most of his suppliers were located in the Arab countries which had severed their relations with Israel. For a while, he struggled on but his business kept declining. As early as 1950, he moved back to Vienna, with the hope of re-establishing his former business. His design was realistic because after the end of WWII, in 1945, Austria actually encouraged those who had fled from the Nazis to return to their pre-war homes. I believe my grandfather was reasonably successful after he moved back.

Father was in a similar position. As from about 1947, he started to spend months in Italy, seeking to launch a new export and import agency. However, he returned to us in Tel Aviv regularly. Still, it became clear that, in Israel, he had no future. Mother, though, was opposed to a move away from our newly found home. Father, too, had his reservations about leaving Israel. Vienna was still divided into four zones (impressively depicted in *The Third Man*), with a general fear that the Soviets would attempt to install a puppet regime to control a major part of Austria. Father was loath to return to a divided Vienna. He traded mainly from Bologna. Mother and I remained in Tel Aviv.

It is difficult for me to explain why Mother and I stayed put. All in all, Mother wanted me to complete my education in Israel. Further, all her friends were members of Yahad. In a sense, she did not want to experience yet a further uprooting.

She was active in business, keeping the remnant of Grandfather Feuer's enterprise going and dealing in stamps and gold coins. Life was not easy for her. However, sparks of her early Zionist orientation remained intact. I do believe that she had come to regard Israel as her home. I, too, could not envisage life in any other place.

The position underwent a subtle change when Grandmother Feuer passed away in Vienna. Mother flew over to hold Grandfather's hand and, in the event, took him back to Tel Aviv. He had retained his flat, but his Israeli business was practically gone. The once successful businessman and high calibre entrepreneur now had to live on his savings. I recall visiting him from time to time and taking him for walks. He had by then become a broken old man. Before long, he suffered a stroke and passed away. His funeral was sparsely attended; and, for the first time in my life, I saw Mother cry.

At about the same time, the Soviet Union withdrew from Vienna. I am aware that officially the Soviets left Austria in 1955, but the negotiations and preliminary discussions started earlier on. Father's Italian clients pressed him to return to Vienna and I suspect he had had a hidden wish to return to his original hometown right from the foundation of Israel. In 1953, he started to frequent Vienna and laid the base for his resettlement. He still stayed in pensions, but, at around 1955, purchased a studio flat from a friend. I believe the die had been cast. In 1956, he renewed his Austrian citizenship. Mother remained in Tel Aviv. I was at that time enrolled in the law course at the Hebrew University and was employed as a cadet by Bar-Shira.

Before returning to my odyssey, I consider it important to sum up in this letter the political climate and policy which had emerged in Israel. It will be recalled that the Zionist Movement preached equality and social unity. David Ben-Gurion's party — Mapai — embraced the same orientation. In consequence, it discouraged private enterprises and attempted to control all substantial business enterprises. I recall they often demanded to have a share in any promising deal and — even in the case of modest enterprises — sought to instill government nominees in well-developed private sector firms.

I recall, for instance, that when Mother secured a lucrative contract for business with a South American entity, the government insisted that she share the venture with a Mapai nominee. Mother declined. She was thereupon refused the required import licenses. In the event, the project fell through.

Another change was of a demographic nature. The new *Olim* from Europe tended to support the centre parties. They were not attuned to Zionism or socialism. In consequence, I noted a move away from the leftist parties (including Mapai) towards the capitalist or centrist parties. I am convinced that the notion of sharing alike was alien to the European *Olim*.

I am less certain about the orientation of the migrants from the Orient. I am satisfied that the European Zionist Movement was not within their horizon. The political systems they knew were all based on materialistic and capitalist thinking. Further, they were strongly inclined to hero-worship a leader. David Ben-Gurion had the requisite charisma. His successors paled in comparison.

Despite the negative trends I have noted, Ben-Gurion's government achieved its proclaimed objectives. Under his leadership, the Yishuv, which constituted a minority of the population of mandated Palestine, turned itself into a sovereign state which welcomed the ascent of Jews from all over the world. For the first time in two thousand years — as from the destruction of Jerusalem by Flavius Vespasian and his son Titus (71 CE) — the Jews had an independent land of their own.

Although I have migrated and am now living in Singapore, I continue to feel a distinct allegiance to the country in which I grew up and obtained my primary, secondary and tertiary education.

I have already recounted my memories of my education and growing up in Israel. My next letter will turn to my remaining years in Israel.

In the meantime, all the best.

As ever,
Peter

15 November 2017
Singapore

Dear Friends,

Letter 9: The Hebrew University — A Legal Cadet

When I finished my studies in Tichon, I enrolled in the Law Faculty of the Hebrew University. Although the University of Tel Aviv had already been founded, the only law school was in Jerusalem. I matriculated in June and the semester in the university was not going to commence until September. Mother thereupon suggested that I enrol in a course in the Pitman School of Secretaries. I liked the idea and went ahead.

The course at Pitman was useful for the organisation of an office. I learned how to open files and organise a filing system. In a period in which computers and the network were still unknown, this enabled me to come to grips with the basics of office running. In addition, I became a touch-typist, which meant that I could transcribe texts to the typewriter without looking at the keyboard. In an era in which word processing was still unknown, this was a major gain.

Another advantage was my first meeting with David Sassoon (Sasske). David's family was patrician. Members of it became leading merchants in Iraq, India and Singapore. They also had close ties with Oxford. The poet Siegfried Sassoon was amongst their kin.

Sasske and I became close friends. When I discussed the Canaanite doctrines with him, I soon realised that I was preaching to the converted. Before long, he started to frequent our flat and I became a regular visitor to his place. His house, incidentally, had an English upper-class milieu, instilled by his late mother who was an English Jewess.

As we enrolled in the same faculty, we often went out together during the term. Like me, Sasske was an ardent patron of chamber music and of amateur theatre performances. We remained in close contact until his unexpected demise, many years later, from lung cancer caused by chain-smoking. Until that sad moment, his career was a set of staggering achievements. He went from strength to strength both as a diplomat, as a member of the World Bank and, finally, as an independent entrepreneur.

Before I turn to my days in Jerusalem, I consider it important to discuss life in Tel Aviv and in Israel in general. It is possible that during its early years the Yishuv was a cultural backyard. However, with the mass ascent of migrants from Eastern and Central Europe, it was joined by many artists, musicians and actors of Jewish origin. Thus, the philharmonic orchestra was founded in 1936. Even before the foundation of Israel, we were visited by celebrities such as Bronislaw Huberman, Leonard Bernstein, Zino Francescatti and Arthur Rubinstein.

Tel Aviv had three major theatres and two minor ones. The shows I saw included *Othello*, *Peer Gynt* and *Death of a Salesman*. Amateur ensembles performed pieces like *The Good Person of Szechwan* and *Mourning Becomes Electra*. I had a particular liking for *The Broomstick* (המטאטא), a satirical theatre which lampooned politicians and questionable events. Even at the time of writing, I am able to chant some of the doggerels from its repertoires.

All performances I attended were in Hebrew. There was, however, a Yiddish-speaking theatre, founded during the early years of Israel. Friends of mine attended some shows and came up with favourable reports. Regrettably, people like my parents, who did not speak Yiddish and never mastered Hebrew, had to be satisfied with the cinema. French and Italian films were common. I recall watching *Les Vacances de Monsieur Hulot* and *The Wages of Fear*. Some German films were also shown. One of them was *Fuhrmann (Drayman) Henschel.*

Earlier on, I have noted the general deterioration in the standard of Hebrew. Nevertheless, a new, genuine Israeli literature was emerging. Over the years, it became inspiring even if inward-looking.

Socially, life at the Hebrew University was lively. I met quite a number of interesting people and participated in activities initiated by clubs and by students' organisations. I recall vividly how, on one occasion, we marched through the streets of a well-to-do suburb. One of our fair colleagues rode a donkey and carried a poster reading (in Hebrew): "Respectable Burghers — join us." I believe that not many did! One elderly gentleman got excited, shook his fist at us and yelled that we were "bloody communists". His matronly wife tried to calm him down.

Although the drive from Tel Aviv to Jerusalem took only one hour, I thought it advisable to find a room in a district near our lecture theatres. In those days East Jerusalem — the exciting Old City — was still in the hands of the Arabs so the Mount Scopus Campus was out of bounds. The Law Faculty conducted most of its lectures in the Ratisbon Hall, rented from a Christian foundation.

At the beginning, I attended lectures scrupulously. After a while, I discovered that most of our lecturers were either dull or ill-prepared. They were not as accomplished as my good teachers in Tichon. Further, they did not hand out reading lists and did not conduct tutorials. The process of self-education in Tichon, where you had to prepare yourself for classes, was actually more advanced.

I recall with amusement one incident concerning our lecturer on maritime law. As was the custom, a list of the candidates sitting for the examination was displayed on the notice board. One wag added the name of the lecturer at the end of the list and allocated him a seat.

One interesting lecturer was our professor of public international law. For reasons best known to him, he spent half the term on disarmament. A problem arose because in Hebrew, 'disarmament' is a phrase comprising two words: (i) dismantling of (ii) arms. The classic word for 'arms' — *zayin* (זין) — is slang for a penis. It is hard to know if the worthy professor was aware of the dual meaning of his phraseology; but word of his performance spread throughout the campus. Unsurprisingly, his lecture room was packed. I recall that one young married girl asked him if the *zayin* ought to be dismantled when used too often. The professor opined that this was indeed the case. He looked pleased when all present broke into peals of laughter.

A special problem arose from the complexity of the Israeli law of contract. When the British conquered Palestine, they left the law intact but provided that if there was any void (lacuna), the judge was to fill it by applying English law. The Turkish law was the *Mejelleh* — a codification loosely based on outdated Turkish writings and divided into categories, such as an agency contract, a contract of employment and a contract of sale. All provisions were augmented by illustrations. Thus, a contract of employment was frustrated (vacated) if the employee was no longer able to perform. One of the illustrations was the case of a wet nurse who ceased to produce milk. Needless to say, this illustration was cited whenever a litigator had the chance to refer to it.

The difficulty in mastering this complex branch of law was exacerbated because the lecturer was trained in civil law. Both the *Mejelleh* and English law were outside the scope of his expertise. I had to relearn the law of contract during my years in practice.

Another issue often arose from the fact that the *Mejelleh* was written in Turkish. As no lawyer in Tel Aviv had a command of this language, there were endless arguments about reconciling diverse translations. It remained in force during my years of studies in Jerusalem and practice in Tel Aviv. To obviate the application of this complex law, most contracts included a clause stating that they were to be governed by English law. I drafted some of these clauses when I became Bar-Shira's employee. I gather that all this antiquated law was repealed and replaced.

In sheer contrast to the unsatisfactory tuition I received in most courses, we had two excellent teachers. Zerach Warhaftig conducted an impressive course on *Talmud*. Although we covered only three stanzas of the *Gemara*, we went through them in great detail and analysed each argument. One of the tools used in the *Talmud* is the *a fortiori* (קל וחומר) argument. Another is analogy (מידה שווה). I recall how, on one occasion, I tried to convince our teacher that a given conclusion could be reached just as readily by employing the latter as by the traditional use of the former. In the event, he tore my argument to shreds. His fine analysis has remained fresh in my mind.

The second excellent course was Professor Hugo Bergmann's Logics. Later in life, I used many of the equations and rationalisations taught by him to work out complex points of law. I remain indebted to him to the present day.

There were some other satisfactory courses. I recall how Sasske and I crammed together in the hope of mastering conflict of laws (private international law) taught by the impressive Professor Levontin. We managed to secure good marks, but I failed to come to grips with the intricacies of the subject until my later years of practice.

The real setback in my years of study at the university was the harsh climate of Jerusalem. Occasionally, you experienced all four seasons of the year in a single day. In consequence, my asthma attacks became severe. On two occasions, I had to take a train back to Tel Aviv so as to regain my equilibrium.

This unsatisfactory state of health as well as the lonesomeness resulting from my being away from home induced me to find a compromise. Having worked out that I could pass the examinations by relying on lecture notes of friends, I decided to pay a visit to Bar-Shira. To my delight, he accepted me as a cadet. Before long, I spent most of my time in his firm and went up to Jerusalem only about once a fortnight.

My first task in Bar-Shira's firm was to update subsidiary legislation. In those remote days, amendments to subsidiary legislation were usually made by a new piece of sub-legislation. To remain up to date, you had to add to the original piece of legislation a note referring to every amendment. Today — some seventy years later — the amended piece of legislation is usually reprinted with all the amendments; but this modernised approach was unknown during my days of practice in Israel.

Before long, Bar-Shira gave me more difficult tasks, such as writing opinions on intricate points of law arising in cases handled by our firm. It was the type of work I enjoyed. The skills I acquired in my study of

Talmud and Logic became useful. By the end of my first year in his firm, I acquired the reputation of a troubleshooter.

One of Bar-Shira's employees was an ageing German Jew who dealt mainly with mortgages. As the then existing Turkish law made no provision for securities, Dr. Goldberg had to vest the title to the mortgaged property in the lender, who resold it to the true mortgagor under an installments sale. Naturally, the periodic payments comprised capital as well as the interest on the loan. The law was reformed by the introduction of a system similar to the Torrens law and another law sanctioning the construction of condominiums and the introduction of strata titles.

By and large, I settled well into Bar-Shira's office. The long hours of work — from about 8.30 a.m. to 8.00 p.m. — did not trouble me. My asthma, though, was getting worse during this period. After the preparation of one particularly difficult case, which required me to spend many hours at work, my chest could not take it any longer. My hissing breath and appalling pallor told their story. In plain language, my lungs succumbed, and I had to be hospitalised.

Donolo Hospital was on the outskirts of Jaffa. The Head of the ward, Dr. Brunner, a well-known consultant of internal medicine, decided to make a last effort to break the hold of my asthma. By then, antibiotics and cortisone had become available, but their administration had to be carried out under medical supervision.

Initially, all went well. Then, during a cold spell, I caught a chill. Late one night, I experienced an attack of breathlessness. Dr. Bruner was unavailable. Mahmood Diab, the male nurse in charge of the ward, sat by my side during my struggle. Postponing the administration of an injection, which would have brought instant relief, he insisted I should try to combat the attack on my own. He explained that, if I shook off the ensuing panic, the spell of breathlessness would come under control.

In the event, it worked. When the asthma attack was over, I smiled at him gratefully. He smiled back with patent relief. I then noticed that his hand, which I had grasped throughout my ordeal, was swollen.

Mahmood Diab became a close friend. After my discharge from the hospital, we went out regularly for lunch, dinner or a show. Then one day, Mahmood called on me unexpectedly. I knew something was on his mind but thought it best not to probe until after dinner. I was about to proceed when Mahmood came to the point without any prompting on my part. In a shaky voice, he told me about certain strong-arm tactics that had been committed by the Israeli army in an Arab village (Tayibe). Apparently, the village had been transferred to Israel during the cease fire agreement with Jordan in 1949. Later on, some Palestinian escapees demanded that their properties in the village be restored to them. The inhabitants had, however, been declared 'absentees' and their land had been confiscated under the Law of Acquisition of Absentee Property, enacted in 1950, but with retrospective effect. The inhabitants' attempts to recover the land were forcefully resisted. I had heard some rumours about the incident but had made an effort to disbelieve my ears. Having listened to Mahmood without interruption, I experienced a deep, biting, sense of shame. Was Israel's policy of confiscating 'absentee' land akin to the confiscation of Jewish property during the Holocaust?

"Eli," asked Mahmood, using my Hebrew name, "what are your politicians trying to do? Israel's only hope of survival is to come to terms with us. And the people who demanded the return of their land were not enemies or terrorists. They were peaceful *Falachim* (Arabic for farmers): they demanded the use of their land; all they wanted was to live and let live!"

Mahmood's narration cemented our friendship. I realised he would not have referred to the sordid episode unless he had full trust in the listener's discretion. He knew also that he could count on my empathy.

Regrettably, Mahmood had to leave Donolo. He fell in love with an Israeli nurse. When her brother, who served in the Military Police, found out, he had Mahmood beaten up. A transfer to a hospital in Haifa was Mahmood's best way out. For a while, he remained in Haifa but, eventually, crossed to a neighbouring country. I do not know what became of him.

The period spent in Donolo and my recuperation had an undesirable effect on my course. By the time I had recovered, most of the examinations I had to take were over. In consequence, I had to take an extra year in order to finish my law course. Bar-Shira was good to me. He simply extended my period as a cadet.

In the course of the following year, I prepared two difficult cases for hearing. Another lawyer, Hannah, worked on the cases with me. We often went out together, occasionally to dinner or supper and, on other occasions, to the cinema or the theatre. In the event, Bar-Shira won both cases; Hannah appeared as his junior and conducted some cross-examinations.

My work with Dr. Goldberg entailed many visits to the Registrar of Land and to other administrative bodies. Before long, I started to appreciate the legacy left by the British. Israel's system of courts, as well as the administrative machinery as a whole, followed systems used in British protectorates. We had also inherited the common law system. During my years in Bar-Shira's firm, I realised that, all in all, the British had been good and orderly colonisers. I do believe that even at the time of writing, Israel continues to adhere to many social and political values introduced during the period of the Mandate. Notably, although appeals to the Privy Council were abolished in 1948, British judgments continue to have a strong persuasive standing in the Israeli courts.

During my years in Bar-Shira's firm, Israel was rocked by what was effectively a political trial. Rudolf Kastner was one of the leaders of the Hungarian Aid and Rescue Committee, which had sought to save Jews from deportations to the Nazi extermination camps. Kastner negotiated with leading Nazis and, in the event, succeeded in saving the lives of some Hungarian Jews by paying large amounts of money to the Nazis involved and also by luring other prospective victims into thinking that they too were to be saved. Many of them boarded the train to the slaughter camps in the belief that they were going to be dispatched to Switzerland.

After the end of WWII, Kastner moved to Israel and became a spokesman of the Ministry of Trade and Industry. In 1953, Malchiel Gruenwald, a freelance writer, published a pamphlet accusing Kastner of having collaborated with the Nazis. An action of criminal libel instituted against Gruenwald by the Attorney General was dismissed by Justice Benjamin Halevy. In a highly emotive judgment, he found that Kastner had indeed been a Nazi collaborator as asserted by Gruenwald and described Kastner as having sold his soul to the devil.

Thereafter, Kastner was shunned in Israel. He became a recluse while awaiting the outcome of an appeal against Halevy's judgment. In 1957 — my very last year as a student — Kastner was murdered by three extremists. I was horrified to discover that Ze'evik Eckstein, the very fellow who pulled the trigger, had been one of my friends in primary school.

A year later, Halevy's judgment was overturned on most counts by a majority of the Supreme Court. I compared the detached and judicially sound decisions of the members of the Supreme Court with Halevy's outburst. I concluded that Halevy did not have an appropriate judicial temperament. In point of fact, his tirade in the Kastner trial was not his first immoderate decision. I was taken aback when some ten years later, he was elevated to the Supreme Court.

I believe that Israel has remained divided on the issues involved. Notably, the assassins were released after serving part of their sentence. I gather that Ze'evik became a respected businessman. I recall him as a highly temperamental, perhaps even unbalanced, boy.

Later, in 1958, a few months after the Kastner tragedy, I stayed in Jerusalem for the examinations period. I had no difficulty with the papers. Whilst we were waiting for the results, I took a short cruise to Turkey. The ship proceeded through Anatolia to Istanbul. I went ashore as often as possible. As we toured Iskenderun, I saw, for the first time in my life, women in *Purdah*. I realised that the Palestinian girls I had met were far more liberated than the women in the Anatolian backwater.

An amusing incident took place in Izmir. The taxi that drove us to the mountain peak descended back to town in a strangely tortuous manner. When I asked the driver, in German, what was the problem, he explained that his brakes did not function. It seemed best not to explain to my fellow tourists what was taking place. I was relieved when we arrived safely back at the pier.

On arriving in Istanbul, I took in the crowd waiting for passengers. To my pleasant surprise, I spotted my father. I had not expected his arrival and was thrilled to see him: I had loved him dearly all my life. It turned out that Mother had written to him about my cruise and urged him to come over from Vienna and spend a few days with me. Father and I had a pleasant time together. I recall our visit to the Porcelain Museum, to St. Sophia and to the Blue Mosque. We also went, in the company of Turkish friends I had made on the cruise, to excellent restaurants.

After a few days in Istanbul, I sensed that Israel was doing well in terms of culture and sophistication. We went to a performance of the local philharmonic orchestra and actually found it unsatisfactory. The Israeli orchestra was, indeed, of a different standard. It was good to realise that the pioneering spirit of the Yishuv and of the newly founded Israel led us in the direction of becoming a first-world country.

Back in Israel, I was pleased to find that my examination results were satisfactory. Thereafter, my status in Bar-Shira's firm was changed from that of a cadet to a 'pupil'. My work, though, remained basically the same.

During that period, my erstwhile pleasant relationship with my employer started to deteriorate. The main reason for this concerned our office's administration. In 1956, the manual typewriter was still the tool of trade. If a document had to be typed in more than one copy, the typist had to use carbon paper. Most of our typists could produce only four copies at a time. If more copies were required, the document had to be typed twice.

Photocopiers had not arrived and so, occasionally, a document had to be taken to a photographer. Precedents were usually incised on stencils: sheets of wax-covered folio papers. The typist had to type (incise) on them by removing the ribbon from the typewriter and typing — or rather, 'cutting' — the text into the stencil. The final product could be rolled on a machine and, in this way, produce as many as eighty copies.

The one typist in our office who could produce eight copies in one go typed only documents to be signed by Bar-Shira. The rest of us had to write our documents out by hand, send them to the typing pool and then wait for them to be typed. Senior Associates often demanded priority. In consequence, 'pupils' had occasionally to wait for two or three days for a document to be typed. After a while, I used the skill I had acquired in the Pitman School, typed my own documents and occasionally 'cut' stencils so as to compose 'precedents' required for my work with Dr. Goldberg. As I firmly refused to type documents needed by others, some started to write negative reports about my performance as a pupil. Occasionally, Bar-Shira listened. In due course, he formed the impression that I could be uncooperative.

At the end of my period as 'pupil', I was called to the Bar (on 3 December 1958). Shortly thereafter, I had a frank chat with Bar-Shira. In the event, I left his firm and started my own practice. Initially, I worked at home. Later on, I managed to secure premises in town.

I shall be discussing my experience in private practice in my next letter. But before I turn to it, I have decided to recount the most important political event of the period, namely the Suez Canal Crisis.

Until I am ready to post my next letter, all the best.

As ever,
Peter

27 November 2017
Singapore

Dear Friends,

Letter 10: Nasser and the Suez Crisis

It is time to discuss the interesting developments in the Middle East during the years of my university studies and my employment by Israel Bar-Shira. These years coincided with the meteoric rise of Gamal Abdel Nasser.

In 1952, Nasser deposed King Farouk, who was effectively a British puppet, and became the ruler of Egypt. Although Egypt had never been ruled from London, it was of great economic value to Britain as a trading post. The Suez Canal, in particular, brought healthy revenues to the holding company's shareholders, which were principally English and French entities. Notably, some British troops were still stationed in the Canal zone.

Initially, Nasser used a senior statesman, known as Naguib, as a camouflage. In due course, he assumed the political leadership openly. Nasser's principal reforms involved the abolition of an outdated feudal system as well as reforms of land law. In 1954, Nasser and Israel had some confidential talks about peace. Notably, the Minister of State in

Nasser's government was Anwar Sadat, who decided to enter into a peace treaty with Israel years later. Regrettably, the 1954 negotiations were unsuccessful: Neither side would budge.

I pause to add that David Ben-Gurion (born in 1886), who still held the reins in Israel, was past his prime and had become inflexible, and that the then Prime Minister, Moshe Sharett, was not renowned for his intelligence. Further, the shameful Lavon Affair, in which Israel sought to plant bombs in Cairo with the view of shifting the blame to political organisations in Egypt (such as the Muslim brotherhood or the communists), led to increasing distrust and tension between Nasser and the Israeli leadership.

In 1955, Indonesia held an International Conference of Asian and African countries in Bandung. Nasser attended and made stops in India, Pakistan and Afghanistan on his way there. In the course of the Conference, Nasser emerged as the spokesman of the Arab world as a whole. At his instigation, the Conference passed a resolution calling on Israel to repatriate Palestinians who had fled during the 1948 War of Independence. In effect, the resolution affirmed earlier ones made by the United Nations Assembly.

In the succeeding years, Nasser entered into treaties with some countries in the Arab world and, eventually, managed to form a United Arab Republic comprising both Egypt and Syria. His manoeuvres posed a serious security threat to Israel, who was now facing a joint enemy on its northern and southern borders. Further, King Hussein of Transjordan — the threat from the East — had a friendly relationship with Nasser.

Emboldened by the progress he had been making, Nasser nationalised the Suez Canal in 1956. Thereupon, France and Britain entered into a secret agreement with Israel. They bombed Port Said with a view to taking command of the Canal. Israel invaded the Sinai Peninsula, which had been under Egyptian suzerainty, and Israeli forces reached the northern bank of the Canal. Nasser thereupon sank ships which were about to enter the Canal, rendering it impassable.

Order was restored by the intervention of the Eisenhower (United States) administration. The end result was that the nationalisation of the Suez Canal was internationally recognised. For the time being, though, the Canal remained impassable. In due course, after Nasser's demise, the route was opened again to international shipping.

The closure of the Canal did not affect Israel. About 90% of its oil was delivered at the Port of Aquaba (Eilat) from ships navigating through the Straits of Tiran — a narrow channel at the tip of the Red Sea separating Egypt from Saudi Arabia. When Nasser threatened to close the Straits to ships bound for Israel, he was told that such an act would constitute a *casus belli*.

In hindsight, I am satisfied that Israel's decision to cooperate with Britain and France was misguided. If Israel had stayed out of the conflict, its image would not have been tarnished by joining two colonial powers against Egypt. Moreover, Israel's cooperation with Britain was inconsistent with the Yishuv's earlier bid for independence and of driving alien masters out of the region.

Israel's military proved its efficacy and strength. All in all, though, the war was of no political value. The Sinai Peninsula was practically neutralised by a force of international observers. All the same, Israel now had to keep a larger mobilised military presence in the area. It gained nothing but helped to unify the Muslim world.

The far-reaching effects of the Suez Crisis influenced my own life in the long run. To a certain extent, they encouraged me, years later, to look for a career overseas. However, at the time the conflict unfolded, it did not have a major impact on my life. As mentioned earlier, I was exempt from army service and hence was not called up. Still, two of my colleagues in Bar-Shira's firm were mobilised. I had to take over some of their work.

Nasser remained a leading figure in the Muslim world until his death in 1970. His main aim throughout was to unite the Arab world under his banner. I have since come to the conclusion that his policy was misguided. Nasser assumed that a united Arab world would stand, whilst if it remained fragmented it was bound to fall. A historical analysis suggests that this is simply not so and that the very opposite is true. The Arab world had been divided for generations, possibly since the repulsion of the Arab advance by Charles Martel at Tours in 732 CE. In the ensuing generations, their world was neatly divided into specific sovereign kingdoms. In effect, as divided they stood; an attempt to unify trod on too many sensitive toes.

No further unification attempt has been made since Nasser's demise. His successor, Anwar Sadat, entered into a peace treaty with Israel, which led to further divisions in the Arab world. Still, Sadat's wise policy achieved more progress for Egypt than Nasser's belligerence.

The Suez Canal crisis took place during my years of employment by Israel Bar-Shira. When I left his firm in 1958 and started to practise on my own, I found the going tough. I had not established a clientele of my own, and, of course, the market for legal advice in Tel Aviv was saturated. Most commercial enterprises used established law firms, which had acquired a sound reputation and standing.

Initially, I practised from home. I handled a few simple matters and, naturally, accepted that my charges had to remain modest. In a sense, my clients received excellent service for modest fees. It dawned on me that when clients engaged well-known firms like Bar-Shira's, the work was often delegated to one of his associates. In reality, they paid an extra charge for obtaining Bar-Shira's signature.

To my utter surprise, work was occasionally referred to me by Bar-Shira, especially in situations where he was 'conflicted' out. I recall one case in which Bar-Shira was asked to handle an industrial accident case, but had to turn down the brief because he was a member of the Board of Directors of the insurance company involved. It was a pleasant experience to go with the clients to his office and negotiate a sound settlement. It was one of the few cases in which I was paid well. Bar-Shira, I suspect, knew and was pleased.

Other briefs were sent to me by Hannah, with whom I had used to prepare cases when both of us were employed by Bar-Shira. She too left his office and became an in-house counsel of the very insurance company that appointed Bar-Shira as a member of its Board. Hannah had good friends in a leading bank and helped to get simple matters, such as debt collection and bouncing cheques, referred to me. Big cases, though, remained out of my reach.

Throughout that entire period, the skills acquired in the Pitman School stood me in good stead. I knew how to open files, how to arrange schedules and how to write short and succinct letters. Further, my takings were not adequate for the employment of a secretary. My touch typing and secretarial skills helped to keep me afloat.

One particularly interesting case was referred to me by a fellow Canaanite, who was asked to advise on the restoration of land to an absentee owner who had originally fled from his village. As my client's papers were in order, he was entitled to compensation under the Law of Acquisition of Absentees' Property of 1950. However, the price of land had doubled by the time he dared raise his claim and so the statutory compensation would not have enabled him to buy suitable land elsewhere.

Initially, the staff-in-charge was unwilling to pay a larger amount. The government refused to return the land to the owner because the entire area was covered by a redevelopment plan. After I threatened to apply for an Order Nisi, which was bound to lead to unwanted publicity, my client was given the chance to present his case.

I recall the meeting, in which I compared my client's position to that of Austrian Jews who were offered a pittance by way of reparation for their Holocaust losses. In the event, the amount paid to my client was doubled. I sensed that my argument — which was in all probability highly emotive — had left an impact.

After some five months in practice, I contemplated teaming up with three other young practitioners with a view to renting a space in town adequate for four separate offices. We also considered engaging a secretary to be employed by the four of us. Fate, though, had other plans for me.

To start with, the bank that kept sending me work was considering expanding its in-house legal team and asked me to join. The salary I was offered was equal to the amount I had expected to earn after two years in practice. Further, the work was well within my grasp and expertise. Difficult cases would, of course, continue to be referred to the bank's panel of established law firms.

I was tempted. To clear my mind, I discussed the offer with Hannah. I have a vivid recollection of our conversation.

"I think you should accept, Eli. The starting salary is OK, and you will rise through the ranks."

"But would I get interesting cases, or will those be sent out?"

"They will be sent out; but the lawyer engaged by the bank would be chosen by you and, more importantly, you would have a chance to look over his shoulder."

"What do you think of my chances as a sole practitioner, Hannah?"

"Frankly speaking, I have my doubts. You can be blunt and ungracious. You may find it difficult to keep clients. Also, Eli, you have the outlook and character of an employee. You are not an entrepreneur. You would like to have a fixed income at the end of every month. I am the same: this is why I went in-house and not to private practice."

This conversation left an impact on me. Mother assessed the situation in the same way. I was about to accept when events took an unexpected turn. It was a direct result of my friend Sasske's victorious return from Oxford.

After finishing his course of studies in the Hebrew University, Sasske had proceeded to Oxford. He had actually finished one year before me and decided to proceed to postgraduate studies before completing his pupilage in Israel. His family's contacts in Oxford had stood him in good stead. After just three months of probation, he was accepted as a D.Phil. candidate. Having finished his doctoral thesis in record time, he returned home, accepted a post in Israel's Foreign Service and, for the time being, remained in its legal department.

I saw him regularly and listened open-eyed to his enthusiastic accounts of Oxford and of London. He told me a great deal about shows he had seen in the West End and in the Sheldonian Theatre and about concerts put up by the Royal Philharmonic Orchestra. He also described his visits to the British Museum and the Barbican. It became clear that he and his wife had thoroughly enjoyed their three years in Oxford.

Another point made by him concerned the advantages of working solidly on a lengthy and well-defined project of your own. He thought this type of work would suit my temperament. His words struck a chord. During my years of employment in Bar-Shira's firm, I blossomed when I had to work out the best approach for handling difficult issues arising in specific cases. On quite a few occasions, I managed to convince my employer to tackle a matter in an unorthodox way.

Yet another relevant experience was the writing of my Masters dissertation, which dealt with the legal nature of a banking facility known as the Letter of Credit. I had enjoyed working on my own and had made a point of dealing with every treatment of the subject. I knew that the production of the final product established the writer's ability to adhere to his point and, where necessary, to depart from the trodden path. Sasske's description of his own work convinced me that it was akin to the writing of a Masters dissertation but had to deal with a subject from a broader perspective.

Sasske was forthcoming with advice respecting admission to Oxford. Before long, his words captivated me. I sensed that a period overseas could lead me to a bigger world I had not explored.

Mother had her doubts about the merits of spending time on postgraduate studies at Oxford. In her opinion, I had established my academic credentials by completing my law course in Jerusalem and by submitting a fine Masters dissertation. In addition, I had done reasonably well in private practice. She thought that a career in the legal department of a bank would be fine.

Father, who was at that time spending a few months in Tel Aviv, took the opposite view. He thought that Oxford might open many doors that would remain shut to a lawyer whose only experience was in Israel. I suspect that Father's real fear was that my existing work experience would turn me into a parochial legal practitioner. He promised to see me through if I decided to proceed to Oxford.

Both Hannah and Bar-Shira agreed with my father. Bar-Shira opined that I was best when tackling a complex issue on my own. He was satisfied that, in due course, I would in any event devote myself to writing treatises. He thought that an overseas qualification would be a better springboard than the M.Jur. conferred by the Hebrew University. Hannah told me that the work overseas might enable me to produce an original piece of writing.

For a while, I was in two minds. Then, to my surprise, I had a call from the bank. It was prepared to keep the offer made to me open for three years if, in the meantime, I had a spell of postgraduate studies overseas. I suspect that Hannah had mentioned to them the possibility of my proceeding to Oxford. This telephone call eliminated my remaining misgivings. It meant that I would have a suitable opening in Israel upon my return from overseas. Further, my trips to Italy and to Turkey had whetted my appetite to see the world. They had also convinced me that Israel was not the only centre of culture and of learning.

I pursued the course proposed by Sasske. I was enrolled in a probationary course leading to admission to a D.Phil (doctorate). My basic objective was to be awarded the degree and then return to Israel with a view to taking up a position with the bank.

In the course of the next few weeks, I settled some pending cases and then handed my few remaining files to a colleague who had also done his pupilage in Bar-Shira's firm. To my delight, Mother, too, came round and supported my plans. She concluded that a postgraduate degree would stand me in good stead and looked forward to my return to Israel and to my joining the bank. Although Father wanted her to join him in Vienna, she decided to stay put.

All that needed to be done was to take my leave from some close friends and associates. Naturally, I went to see Bar-Shira and two of his associates. To my surprise, they encouraged me to consider private practice. Bar-Shira, in particular, thought that a position as an in-house counsel might, in due course, become boring. I also called on two of my teachers in Tichon. Both were pleased to hear that I was contemplating further studies.

About two weeks before my impending departure, I spent an evening with Hannah. When I told her I already had the tickets for the theatre, she insisted on hosting our dinner.

"I am really glad you have decided to take the great leap forward," she told me.

"I'll keep writing to you from Oxford."

"Perhaps not too regularly, Eli. You will be away for at least three years. When you come back, if you do, I shall be close to fifty."

"Will you remarry? Your Tali will by then be of marriageable age."

"She already has a boyfriend; and she will hold on to him."

I looked at her with concern. I knew that Hannah had married young and that she had seen her husband through. He then left her and married a younger woman. He had willingly agreed to Hannah being given custody of their daughter, Tali. I knew also that he had departed from Israel and had severed all contacts with his ex-wife and daughter.

"If I find a suitable widower or divorcee, I may decide to remarry, Eli. A second marriage can be good, provided the spouses are open with one another and do not expect too much."

"I always enjoyed going out with you, Hannah."

"I know; both of us are mid-European Jews. We have the same breeding and cultural heritage. But if you come back, you'll have to find a wife in the correct age group. And I am not sure that you will fall for an Israeli girl!"

"Why do you say this?"

"You are not a typical Israeli, Eli. Your mother has moulded you into a mid-European Diaspora Jew. You may find an Israeli girl too dominant and culturally alien. I won't be surprised if you married an Austrian or English girl."

Hannah's words struck a chord. I knew that, all in all, I might feel more comfortable if I settled overseas. I further knew that keeping in touch with friends and with associates was going to be difficult. The bonus conferred on people with the advent of the email and of inexpensive overseas phone calls came years later. When I planned to proceed to Oxford, communications were still by means of airmail letters. Normally, an exchange of correspondence took at least three weeks. Telegrams and overseas calls were used only in emergencies.

My last call before my departure was a consultation with Dr. Bruner, who had treated me in Donolo Hospital. After listening to my chest and checking my heartbeat, he opined that a spell overseas would be beneficial. He had concluded that although my chronic asthma was a lung disease, it also had psychological components. Whilst settlement in a European or North American country would be unwise, a spell away from home was advantageous. He also observed that chest infections were common in England and so British physicians were familiar with them. Further, medicine was making advances. He hoped that, before long, some pharmaceutical companies would come up with cortisone inhalers and improved antibiotics. He advised me to stay indoors when the weather was increasingly foggy and to avoid contact with people who suffered from chest infections or severe colds. My immunity was poor.

"The asthma is stronger than you," he explained, "so avoid situations which may lead to the onset of an attack. But you must not allow your asthma to affect your life. England does not have a good climate, but I am sure you can come to terms with it."

He ended our session by asking me not to forget Israel. He, himself, would never return to Germany, which had expelled him. I knew he believed in what he said. Generally, some people were prepared to take the road back. Others, like Dr. Bruner, regarded Israel as their new and only home. Still, as I had come to him only in order to obtain medical advice, I was not unduly affected by his political philosophy.

A few weeks later, Mother accompanied me to our airport in Lydda. In my next letter, I propose to tell you all about my trip and my first few months overseas.

Till then, all the best to you.

Yours ever,
Peter

Part II

A YOUNG ACADEMIC

2 December 2017
Singapore

Dear Friends,

Letter 11: Oxford

My first stop was Vienna. I spent a few weeks with Father. We visited the homes of friends who had also returned to Vienna. Loyal Israelis called anybody who went back a 'deserter' (*Yored*: יורד). It did not matter that many a 'deserter' could not make ends meet in Israel and could live comfortably overseas.

I recall watching television in the Viennese home of such 'deserters'. It was a new experience: Israel had no television in those days. I realised that if television channels presented good programmes, or showed films, people might prefer to stay at home and watch them on their screen rather than go out to the cinema.

I also visited the Ferris Wheel, the palaces and the museums. Father and I went to the opera, to theatres and to the fresh-wine evenings (*Heurige*) in Grinzing. I really enjoyed myself. My only surprise was to discover that some flats in Vienna did not have running water; it had to be carried by pails from a common tap, known as the *Bassena*. Most flats of this type were in older buildings constructed in the 19th or early 20th centuries.

My father's generosity enabled me to make stops in Paris and in London. I remember Malmaison, the Louvre and the evenings in Montmartre. I spent days in the Egyptology Department of the British Museum. Naturally, I also went to theatres in the West End and generally saw as much of London as one could in a few weeks. After a visit to the National Portrait Gallery, I spent some time in Trafalgar Square. I had once been told that the famed lions roared if a virgin passed by. Well, they remained silent although many attractive girls were in the crowd.

One grave disappointment was my realisation that although my reading knowledge of English was fine, I had problems with everyday communication. I recall my disappointment when I had difficulties coping with the menu in restaurants and when ordering tickets at cinemas and theatres. One particular surprise took place when I ordered a 'Todd in the Hole'. I had anticipated an exotic dish with frog legs; the sausage roll that arrived was rather ordinary. A Welsh Rarebit was another cause for bewilderment. It soon dawned on me that I had to come to grips with contemporary spoken English. I tried to do so by frequenting pubs and taverns.

After a few weeks in London, I had to travel to my final destination. The train from Paddington to Oxford took about one hour. Having settled the admission procedures of my college, St. Catherine's, I called on the Delegacy of Lodgings, an inter-collegiate body helping newcomers to find diggings. I saw quite a few nice rooms in fashionable Summertown but they were too dear for my purse. After three days of walking around, I found a pleasant room in South Oxford, off Abington Road. As often before, Fortuna was with me. The landlady was a pleasant matron, who lived on her pension plus the rentals on rooms. I only had to pay £2.10 a week for bed and breakfast.

The location of my room had yet a further advantage. There was a bus stop around the corner, which meant that on rainy days I could avoid the 20 minutes walk to the library. I recall with amusement that one dreary morning, when I waited for the bus, my landlady, who was over eighty, passed by on her moped and greeted me, her young lodger, rather loudly. I was not surprised when other people queuing for the bus looked at me with unconcealed amusement.

In those golden days, the Law Reading Rooms were still located in the Old Bodleian Library. Radcliffe Camera, a round building constructed in the 18th century, was in the centre of the square and Brasenose College by its other side. I was amused to hear the anecdote about the famous Professor of Mathematics, who, having had a few drinks too many, was discovered one morning walking in a state of exhaustion around the Camera with one finger attached to the outer wall. When asked what he was doing, he explained — between hiccups — that he was trying to prove empirically that a circle had no beginning and no end.

Although term was not to start until September, I thought it prudent to get my reader-card for the library. My first task was to find a suitable topic for a doctoral thesis. Before long, I discovered that many topics which appealed to me had been covered. One possible topic was a study of the records of the Exchequer of the Jews, dealing with clipping of gold coins. Regrettably, my grasp of Medieval Latin was inadequate. Another possible topic concerned the standing of customs and usages as a source of law. However, I sensed that I had little to add to the excellent works available. In the end, I decided to write a comprehensive thesis on the very subject I had studied for my Masters dissertation and to compare the treatment of letters of credit in different legal systems.

Having chosen my topic, I had to ascertain the location of all relevant legal publications. English materials were, of course, available in the Law Reading Rooms or in the stacks. French legal texts were available in the Codrington, the library of All Souls College. A full collection of American law reports was not — at that time — available in Oxford. I had to obtain admission to the Middle Temple Library on the London Strand in order to collect the required materials.

In Oxford, the Duke Humphrey's Library was a gem located within the Old Bodleian. It was founded in 1450 and renovated in 1598. It still housed medieval books, chained to the alcoves. I had to use it when the Bodleian borrowed for me books not available in England. Generally, the Duke Humphrey's was desolate: the creaking floors discouraged readers and visitors from walking through it.

Unlike the Hebrew University, which divided the academic year into two semesters, Oxford had three terms: Michaelmas (fall term); Trinity (winter to spring); and Hilary (early summer). Each term comprised eight weeks followed by a break. By the time term started in 1959, I had developed a routine. I would get up at 7.30 o'clock, take my breakfast and by 9.00 o'clock arrive at the Bodleian. Initially, I had to spend a great deal of time in the catalogue room so as to ensure that I was not going to overlook any relevant publication. I then went to the Law Reading Rooms and read the relevant law reports.

As there were — as yet — no photocopying facilities, I had to summarise the facts of every relevant case and copy by hand all seminal passages. It was a slow process, but I tended to absorb and remember everything I had jotted down. Back in my lodgings, I used to index all materials covered. This too had to be done by hand.

About twice a week, I had to travel to London. On such days, I had to leave home by 8.15 a.m., walk to Oxford's train station and catch the 9.00 o'clock express train to Paddington. From there, I proceeded by tube to Holborn or Strand, which were the stops nearest to the Middle Temple Library. Late in the evening, I returned to Oxford.

After a while, I realised that many of the applicable legal principles were based on the courts' construction of the forms used by banks. I further realised that these changed from time to time. In the event, I visited some exclusive banks which were prepared to show me their forms and gave me access to their archives. Glyn, Mills & Co. — a patrician bank now absorbed by the Royal Bank of Scotland — was particularly helpful and a good source of commercial practice.

After a few weeks of work in the library, my supervisor, who wrote a leading text on contract law, asked me to write the first chapter of my thesis. The draft I presented was unsatisfactory. The difficulty was that my thought process was in Hebrew which I unconsciously translated into English. The result was that many sentences were poorly constructed and some idioms inappropriate.

Guenter Treitel corrected my grammar and dealt methodically with legal points I had made. One of his main concerns was that many of my sentences comprised too many subsentences. As a result, their readability was impaired. Under his patient tutoring, I was able to switch from translating Hebrew sentences into adopting English as my main language of thought, composition and expression. I was also advised to write short sentences. Under Treitel's guidance, my writing ability improved.

My social life was fulfilling though not exuberant. There were many interesting clubs in Oxford which welcomed newcomers. In addition, I often went to St. Catherine's Common Room to play bridge or to take part in debates on political and social topics. After a while, I joined the Oxford Union, which had, inter alia, excellent luncheon facilities.

Although my college — like most colleges in Oxford — was 'men only', I met some interesting girls in different clubs. Notably, five colleges in Oxford admitted only women. Over the years, all colleges modernised and became unisex.

Before I left Israel, Sasske had advised me to mix with local people and to avoid becoming part of the Israeli community in Oxford. His main concern was my need to acquire a good command of spoken English. I acted on his advice but for a different reason. Ideologically, I was not committed to the Israeli policy of the day. Accordingly, it seemed best to avoid social and political circles where issues respecting Israel's future dominated. Further, I felt more at ease in multiracial and multicultural circles than with groups idolising Zionism and the supremacy of Israeli norms.

I recall one specific visit of a fellow Israeli, who asked me to attend the Shabbat eve service. When I explained that the meeting place in North Oxford was too far, he asked whether I might perhaps attend the morning prayer session. He assured me that my plan to go to the library was unrealistic. The Bodleian was closed on Saturdays but open on Sundays. It took me some time to convince him that in Oxford the libraries were open on Saturday morning and remained closed on Sunday because that was the resting day in the United Kingdom. The experience left a bitter taste in my mouth. I realised that some Israelis reading for a postgraduate degree in Oxford found it difficult to detach themselves, even temporarily, from their heritage.

To the present day, it is frequently said that Oxford and Cambridge are exclusive universities and that admission depends to a large extent on an applicant's background. Whilst I am not in a position to express a view as regards admission to the basic B.A. course, I recall that each of the undergraduates I met had excelled in his 'A Level' examinations.

Admission to the prestigious postgraduate B.C.L. ['Bachelor of Civil Law'] Degree and to the D.Phil. was restricted to applicants who had excelled in their undergraduate course. These postgraduate degrees attracted many bright applicants from overseas countries, such as Australia, New Zealand, South Africa, India, Sri Lanka, Pakistan, Bangladesh, Nigeria, Israel, Transjordan and Singapore. Those who found the going too difficult usually left within a few months. All in all, Oxford was — and has remained — a place of academic excellence.

A candidate reading for the D.Phil. has to concentrate on a well-defined topic. To remain visible, I decided to enrol in two courses offered for the B.C.L. I really benefitted from the excellent course on trusts and from the course on comparative law. As Professor Lawson was principally conversant in Romance languages, I was able to contribute by identifying relevant materials on German and Austrian law. Fortunately, the Codrington had a good foreign laws collection.

The skills I had acquired in the courses on *Talmud* and on Logic at the Hebrew University were of momentum. They helped me to master the art of summarising the general principles laid down in precedents and distinguishing binding cases if their application in different circumstances would be unsound. In one sense, my studies at Oxford augmented courses I had attended in the Hebrew University. In addition, they taught me how to apply my knowledge at a practical level. I do believe that the excellent teaching method of Oxford played a major role in my development as an academic lawyer. I recall my studies in Oxford with gratitude and warmth.

One of my fellow postgraduate students was Lalith Athulathmudali. When I arrived in Oxford, he was reading for the B.C.L. Lalith had been the President of the Oxford Union. Under his influence, I started to attend functions. I recall in particular the debate on apartheid. In those days, quite a number of politicians believed in the doctrine, which supported the strict separation between Black and White in South Africa. Like most liberals, I disapproved of the policy.

In the debate, Sir Oswald Mosley spoke in support of the doctrine. His opponent was Jeremy Thorpe, who was at that time the icon of the Liberal Party. Sir Oswald's address was excellent: Jeremy was simply outclassed. At the end of the debate, the attendants had to leave through one of two doors. Many of us, who strongly disagreed with Sir Oswald's views, left through 'his' door in recognition of his performance. The next day, one of the dailies had a report decrying the Union's support for a racist doctrine!

Over the next few months, Lalith and I became close friends. I realised that his real interest was not in a legal career but in the politics of his home country, Sri Lanka. On two occasions, we went up to London together. Lalith attended a Sri Lankan forum whilst I spent my day in the Middle Temple Library. In the evenings, we dined together. I recall how, on the second occasion, Lalith took me to a Sri Lankan restaurant. As I was unable to hide my discomfort as I ate the spicy dishes, Lalith took me for coffee in another place. Over the steaming cups, he told me that he intended to make a small fortune and then enter politics in Sri Lanka. I was sad to gather that an appointment to the Sri Lankan Bench would not satisfy him.

By the end of the Michaelmas term, that is, at around Christmas, I decided to take a break and visit my father in Vienna. The cheapest way was to go by train. To my surprise, I faced a problem. I had to change trains in Germany, which meant that I needed a visa from West Germany. My Israeli passport, however, was valid for 'all countries except Germany'. To my relief, the Israeli Consulate removed the restriction without any argument. In the event, my change of trains simply involved walking from one platform to another. A German visa was, in reality, superfluous. Still, I realised that travelling on an Israeli passport could involve travel problems.

Father received me with open arms. To my surprise, he asked me to join his ever growing business. He told me that I was entitled to reclaim my Austrian citizenship. I was tempted to join him, but realised that my inability to write German grammatically was a handicap. Further, I feared the harsh winter of Central Europe and, in any event, had set my heart on a career in law. I declined Father's offer but was keen to regain my Austrian citizenship, especially as dual citizenship had been sanctioned.

Father hid his disappointment. I understood him. He was regaining his original standing in the Viennese business world but was perturbed by the thought that there was no heir to his ever-growing business. Still, we took the steps needed to reinstate my original citizenship.

About two weeks after my arrival, Father asked whether I proposed to return to Israel. He was aware that I had an offer for employment in Tel Aviv but sensed that my heart was no longer there. I told him that I found my existence as an outsider more congenial than being part and parcel of a struggling nation. As an outsider, I would be able to remain on the sidelines and be left in peace as long as I did not break the law. Back in Israel, I would have either to conform to certain norms and precepts with which I was not in real agreement or take a stand. Neither option suited me. I added that I hoped to find a suitable research scholarship or a teaching job in the United Kingdom or in a Commonwealth country.

"You have not accepted British norms, Peter'le?" asked Father.

"Not really. But I find the British tolerant and easy-going; and they have a good sense of humour. One more point: English is becoming my main language. I am comfortable with it and like its rich idiomatic base."

"You are an Oxford convert," muttered Father.

"Guilty as charged," I conceded.

I spent another two delightful weeks with him. A visit to the office he set up convinced me that he had fallen on his feet. At the same time, I was aware that the old world, which he had known before the outbreak of WWII, was gone forever. In the post-WWII era, Vienna had come under American influence.

On my way back to Oxford, I broke my journey in Munich. I enjoyed the good food and the sights. However, whilst driving through the town in a rental car, I encountered a signpost directing traffic to Dachau. It gave me a jolt and spoilt the day. I realised that some memories could not be erased from one's mind.

Two days later, I was back in Oxford. Once again, I frequented the pubs and eateries I had come to like. I recall, in particular, an eatery in Carfax — Oxford's town centre — where I enjoyed an excellent steak and kidney pie for a token sum.

After the end of the following Hilary term, I spent a few working weeks in London. Having completed the collection of the relevant American materials, I returned to Oxford. Most of my friends were at that time busy cramming for their examinations. Many were planning to leave Oxford and embark on their professional careers. Lalith, too, was planning to leave. He had secured a teaching post at the newly founded Faculty of Law at the University of Malaya in Singapore.

During the long vacation, I spent a fortnight in Paris. I had a pleasant time and then went on for yet another visit to Vienna. Mother flew over from Tel Aviv. She was disappointed to hear that I had no wish to return to Israel. In her opinion, Israel had become the real home of all who had found refuge there during the Holocaust. She knew Father was also most unlikely to return to Tel Aviv. She decided to return and keep our roomy flat in Tel Aviv for the time being. She took a flight back two days before I returned to Oxford.

Nowadays, I keep asking myself why Mother did not join Father in Vienna at that time. Mother's own explanation was her desire to maintain our Israeli identity. She had followed Father to Israel but had no wish to return to Vienna, from which they had had to flee. Father never discussed the subject, at least not with me. He was, I am satisfied, a very private sort of person, who invariably kept his own counsel. My friend Zvi (Paul) mentioned to me in one of his letters from Canada that his impression was that Father had wanted to live apart from Mother but did not wish to separate officially. In Zvi's view, I was the glue that kept them together.

As far as I know, my parents never discussed separation, let alone a divorce. They simply maintained their separate existences but remained a married couple. To tell the truth, I always regarded them as a unit. I shall be telling later on why and how Mother left Israel and joined Father in Vienna. Both of them are buried there.

In my next letter, I shall have more to tell about my remaining months in Oxford.

Till then, all the best to you,

From,
Peter

10 December 2017
Singapore

Dear Friends,

Letter 12: From Oxford to Singapore

At the beginning of the Michaelmas 1960 term, I was back in Oxford and was working in full swing. Chapter after chapter of my thesis was knocked into shape. Treitel was satisfied with my progress. St. Catherine's, too, recognised my labours. As I was running short of funds, I applied for a scholarship, which, to my delight, was granted.

I could also sense that my command of English had improved and that, for all purposes, English had become my working and everyday language. Apart from Treitel's guidance, I benefitted greatly from my reading habit. Back in Israel, I still preferred reading texts in Hebrew and in German. In Oxford, I read English literature in its original version. One of the authors I discovered was Joyce Cary. Further, I revisited Charles Dickens, whose novels I understood far more clearly than I had back in Israel.

English also became my written language. I derived great satisfaction when my first case note — dealing with an Australian judgment — was accepted for publication by a renowned periodical. My pleasure, though, was short-lived. A full-length article, sent to another leading law review, was summarily rejected. However, in this instance, I had the last laugh. Some twenty years later, when my academic and professional credentials had been established, the new editor of the same review invited me to submit an article. He readily published an updated version of the very same composition.

By the end of the term, I went to Peterborough in East Anglia and spent a few days with one of Father's friends. He had sent me a return ticket and suggested I spend *Rosh Hashanah* (the Jewish New Year) and *Yom Kippur* (the Day of Atonement) — the Jewish high holidays — with his family. I accepted his invitation gratefully.

To my surprise, the small town had an established Jewish community. The synagogue struck me as traditional Ashkenazi and the prayer book was familiar. They had invited a cantor from Israel. I had never been to a synagogue with my parents, who were assimilated, but occasionally had accompanied friends. The small congregation in Peterborough was considerably more traditional than secular Jews in Vienna. I had no doubt that the members of this congregation regarded themselves as Jews living in England; not as Englishmen of the Jewish faith.

I spent both the eve and the first day of *Rosh Hashanah* with my host. During the morning service, which included the blowing of the horn, I studied the members of the congregation. I was satisfied that none of them would give up a lucrative existence in the United Kingdom and migrate to Israel. All the same, they were avid supporters of Zionism and of the Jewish dream of a fatherland.

In a sense, this visit gave me an understanding of the roots of anti-Semitism. I had no doubt that once a congregation or group set itself apart from the rest of the community or common people, it became open to xenophobia and discrimination. It was unrealistic to opt for a segregated existence and, at the very same time, to insist on being treated as being part and parcel of the population. It was not the alien religion that mattered. A country could tolerate many religions and actually encourage broad-mindedness in everyday life. It was the clannish existence of the Jewish population that set it apart.

When I excused myself from accompanying my host to the synagogue on the second day of *Rosh Hashanah*, his wife told me that her husband was disappointed. In the circumstances, it seemed best to return to Oxford the next day. In any event, I had no wish to observe the *Yom Kippur* fast.

Back in Oxford, I accepted an invitation to a bridge tournament. I was so taken up with the prospect of shining that I ignored the fact that many competitors were coughing badly. I ended up with a virulent attack of bronchitis and a bout of high fever. I was about to be hospitalised when Mother flew over and nursed me back to health. She looked after me as I was recuperating. I was extremely feeble and found walking difficult. Still, I managed to take Mother to a fine concert at the Sheldonian Theatre and to a visit of the Ashmolean Museum. Mother stayed in Oxford for three weeks. I felt sorry for her and also extremely ashamed: I was 27 years of age and still in need of help. I gave Mother a lovely farewell party in my favourite restaurant: the Elizabeth in St. Aldate's.

By the time I had returned to the Bodleian Reading Room, I realised that my ability to work hard had suffered. I tired easily and found my routine of going to London in the morning and returning to Oxford in the evening too difficult.

Still, in one way, my mother's visit helped me to improve my writing technique. Up until then, I used to write out my chapters in long hand, which I then took to a secretarial office for typing. It was an extremely slow process. Mother brought me a tape recorder. Thereafter, I was able to dictate my text and bring the tape to the typist. Initially, we had some problems arising from the incompatibility of British and Continental recording machines. But once this hurdle was overcome, my speed improved enormously. It also established — to my satisfaction — that I had come to grips with spoken English.

I knew that with the assistance of the tape recorder, I could finish my doctorate in about one year but did not like the idea of spending yet a further winter in England. Many of my undergraduate friends were at the time looking for an opening to pursue further studies. The book used by all of them was an American publication entitled *Further Studies Overseas*. It was a sort of encyclopedia, which listed all scholarships and bursaries available for studies in the United States. I acquired a copy but soon realised that most openings were of no relevance. Many were in universities in the freezing Northeast of the United States; others were in the Midwest of the country and others still in centres of little reputation. Another defect was that all of them, without exception, were for further coursework studies. Having become used to working on a project of my own, I felt disinclined to go back to a classroom. I had crammed for exams most of my life and saw no point in another stretch. Further, the designation of 'eternal student' was disturbing and unappealing.

My initial plan was to work on my project until the end of the summer and then apply for leave of absence. I intended to take up the in-house counsel post in Tel Aviv and then return to Oxford with a completed thesis. Mother, with whom I discussed the idea, was supportive. I know she was keen to see me back at home. Father suggested that I brave another year in Oxford and assured me he would see me through.

I was in two minds. On the one hand, I enjoyed my life in Oxford. The excellent luncheons in choice pubs and in the premises of the Oxford Union, the stimulating debating societies and clubs and the proximity of London were enthralling. They exerted on me a magnetic pull. On the other hand, the unfriendly climate and the endless toil on a narrow subject dictated a change of venue and of existence. Private practice, even as an in-house counsel, became alluring.

Then — unexpectedly — I received a letter from Lalith. He described his experience as assistant lecturer in Singapore as stimulating and sang the praises of that city. I have to confess that, in those remote and golden days, I knew very little about Singapore. I recalled that during WWII this British colony was overrun by the Japanese but was later on retaken by the British. A perusal of maps confirmed that Singapore was located at the tip of the Malayan peninsula and that it commanded a strategic position in international maritime trade between East and West via the Straits of Malacca. I then recalled that Joseph Conrad's *Lord Jim* dealt with this part of the world.

From Lalith's letter, I gathered that Singapore had attained virtual independence (internal self-government). Lalith further mentioned the pleasures he derived from visiting the hawkers' stalls and Indian restaurants and said that the town boasted fine antique shops. The last sentence of Lalith's detailed letter indicated that he thought that a spell in Singapore would be good for me and that my reading for the Oxford D.Phil. would give my application for a teaching job a good standing. I was tempted.

A few days after my receipt of Lalith's letter, another friend — Patrick Davis — invited me to spend a week in his home. I accepted gratefully and before long took the train to Edinburgh.

Patrick met me at the railway station. I was so fascinated by the town that I made a blunder. "Edinburgh is the most beautiful place in England," I exclaimed at the top of my voice. Startled by the ominous looks of those who listened, I looked bewildered at my host.

"You mean 'Britain'," Patrick spoke gently, "we are in Scotland!"

"Oh..." was all I managed to mutter.

It turned out that Patrick's father was an Englishman, who had settled in Edinburgh for business reasons. I enjoyed myself thoroughly, but, for the life of me, could not see any cultural difference between England and Scotland. The pubs and eateries served the type of food and drink I got used to in Oxford. One evening I tried the national dish — Haggis. It is possible that one day I will come to like it.

Two days before I returned to Oxford, I discussed Lalith's letter with Patrick. He took the view that, as I did not like Oxford's winters, a few years in a tropical climate might be my best option. He, himself, had decided to have a go at journalism. I understand that, in due course, he became successful and that many of his articles appeared on the front pages of leading English newspapers.

After my return to Oxford, I applied for the post of an assistant lecturer in Singapore. In addition, I also lodged applications for further studies in some American universities. For the rest of the term, I immersed myself in my thesis. Treitel's reserved but supportive comments assured me that I was getting there. I was particularly pleased when he confirmed that my style and grammar had reached the required standard.

One of my applications to American universities was successful. I suppressed the urge to accept by putting it on hold. In reality, I was awaiting the outcome of my correspondence with Singapore. I knew that the fact that my Oxford qualification was still in abeyance would be a negative factor. Still, I did not lose courage. From Lalith's letters,

I gleaned that my application was pending. It seemed best to concentrate on my thesis.

I was still waiting for a reply when I received a letter from Father, who wanted to visit me and see Oxford. We went straight from Heathrow to Oxford, where I had secured a room in The Randolph.

I had by then made a full recovery and so I was able to take Father, who was an outdoors man, to Addison's Walk. I recall how we proceeded from Magdalen College, along Merton and Christchurch Meadows to St. Aldate's. On the way, a squirrel hopped onto my shoulder. Regrettably, I had no nuts with me, and so, disappointed, it jumped back to its tree trunk. As my gaze rested on Father, I noticed that his glasses were getting misty.

"What is the matter, Papa?"

"I only hope you will not disappear from our lives like that squirrel."

We walked back from St. Aldate's to Carfax and down the High. Father cheered up over a pleasant meal in Town and Gown Restaurant. After lunch, I took Father across the street. The librarian allowed me to take him to see the Duke Humphrey's and the porter in Brasenose College permitted us to stroll in the main quadrangle.

Two days later, we went for a day tour to Woodstock. Father was not impressed with Blenheim Palace. I, too, thought it was bombastic and lacking in charm. We had our lunch in a pleasant eatery in a small hotel. The attractive young woman and good-looking man sitting at the next table struck me as the epitome of a happily married couple. To my surprise, Father looked amused. The reason became clear when the waitress served their coffees.

"How many spoons do you take with your coffee?" asked the girl.

"So, you see, Peter'le: they are not married. They just came here for fun," grinned Father. "I thought as much as soon as I spotted them. A husband would not be so solicitous and excessively polite to his wife!"

We had an excellent dinner in The Old Parsonage. The bells of St. Giles Church were chiming. We then walked at leisure to The Randolph.

A few days later, I went with Father to Heathrow and then stayed in London for some three weeks. My objective was to read the most recent American cases and to collect additional banking forms. Having finished my research, I returned to Oxford.

The indexing of my new materials took a few days. Then, one foggy and rainy evening, when it would have been best to stay at home, I had a sensation or expectation of news from Singapore. On my way to St. Catherine's, I almost collided with a chap who was crossing Foley's Bridge, which connected Abington Road with St. Aldate's, in the opposite direction. Having muttered my apologies, I proceeded to St. Catherine's. As expected, a formal letter of offer for a three-year contact was in my pigeonhole.

Many years have passed since this event. Nowadays, living in Singapore in retirement, I often turn back to that fateful event which paved my way and determined my future. For all practical purposes, I have remained a sceptic. Whilst I would not describe myself as atheist, I am a staunch agnostic. I have remained unimpressed by rituals, by horn-blowing and by preaching. All the same, I cannot deny that throughout my odyssey — which I believe is drawing to its end — I sensed the presence of a guiding hand. It induced my parents to escape from Europe to Palestine; it drove me to the law; it encouraged me to start my own practice and move to Oxford and then, at exactly the right moment, directed my feet to Singapore. Naturally, pure chance may provide another explanation of the events. I am not sure what or which is the correct answer.

I dispatched my letter of acceptance within two days. I then had to apply for leave of absence for a period of three years to complete my thesis. The Oxford Board of Studies granted the application, subject to my sending to my supervisor at least one penultimate draft of a chapter every three months. I realised that the Board appreciated that I had not lost my zeal.

My application for a post was approved by a Selection Board of the Faculty of Law in Singapore. The arrangement of my trip was in the hands of a long defunct body, called the Inter-University Council for Higher Education Overseas. I understand that in previous eras, this body also acted as recruitment-cum-selection board. I knew that quite a few of my future colleagues had been appointed by it. However, in 1960, staff was appointed by local selection boards. The Council's role was then confined to the execution of new contracts.

To my surprise, the Council sent me materials indicating that male staff members were supposed to wear white shirts and long trousers. Shorts were forbidden. Female staff members were expected to don skirts; in their case, trousers or short skirts were precluded. The pamphlet further indicated that staff members were to keep their distance from students and that fraternising with them was prohibited.

Lalith, to whom I referred this pamphlet, was amused.

"In the past, they wanted staff to be Pukka Sahibs. We are well past that stage. Let them arrange your trip and don't pay any attention to what they say. They are out of date. You might find a T-shirt and shorts more suitable to our tropical climate than formal clothes. And you better buy new things here; the prices are lower."

I took Lalith's advice. In any event, I was running out of funds and so decided not to make unnecessary purchases. Then, to my surprise, Lalith wrote to urge me make notes of cases I wanted to use.

"Our library does not have American reports or the *Lloyd's Law Reports*." I was stunned. *Lloyd's* was the leading set of reports of English commercial cases. Personally, I was not concerned. I had covered all the relevant cases in *Lloyd's Law Reports* in Oxford. However, I was convinced that this set ought to be made available to students studying English commercial law in any respectable university. It dawned on me that the law library in of the University of Malaya in Singapore might require additional materials and building it up would be one of my tasks.

Before long, my preparations for the trip were complete. The airplanes then in use were Dakotas, which needed to refuel every three or four hours. My flight involved four stops: Istanbul, Tel Aviv, Teheran and Bombay. This was during the Shah's regime, when Iran had friendly relations with Israel. Today, a plane which stops over in Tel Aviv would not be allowed to land in Iran. However, nowadays there are direct flights from London to Singapore and vice versa.

It took me a few days to pack my things. I had by then acquired a collection of books on the law of letters of credit in different jurisdictions. In addition, my detailed notes of cases, summaries of leading articles and index card boxes were precious: They had to be packed meticulously, and I felt the need to take them with me as part of my luggage. My clothes fitted neatly into a substantial suitcase to be sent by sea.

Before I left, I took my leave from Treitel, Professor Lawson and a few other dons who had been kind to me. I also called on the banks that had helped me and wrote a letter of thanks to the Middle Temple Library.

As I boarded the plane in Heathrow, I looked eagerly forward to a new future. I had no misgivings or fears. I knew — or perhaps sensed — that my future was destined to be that of a law teacher.

After I had received the offer to spend three years in Singapore, I managed to read Wallace's *The Malay Archipelago*, an English translation (from classical Chinese) of *Dream of the Red Chamber* and Barber's *The War of the Running Dogs*. I gleaned from Wallace's book that the tribes and communities he had visited had their own ethos and internal hierarchy. The Chinese epic, too, excited me. Obviously, a Chinese society had its own beliefs, values, norms and traditions. The *Running Dogs* confirmed that Malaya had to grapple with communist insurrections. Was the insurgency really over? I knew I was in for an exciting and rewarding time: I had to keep my eyes open and learn.

Nowadays — when I write these memoirs — I am surprised by my ability to take tough decisions when needed. I was aware of my medical and physical limitations. I knew that I had a poor constitution and that my weak lungs would lead to occasional relapses. All the same, I had had no qualms when I gave up a sound post in Israel or when I decided to leave Tel Aviv in order to further my studies in Oxford. Further, I did not hesitate when I decided to prefer a teaching post in an alien country to an appointment as in-house counsel at home and was not deterred by the fact that my teaching contract was for a probationary term of three years. Despite my indifferent health, I had retained my courage and knew how to grab a lucky break when it materialised.

My next letter will show you that I had made the right choice.

Till then, all the best,

Peter

20 December 2017
Singapore

Dear Friends,

Letter 13: Singapore — First Year

I changed planes in Bombay (Mumbai, as it is now called) and proceeded to Colombo. Lalith welcomed me in the airport. I was happy to meet his mother and younger brother. Whilst the dishes were spicy — that is, too hot for my palate — I enjoyed the rice hoppers and the milder curries.

On the second day of my visit, we toured Colombo. It was a huge town, lacking in any charm. It was a third-world town. I felt the need to wash my hands after every outing. Colombo appeared even less modern than Izmir in Turkey.

Later in the week, Lalith drove us up to Nuwara Eliya, a cool mountain resort which, Lalith told me, had been a favourite haven of the British Civil Service during colonial days.

As he drove me to the airport, Lalith briefed me on the affairs of the Faculty of Law in Singapore. It was clear that he felt intellectually superior to most of his colleagues. He basked in Oxford's glory. It was further clear that, from his point of view, Singapore was a provisional haven. He had set his heart on a political career in Sri Lanka.

Dean Lee Sheridan and two colleagues met me at Singapore's 'new' commercial airport, which eventually moved to Changi. I recall the drive to the university campus and the delicious smell of food prepared at the hawkers' stalls. I should have liked to stop and partake. My hosts, though, drove me straight to the Wolverton Mess, where I was allocated a pleasant room with an attached bathroom. I was going to be housed there until a staff apartment became vacant. Shortly after my arrival, I fell asleep. I was exhausted.

At the time of writing (2022), the Wolverton Mess had long been swallowed up by the ever-expanding Botanic Gardens, which is now a UNESCO world heritage site. When I arrived in Singapore on 27 April 1961, the first floor of the Mess had some eight rooms occupied by visitors or new arrivals. On the second floor were two roomy apartments, let to staff at a subsidised rate. Other apartments were located in an adjacent building and yet another apartment block was within a comfortable walk.

Breakfast was served in the Mess from 8.30 till 9.30. David R., a lecturer in the English Literature Department who lived in one of the flats, walked me to the university's campus. It took us some ten minutes to get to the main building. Shortly after my arrival, Dean Sheridan discussed with me my teaching commitments. He had assigned me 12 tutorials in an introductory course, entitled Courts and Precedents.

I had lunch with David R. in our staff cafeteria and then went to see the town. The impression I formed was that Singapore was neither a first-world nor a third-world town but somewhere in between. The central part of the town boasted excellent restaurants and fashionable hotels. It had a fine theatre and the philharmonic orchestra, in an adjacent building, was of a good standard. Orchard Road was then a two-way street. Orchard Boulevard did not exist. There was room for development, but I was satisfied that this part of Singapore was first-world.

There were at the same time poorer parts on the outskirts as well as *kampongs*, that is, small settlements in which people had their own quarters but shared many facilities, such as a common tap. Some did not have electricity. I reasoned that these were indicative of a third-world area. As yet, there were only a few Housing and Development Board blocks ('HDB blocks'), the flats of which were built and sold by the Government to locals at a subsidised price. Skyscrapers were conspicuous by their absence. The 19-storey Asia Insurance Building downtown — today a relatively small and low office block — was at that time the tallest building in Singapore.

When I arrived in Singapore, the university was still reeling from what became known as the 'Enright Affair'. It was sparked off by the Professor of English Literature's, Dennis Enright's, inaugural address, in which he had made some remarks about the slow development of culture. He observed that the process could not be sped up by governmental intervention. Back in Israel, such observations would have been ignored or ridiculed. In Singapore, the local government took offence and reacted. In the event, the matter was smoothed over and peace was restored. David R., an avid member of Dennis' Department, thought that the entire matter was insignificant and had been blown out of proportion by the local media. He convinced me. At the same time, I realised that teaching should be kept apart from local politics.

Having settled comfortably in the Wolverton Mess, Geoffrey Bartholomew, who became a lifelong friend, helped me to search for a car. He also took me to some excellent and reasonably priced restaurants. After a few days, I purchased an Austin Metropolitan convertible, which was inexpensive as it had been used by an up-country owner in Malaya.

The acquisition of the car enabled me to tour Singapore. Geoff accompanied me on a trip to Changi Village. In those days, the only route wound through the Merdeka Bridge to the East Coast and from there on to our destination. As yet, there were no highways and the Sheares Bridge, currently connecting the city with the East Coast, had not been constructed.

Changi Village was one of the stops on the way to the British Base. The small shops crowding the road sold consumer goods, such as photographic equipment (e.g., telescopic and wide-angle lenses) and gramophones, at bargain prices. They catered both to the local population and to the British army personnel. There were also excellent food stalls. Nowadays, the trip from the centre of the town to Changi Village takes approximately 20 minutes. In those days, it took at least 45.

On another day, I went with David R. to Raffles Place, the heart of town. We parked in the ground-level carpark and proceeded by trishaw — a bicycle with an attached small carriage for two passengers — to Chinatown. I loved the antique shops and enjoyed the food in the excellent and reasonably priced Chinese restaurant. After we returned to Raffles Place, we gave Robinsons, the fashionable and famed department store, a miss. It was too pricy for us.

A few days before the beginning of term, Geoff, David R. and I spent a day in Johor Bahru and Kota Tinggi. In those days, there was no checkpoint between Singapore and Malaya and vehicular traffic flowed smoothly between the states. A chain of rest-houses, used during the British period, continued to operate and provide their traditional inexpensive lodging and food.

Having toured Singapore and the surrounding region, I started to prepare the reading list for my course. As there were still no photocopying machines, students had to read the relevant cases in the library. The librarian warned me that her experience with students was bad. Some hid books on inappropriate shelves to make them unavailable to other readers. Other students simply vandalised books by cutting out the relevant pages with a knife or razor blade. The personnel were unable to police the library. One way to combat the problem was to put books on 'red spot', which meant that a reader could borrow them for a restricted time only. Regrettably, the library could not reserve too many books. This problem continued to plague us until the advent of photocopying machines. Thereafter, relevant materials were 'zapped' and copies distributed to the students.

The course went well. As term progressed, I started to wonder about the status of my new home. The British armed forces were still present, and matters respecting defence, security and foreign affairs were controlled from London. Internal affairs, such as education, home affairs and immigration were in the hands of the local government. In reality, the state of affairs reminded me of Palestine under the British mandate. I concluded that, all in all, Singapore was semi-independent. I then attended a lecture delivered by a recent graduate — Tommy Koh — who took the view that Singapore was still a Crown Colony. This made sense, but I was not convinced. Even in matters respecting security and defence, London would consult the local government before it took a stand.

My social life during these early days was confined. I had to spend many hours in the library both on my teaching course and on further research on my doctoral thesis. About once a week, I went out with the Enright crowd, which meant joining David R. I admired Dennis' sparkling conversation and recall with admiration his analysis of *Ulysses* and of some of D.H. Lawrence's books. Dennis was an accomplished and natural teacher. Reading works of these authors improved my command of literary English. Odd to say, David R. took a critical approach to Shakespeare. His words fell on open ears because I had disliked the Fair Swan of Avon since my days in Tichon.

Our existence, though, was not restricted to literary analysis. Occasionally, we had drinking bouts. At times, I went with David R. and other bachelors of the Department of English Literature to the notorious Guan Guan Bar. The hostesses were liberal in their favours.

On other occasions, I joined Lalith, who had forged close links with the local Bar. We used to take lunch in the G.H. Café in Battery Road, which stood on the site currently occupied by the Standard Chartered Bank. The attendants usually talked shop or gossiped, which made me realise that saints were as rare in Singapore as in England or Israel. I would just listen, but had nothing to add. The dish I favoured was the gado-gado, an assortment of vegetables and potatoes spread over with a pungent peanuts sauce. Today — alas — my physicians have proscribed this excellent dish, which is available in all Indonesian restaurants.

By the end of the first term, Dean Sheridan sent Lalith to Malaya on a recruitment trip. In those days, ours was the only law faculty in the region, and, of course, it was new. Lalith's task was to encourage school leavers from all over Malaya to apply for admission. By and large, half of our intake came from Malaya, mainly from Kuala Lumpur, Ipoh, Penang and Johor.

I accompanied Lalith, who was an excellent salesman. What impressed me most was the fine standard of English of the school leavers. Further, some of them gave Lalith a hard time. I recall that one listener asked whether it was true that "every lawyer is a liar". Lalith turned the question into a joke. Still, it gave me an insight to our profession's reputation in some local circles.

The trip took us to the Malay heartland of Kelantan and Terengganu. I noticed that in these two states the standard of English was lower than in Johor and Selangor. All the same, Lalith had some lively sessions of questions and answers. One boy impressed me by asking whether a person of his background would have a chance at the Bar in places like Kuala Lumpur or Singapore. Lalith assured him that if his results were satisfactory, the doors would open themselves. To my delight, this very boy enrolled in our law school. Some six years ago, he retired from a lucrative practice.

When we completed our trip, I realised that both in Malaya and in Singapore, the population was divided into different ethnic groups. Singapore boasted a Chinese majority, which, however, was itself broadly divided into two sects. One was the Chinese-educated world, with a stronghold in Chinatown. Many of these Chinese were not conversant in English. Their lingua franca was their ethnic dialect, for instance, Hokkien or Cantonese. The other sect encompassed the English-educated Chinese population. They spoke English at home, although most of them were conversant in their ethnic dialect. I believe that very few English-educated Chinese knew how to read or write Chinese properly.

The other ethnic groups in Singapore were the Malays, the Indians (who migrated mainly from South India and whose language was Tamil or Malayalam) and a small well-defined Eurasian community, which encompassed mainly the second or third generation of Portuguese migrants and Anglo-Chinese as well as Anglo-Indian people. There was also a small European community and, of course, a miniscule group of Jews.

The position differed in Malaya. In all of its states, the Malays constituted the majority. The Chinese were a substantial minority, but, in point of fact, controlled the economy. The Chinese lived in towns or urban areas. For instance, Ipoh — the capital of the tin industry in the early 20th century — was a Chinese-populated town. Similarly, Penang and Kuala Lumpur always had a large Chinese population.

Effectively, all the states of Malaya were still under British influence to a large extent. By the time I arrived in Singapore, the communist insurgencies had been largely contained. All the same, the Malayan and Singapore governments continued to fear a resurgence of communist activities. I am not certain if the danger was real.

Back in Singapore, I got ready for my second term course. I had to lecture on the political structure of Malaya. In reality, most students knew more than I about the subject. I felt frustrated and decided that I had to move to some other courses such as the law of contract.

In the course of this term, I got in touch with the Jewish community. Here, the catalyst was a colleague — the Professor of Public International Law — a London Jew. Leslie Green took me with his family to the house of the head of the community, the daughter of its founder. When we went to Mrs. Nissim's house, we wore jackets, but then took them off. This was necessary because there was no air conditioning. The cantor was an Israeli émigré, and we had a semi-Orthodox Shabbat prayer. Mrs. Nissim invariably gave us a good meal, which was some compensation for the cantor's ramblings. I recall with delight the succulent mangoes served as dessert.

In the course of this second term, I also met a number of Israelis who had come over to Singapore. Some took up a three-year contract as government consultants; others were sent by Israeli firms, with a view to using Singapore as a bridgehead for investments in the region; and others still came over as migrants, who intended to build up a business. Many of them were engaged in the diamond trade.

To my surprise, I discovered that Singapore had two synagogues. I was told that the two most prosperous Singapore Jews did not get on with each other. In consequence, each launched his own centre. Mrs. Nissim's synagogue, founded by her father, was in Oxley Rise. The other was in Waterloo Street.

As most Israelis frequented the latter, I joined them from time to time. In reality, the two synagogues used the same Sephardic prayer book. Nowadays, the Oxley Rise synagogue is not as popular as the Waterloo Street one. A generous donation by a Jewish stockbroker led to the establishment of the Jewish Welfare Board, adjacent to the Waterloo Street synagogue. Currently, this is the effective centre of Judaism in Singapore.

Three further positive developments took place in 1961. The first concerned my lodgings. Although my room in the Wolverton Mess was spacious, I was getting tired of the need to share meals with others. I craved to have a place of my own with the resulting privacy. Dean Sheridan came up with an excellent solution. He secured for me a Residential Fellowship at King Edward 7th Hall ('KE.VII'), the dormitory of the students of medicine. This meant that I had free lodgings: effectively a flat of my own. As the university expected its fellows to mix with the students, the flat did not have a kitchenette. The food, though, was fine and the breakfast and dinner hours most liberal.

I enjoyed my new position and mixed well with the students. About once a week, our corridor would have a 'tug of war' with the adjacent one. Being a heavyweight, I tended to take a place at the end of the rope. Frequently, sheer weight led us to victory.

Regrettably, I also ventured into the *mahjong* room of the hall. From my experience in Tel Aviv, I regarded myself a champion player.

In KE.VII, the young players ganged up on me. More often than not, I left the battleground — the room — with my tail between my legs.

KE.VII was near Chinatown. Frequently, I joined students from my corridor on an excursion to the food hawkers there. I remember the splendid Hokkien mee with affection. There were also some moderately priced restaurants with Cantonese cooking. I recall the dishes with pleasure.

The flat in KE.VII made it possible for me to throw parties. Before long, I discovered that many staff members enjoyed playing bridge. Both the Professor of Mathematics and a leading urologist were delighted to join in. We became a multi- disciplinary group. Fortunately, I did not need the urologist's medical attention; although on one occasion, he told me I was not drinking enough water. Our mathematician posed an unusual problem. Although he was able to recall all 52 cards, his bidding left much to be desired. I preferred to partner a political scientist, whom I mollified, whenever I made a mistake, by encouraging him to give us a lecture on John Stuart Mill.

The second excellent development in 1961 was my forging a strong friendship with our American Professor of Constitutional Law. Harry Groves was a Black American, and I regret to have to say that he had a chip on his shoulder. I recall how he embarrassed me when we lunched in the American Club. Out of the blue, he told me:

"You know, Peter, every white American present notes that I am a black!"

"Surely, Harry," I replied too quickly, "this is more in your mind than in theirs. I never fear to encounter anti-Semitism."

"But, then, your skin does not give you away."

It seemed best not to take the matter further. In my heart of hearts, I knew he was right. Suffice it to say that some young white American staff members developed a dislike for him. They regarded Harry as an 'Uncle Tom' (not a 'Martin Luther King') and took exception to everything he did.

Another rather amusing incident took place when Harry came back from a break in India. Having sent his wife away, he showed me the slides he had taken during a visit to a highly depraved temple ruin.

"I could not do such things," he muttered, as we watched some photographs of exceptionally explicit sexual scenes.

"Neither could I," I conceded.

Up to this point, I covered the dents in Harry's armour. His scholastic ability and contribution to the faculty were great. To start with, he was an excellent teacher, and I do believe all his students have remembered him. In addition, he helped junior colleagues with their research and drew their attention to American materials. In my opinion, he started the faculty's leap into the international arena.

The third development that took place in 1961 was the split between the University of Malaya and our university. Thereafter, our institution, the University of Singapore, attained independence. We could now pursue interests of our own. I used the occasion to convince Dean Sheridan that a course on banking law was necessary as Singapore had the making of a regional banking centre. I secured his promise that, in due course, I would be allowed to launch a course on this subject. I was now able to look forward to a future as a law teacher.

The split of our university from the Malayan institution brought to the foreground a problem I had noted shortly after my arrival. It concerned the expatriate allowance that was, in those days, granted to every staff member recruited from overseas. As all staff enjoyed, in addition, subsidised housing, it was difficult to justify the extra amount paid to foreigners. Expatriate staff members used to point out that the

United Nations, too, granted an extra allowance to staff posted overseas. However, this allowance was aimed at assisting staff to meet the increased cost of living. Our university's financial arrangement was different because not only was subsidised accommodation provided to staff, but in addition, the university leased out the premises occupied by the staff house, which had a cafeteria, at a nominal rent. In consequence, meals were effectively subsidised and, hence, inexpensive. Both local and expatriate staff went there for lunch. In reality, the cost of living of the expatriate staff was low. Many locals felt that expatriates were pampered ("fat cats"). I am pleased to say that the position was changed later on; but, in 1961, the expatriate allowance was controversial.

After the split, another memorable event occurred. Shortly after the final examination results were made public, the Law Students' Club arranged an end-of-year party. Lee Kuan Yew ('LKY'), the Prime Minister then, was the guest of honour. The first speaker was the Club's president. I had expected him to welcome LKY and to express confidence in and support for the government. To my dismay, the student took a different approach. After a brief and formal welcome, he delivered a speech in which he demanded certain improvements to the faculty, such as additional books for the Law Library, and followed this up with an elucidation of Western liberal principles. LKY's face remained inscrutable, but I noted that he appeared tense.

To my relief, the next speaker delivered an appropriate welcome speech. LKY seemed to relax but his face remained blank. I hoped that in his response, he would either ignore the student's speech or gloss over it. Instead, LKY tore the student's speech to shreds. He made it clear that the task of a local university was to serve the interests of the community. If there was a clash between these needs and some foreign political philosophy, the former had to prevail.

LKY's message was clear. I noticed that Dean Sheridan, who was sitting at the same table, did not smile. Neither did Geoff. In contrast, Harry nodded approvingly and clapped. I must confess that I shared LKY's view. His policy was unexceptional. The task of any public-funded university, or other institute of learning, is to serve the interests of the people. Indeed, this has always been the approach of the Hebrew University and the majority of the European institutes of learning. Although I had personally come to embrace the liberal philosophy and precepts of Oxford, it was clear to me that these were not universally applicable, especially to newly independent countries.

I believe that in this pungent and clear speech, LKY set the intellectual direction that our university was expected to follow. I shall have more to say about the issues involved in my next letter.

With kind regards,
Peter

2 January 2018
Singapore

Dear Friends,

Letter 14: Courting and Tying the Knot

Towards the end of the long vacation, Father paid me a visit. I was glad to see him. The Master of KE.VII arranged accommodation and so Father and I stayed in the same building. His sister, my Aunt Ida, flew over from Sydney in order to meet him. It was their first reunion since the Holocaust. It will be recalled that during that horrible period, many families were scattered by the Third Reich's 'final solution' to different parts of the world and Aunt Ida and her family were lucky to obtain visas to Australia. They had fled from Vienna before us and had lived in Australia ever since. Father discovered their whereabouts through a Jewish Agency, The Joint, which was instrumental in re-establishing contact between members of dispersed families.

Once again, I consider it important to reflect on the enormous advances humanity has made in both technology and communications. Today, it is quite common for people to 'hop on a plane' and fly, say, from North America to Australia. In the sixties, flights took longer and were far from commonplace. I recall how Father expressed his concern when

I contemplated applying for a scholarship in Australia. He feared he would never see me again. At present, of course, many North American holidaymakers fly as far as New Zealand so as to distance themselves from places in which crime and acts of terror are on the increase.

I picked Ida up at the airport. She was easily recognisable from family photos. As Ida was not wealthy, I managed to find accommodation for her in the house of a colleague, who had flown for two weeks to Burma (as it was then called). I spent the two weeks she stayed in Singapore by taking her and my father to see the Chinese temples and Malay shrines. Regrettably, it was difficult to explain to Ida that Malaya and Indonesia were separate countries. As far as she was concerned, we were in the 'Orient', which, in her view, was far less advanced than Australia.

One point I noticed then — and still regard it a valid observation — is that my father and aunt had distinctly Aryan features. Both were fair-haired and had blue eyes. I suspect that Jewry all over Europe had mixed blood. It is true that one Turkic kingdom, the Khazars, embraced Judaism in the 8th century. I suspect, however, that their conversion and resulting intermarriage with the Jewish community is not the only explanation for the manifestation of Aryan traits in Jews of the Diaspora.

When Father flew back to Vienna, I had to get ready for my teaching in the forthcoming year. At my request, Sheridan reduced the number of tutorials I had in the introductory course and assigned to me three tutorials on the law of contract. To my surprise, the colleague who delivered the lectures on the subject performed his task by reading out in class a well-known text on the English law in point. He ignored the applicable Malayan law, which was codified and which differed in certain regards. I sorted out my dilemma by drafting tutorial problems confined to issues governed by the law of Singapore. This way everybody was happy. Harry alone made an appropriate snide remark. Sheridan ignored it, and Lalith smiled slyly. He thought my 'one-eye' approach was true to my character.

One of my students in my new course was James Puthucheary. He was a part-time lecturer in the Department of Economics but wished to qualify for legal practice. James was a well-known figure in Singapore. Initially, he was a member of the People's Action Party ("PAP") but joined the Barisan Sosialis when they split from the ruling party. During his years in the PAP, he had risen high in the government service.

James was a brilliant student and a fine debater. He enlivened our tutorials by raising unexpected points and focusing on economic problems hidden behind the legal façade. Before long, we became friendly. I visited his house on Faber's Hill on two occasions, and from time to time, we went out together for lunch. James knew many excellent hawker stalls as well as good North Indian restaurants. I knew that he had a 'left-wing' affinity, but from our numerous conversations, I suspected he was a capitalist at heart.

My teaching duties kept me well occupied. In addition, I became involved in the editorial work respecting our *University of Malaya Law Review* (first published in July 1959 and renamed *Singapore Journal of Legal Studies* in due course). In my spare time, I worked on my Oxford doctorate, sending at least one chapter per term to Treitel. About once a week I joined the Enright circle and on another went out with Lalith's crowd. Regrettably, the latter outings came to an end because, by the end of the first term, Lalith took six months' leave and enrolled in a course at Harvard.

I saw little of Geoff. He had met a pleasant Chinese girl and was going steady with her. By the middle of 1962, they got engaged and set a date for their wedding. In 1961, Geoff had often joined David R. and me in the staff cafeteria. In 1962, we missed his company.

Before long, David R. also started to go steady with another girl. I was not sufficiently close to the Enright circle to join them on my own. I became lonely and feared I might become a recluse. Then, one day, a newly appointed staff member asked me to join him for dinner. He had by error dated two girls and so needed one more male guest. One of the girls was Patricia (Peh Choo) Goh. I liked her and we started dating.

Pat was Chinese-educated. In some ways, her family's story resembled that of Holocaust victims. Her father, Goh Pheng Cheng, was born in Amoy in China (a Hokkien-speaking city). He was driven by poverty into migrating to Medan in Sumatra. Initially, he remained destitute, but, in due course, was taken into the business of a wealthy merchant. Thereafter, he had a steady, even if modest, income. This encouraged him to marry a local Chinese girl. Pat was their fifth child. By the time she was born, her father was constituted a full partner of the firm in which he was working and had made his fortune.

He did not suffer a financial reversal during the Japanese occupation of Indonesia. It is possible that he was a collaborator. Be this as it may, he had to leave Indonesia after the Japanese were driven out in 1945. By then, he had married a second wife — a tsip — and (as was common to wealthy Chinese) maintained two households. He took both families with him when he returned to Amoy. There, too, his fortune held. I am told he was one of the richest men in his hometown. He hoped to remain there for the rest of his life, invested shrewdly in local real estate and, in general terms, felt fulfilled. The future appeared rosy.

Then, an upheaval struck. Mao Zedong defeated Chiang Kai-shek and the Red (revolutionary) Army was bound to take Amoy. Goh Pheng Cheng had to leave most of his fortune behind, but was able to take enough with him as he fled with his two families to Singapore, which eventually granted him Permanent Residence.

During his first few years in Singapore, Pat's father did well. He bought a fine bungalow in fashionable Frankel Street in Katong, invested in two go-downs in the port area and sought to resume his trading. Regrettably, he was unable to service the overdraft granted to him by a local bank. In due course, the latter foreclosed his properties. Once again, Goh Pheng Cheng became destitute. Worse still, his youth was gone. He was drained, felt forlorn and had two families to feed. Eventually, Pat's father moved with his second family to a flat in one of the new HDB blocks. Pat's mother now had the burden of looking after her own offspring. All of them were young and, as yet, unable to earn an adequate income. Fortunately, her erstwhile maid let them a small terrace house. The rent was modest, and, at the very least, the family had a roof over the heads.

In two regards, the Chinese tradition resembles the Jewish. First, both lay store by education. Notwithstanding the family's impoverished condition, the Gohs pooled resources so as to enable some members of the family to acquire decent qualifications. It was understood that if the educated members of the family met with success, they would look after the other members. Secondly, the family members were bound by an unwritten code to look after each other. Neither Chinese nor Jewish families expected to rely on welfare benefits or on third-party support.

There was, however, one marked distinction between Jewish migrants and the Chinese. Although the Jews adhered to their own religion and folklore, they usually became well-versed in the culture of their new environment. In some cases, they even enriched it. Goh Pheng Cheng's Chinese generation adhered to its own norms and failed to adapt. To give but one illustration: Pat's father learnt no English, although it was the language of government, law and commerce in Singapore.

When Pat and I met, she was living in their former maid's house in Happy Gardens East. Before long, Pat told me her own sad story. Back in Medan, they were coached by a private tutor. In Amoy, they had to go to school every morning. It was a long walk. In Singapore, Pat went to a Chinese secondary school and then enrolled in Nanyang University (Nantah), which was a Chinese university. It was founded by millionaire Tan Lark Sye, and its first president was the well-known Lin Yutang. He was living in the United States and was especially recruited to head the institution.

Pat led an active social life and became engaged to a young Indonesian. Then, unexpectedly, she contracted tuberculosis. At the end of her penultimate year, she had to drop out of Nanyang, and, to make matters worse, her fiancé jilted her. I met her after she had been discharged from the hospital and was working as a secretary in an import and export business.

Despite her winding odyssey, Pat had always remained within the same cultural, Hokkien, milieu. Whilst she had a basic command of English, she had remained attached to Chinese culture and values. Unlike me, she did not have to shuttle between different sets of norms and values. Her family's financial reverses had not affected her inborn dignity. She was a beautiful and self-assured woman. However, she abandoned Taoism and became a devout Christian.

On 12 August 1962, we went out together for the first time. I took Pat to dinner and both on the way to the restaurant and on the way back I listened to her story. Pat, in turn, wanted to know mine. She was bewildered by my numerous cultural shifts. To my surprise, she knew little about the Holocaust; even less than what I knew about Japanese brutalities committed during the occupation of Southeast Asia. However, I was surprised to hear that, during the Japanese Occupation, many girls wore male clothes. Rape and rapine were apparently common pastimes of Japanese soldiers. I was of course aware that many members of the small Singaporean Jewish congregation had fled to Australia or even to India so as to escape the brutal Japanese regime. However, I did not realise that sheer lawlessness and brutality were the key marks of the Japanese occupation of Indonesia.

I was captivated by Pat's beauty, natural dignity and demeanour. Further, I realised she had attained high standards in her native culture. For instance, she had a command of some 15,000 Chinese characters, was well read in Chinese classic literature and had, at one stage, taught Chinese language and writing at secondary school level. I was also under the impression that she would be able to make the necessary shift into English literature and culture. She also had the mystique of the East. I felt confident that she would be less bossy and headstrong than an Israeli girl. Within a few months, I proposed.

By the middle of the year, I managed to get a one week break from teaching. I spent it with Pat in Fraser's Hill, a cool and pleasant holiday resort in Malaya, reminiscent of Nuwara Eliya in Sri Lanka. I recall our drive to the resort. We spent one day in Kuala Lumpur and, the next morning, were guided to the highway leading to Fraser's Hill. The final stretch of the road leading to the resort was a one-way lane. For the first 30 minutes of each hour, it was open for vehicles driving down; for the next half hour, cars went uphill. The long wait at the foot of the road and the climb on the poorly asphalted road was tiring. I was exhausted when, finally, we arrived at the rest house. Pat was so disturbed when she noted my fatigue that she was inclined to break our engagement. I managed to persuade her to change her mind.

For the next few days, we toured Fraser's Hill. I recall that at one dinner I made a gaffe. The waiter offered me a dish, anticipating I should take only a portion. Unthinkingly, I took all of it. To my relief, he soon reappeared and proffered a new dish to other guests. Notably, Pat and the waiter could not converse. The waiter's only dialect was Hainanese, of which Pat had no command. Fortunately, they managed to communicate in writing because the Chinese characters in the written language are the same although different dialect groups pronounced them differently.

On the way back to Singapore, Pat and I set the day for our wedding. We agreed that whilst she would retain her faith, I should continue to adhere to mine. We even agreed that if we were blessed with children, they should be brought up as Christians. I further explained to Pat that I wanted to discuss our plans — which involved my marrying out — with my parents. Pat understood and, I think, approved. She told me that her mother had already agreed to the match. Her estranged father was likely to agree. I sensed that Pat would go ahead regardless of his reaction.

Back in Singapore, my marriage plans led to a change in my status. Up to that time, many local colleagues distanced themselves from me. I do believe that the expatriate allowance, mentioned previously, was one reason. The other related to the fact that foreigners were birds of passage. Many local colleagues felt that expatriates had no commitment to Singapore and in consequence were unlikely to make lasting contributions to the emerging state.

When it became known that I was engaged to marry a Chinese girl, my local colleagues started to regard me as a sort of hybrid: a foreigner planning to stay put. The assistant registrar of the university, Mrs. Lu Sinclair, was married to an ex-army Englishmen. They now treated me as one of them. Maurice Baker, a member of Enright's department, was an Anglo-Indian. Both he and some members of his circle now started to treat me as having a foot in their camp. All the same, Maurice advised me against swapping to a local contract.

"At this stage, Peter, you better keep your expatriate allowance. We'll let you know when it's time to swap."

Lu Sinclair took the same view. Her reasoning, though, differed. She told me that many locals dabbled in real estate investments. She knew that expatriates kept away from these. She assured me that, in the long run, real estate and shares were bound to rise.

"If you are going to settle here, Peter, start to invest your expatriate allowance in local stocks and property. You cannot possibly go wrong."

Regrettably, I did not follow this sound advice. Instead, I invested my savings in antiques which, over the years, lost their value.

The only dissenting voice was Lalith's. He wrote from Harvard that in his opinion, I would be unable to contract a happy mixed marriage. In his view, I was far more Jewish than I conceded. He was certain that a Chinese-educated spouse would often see things in a manner differing from mine. It was an advice coming from a close friend who knew me well. In later years, I often recalled his letter.

Interestingly, the same year — 1962 — was a landmark in Singapore's politics. Britain refused to grant Singapore full sovereignty. Instead, Her political leaders came up with the idea of merging the two British colonies in Borneo (North Borneo [Sabah] and Sarawak), Singapore and the Federation of Malaya. Their object was to contain the communist threat and secure their mercantile interests in the East. The PAP (the ruling party in Singapore) supported the idea. In contrast, the Barisan Sosialis, who had split from the PAP, were opposed to a merger. Other minority parties sided with them. In the event, the government held a referendum, which, however, did not include an option of rejecting merger but only the conditions of it. The opposition parties formed a Council of Joint Action which advised people opposed to the merger to cast blank votes. The PAP countered by legislating that blank votes would be treated as supporting the most popular option for merger. The outcome was that the option favoured by the PAP was voted in by the voters.

I knew that neighbouring Indonesia was bound to oppose the proposed merger. The then ruler of Indonesia was President Sukarno, who had his own ideas about the vast island of Borneo, which included Sabah and Sarawak and was called Kalimantan in Indonesia. I believe that he was opposed to the idea of these two territories being incorporated in a federation governed from Kuala Lumpur.

I could sense the gathering storm but have to admit that these regional disputes had little impact on me. I focused on my own affairs and future and, notwithstanding James' tirades against the merger, felt largely indifferent. I was confident that LKY's objective was to gain real independence for Singapore. Like Harry Groves, I concluded that, for me, it was best to concentrate on my teaching courses. I knew that both Sheridan and Geoff took a different view. However, even today — more than sixty years later — I believe Harry and I had our hearts in the right place. We were law teachers, not politicians. I pause to add that, in his own way, James accepted my stand. My warm friendship with him was never affected by differences in political or economic views.

One issue, though, kept bothering me. By 1957, the British had declared their intention to give up their colonies in this region. Why then were they so keen on the merger leading to the creation of Malaysia?

The issue continues to baffle me but one possible answer requires consideration. The British did not wish to leave a vacuum. They had learnt their lesson in the Indian subcontinent and in Palestine. Their objective was to leave a legacy behind them, and the Malaysian Federation appeared the best course.

Having covered the major political developments of that period, I have to return to major events affecting our Law School. The first was an international law conference, sponsored by the Asia Foundation and planned by Harry. Delegates came from all over Asia. Harry chaired most sessions, and, in my opinion, his performance was outstanding.

The importance of this conference was that it placed Singapore on the international legal studies map. I felt confident that in years to come Singapore was bound to be recognised as a hub of learning and scholarship. Regrettably, the debates and plenary sessions that took place during this conference were not published as a book. All the same, I am satisfied that many of the speeches and the brief papers delivered had a lasting influence on law schools in Asia.

The other event was yet another end-of-year dinner, held in an excellent — regrettably long defunct — restaurant in the Lido. I joined Geoff's table whilst Sheridan and Harry were, of course, at the table of honour. On this occasion, LKY was properly welcomed and lauded. Regrettably, the hall was smoky, and, like many others in attendance, I felt dizzy. So did LKY. At one point, he had a fainting spell — syncope — and fell over. Instantly, the then vice-chancellor, Dr. Sreenivasan, rushed to his aid. The rest of us remained in our seats. Within a matter of seconds, LKY recovered, regained his composure and finished his speech. In many respects, he repeated the message he had delivered in the previous year, that is, that the interests of Singapore were paramount and that the university's task was to serve them. I noted that at one point he cast an unfriendly glance at Sheridan. I sensed that the relationship between the two was neither warm nor friendly.

The last, highly disturbing development in our local politics, was Operation Coldstore. In a joint exercise — sponsored by the British, Malayan and Singapore authorities — leading opposition politicians and their supporters were rounded up and placed in detention without trial. One of the detainees was James Puthucheary. Another friend warned me not to visit James in prison. I took his advice, but felt sad to have lost my star student. Further, I wondered — still wonder — about the wisdom of the operation. It is possible that Lim Chin Siong posed a real danger to LKY's PAP. I find it hard to comment. The other detainees struck me as harmless dreamers. In the event, I never visited James. I felt and continue to feel deeply ashamed.

When term was over, I was getting ready to fly to Vienna. Initially, I was concerned about facing Europe's harsh winter after a flight commencing in the tropics. So I postponed my flight until the beginning of March.

Father's reaction after I told him about my plan was simple. He went to a jeweller's shop to buy a rose pin of gold and asked me to give it to Pat. He added, to my surprise, that he would not be perturbed if I decided to convert to Christianity. He knew that I was a sceptic and thought that it might be best if I transferred my doubts to another faith. For the rest of the week I spent with him, we went to his favourite restaurants and variety shows.

I spent the next three weeks in Oxford. The calm and dignified ambience of the place contrasted pleasantly with the imponderables I had experienced in Singapore during 1962.

On my way back to Singapore, I broke my journey in Tel Aviv. Mother listened to my plans calmly.

"So, at long last, you will not be my responsibility," she remarked. "But, Peter'le, you are not going to give up our religion. A Jew is always a Jew: Adolf Hitler made his point there."

"No, Mama," I told her firmly. "I may embrace another religion if I find it convincing. Christianity is not; and other faiths do not make demands."

"Would you really jilt her, if we opposed the union?"

"We shall never know."

Back in Singapore, Tommy Koh, who had by then become a close friend, enabled me to get our marriage license quickly. His mother helped me to choose a suitable engagement diamond ring for Pat. The road was now clear. I shall have a great deal to tell you about my next few years in Singapore. In due course, LKY became the unquestioned leader of Singapore, and the PAP controlled all seats in Parliament.

In addition, I propose to discuss my marriage. With the hindsight of a lifetime, I realise that I failed to appreciate the difficulties posed by Pat's deep Chinese roots. As I failed to make an effort to become conversant in Pat's language, I forsook the opportunity to come to terms with her culture. At the time, I did not realise that I was bound to pay a heavy price.

In the meantime, I wish all of you the very best.

With kind regards,
Peter

15 January 2018
Singapore

Dear Friends,

Letter 15: Early Years of Marriage

When I returned to Singapore, the faculty had changed. To start with, our rooms were air-conditioned. The main building, housing the deanery and some staff offices, had a centrally controlled system. Other offices, mainly in the old Japanese block, had individual units. More importantly, our lecture theatres had installations. They were far superior to the earlier facilities, cooled by fans which often blew your notes away.

The other major change concerned Lee Sheridan, the foundation professor. At the end of 1962, he announced his resignation. Shortly after my return from Europe, he left us and took up an appointment to a newly created chair at the Queen's University of Belfast. One school of thought was that Sheridan resigned because of a misunderstanding with LKY, which arose from Sheridan giving legal advice to Ong Eng Guan, the mayor of Singapore, on issues pertaining to the City Council. Another school of thought took the view that Sheridan had intended to leave earlier but failed to find a suitable opening. My own view remained that the rift between LKY and Sheridan went much deeper than a disagreement on a specific point. Sheridan was an advocate of English liberalism. LKY supported some of the principles involved but felt that the principal objective of a university was to serve the interests of the state that actually funded it. I am satisfied that both views were legitimate; but they could lead to disagreements. Sheridan decided to leave the scene.

Geoff, too, left and joined the Department of Commercial Legal Studies at Melbourne University. Many members of Enright's department migrated to Australia.

Then, the Staff Association, which had been dominated by a small group of vociferous expatriates, split into two: the local association and the expatriate one. The official reason for the split was the allegation by some locals that expatriates spoke better English and dominated important staff committees. As some of the leading members of the local association were writing English poetry and spoke English at home, the argument appeared artificial. I believe the real reason for the split was financial. Our salary structure required revision, and, in a sense, different camps had to tackle separate problems.

It seemed advisable to avoid all these issues and to concentrate on my personal affairs. Pat accepted that in our case a civil marriage was the only option. A Jewish marriage was out of the question, and I made it clear that I was not prepared to marry in a church. Furthermore, I was too poor to arrange the traditional multi-table Chinese wedding dinner. We settled on a formal dinner with Pat's family and a tea reception. Regrettably, my parents did not fly over. Instead, they gave us a '*hongbao*' or '*ang pow*' — a large amount of money far exceeding their airfares — as a wedding gift.

In those days — just as at present — it was common for couples to celebrate their marriage before a registrar. They called this 'registration'. Within the next few days, they had a church or a traditional Buddhist celebration.

We went to our ceremony in a luxury car borrowed from the father of my best man, Tommy Koh. I believe the Registrar of Marriages was surprised when Pat and I appeared before him formally dressed and groomed. He was used to couples coming over dressed informally so as to 'register'. I fear that, to the present day, many Chinese may be unable to realise that this 'registration' is, actually, a civil marriage and that everything else is legally superfluous.

We had a brief honeymoon in a local hotel. I recall with warmth the lovely flowers sent to us by Harry. I had told Pat that, once I completed three years of service, I would be entitled to sabbatical leave. We should then have a lovely holiday trip in Europe.

After a few days in the hotel, we moved into a spacious house in College Green, where university staff members were allocated dwellings. For the first time in my life, I had an entire house for myself. To my surprise, though, Pat (whom I nicknamed 'Susu' — meaning 'sweet milk') asked her sister, B., to live with us. I had earlier on agreed to pay for B.'s university education, but Pat's invitation was extended without my knowledge or any previous mention. I faced a *fait accompli*. Still, the Goh family lived in a different part of town and so it made sense to allow B. to stay with us. This way, she had better access to her lectures. Before long, I gave her lifts when I went to the campus.

Shortly after my wedding, Lalith returned to Singapore. He had done well at Harvard and was all set to embark on a political career in Sri Lanka. We often had lunch together and supported one another on all matters pertaining to academic affairs. To my disappointment, Pat took a dislike to Lalith. It took me some time to realise that she was bound to dislike any person close to me.

Matters at the faculty were tense. On the positive side, Sheridan did complete the teaching allocations and, to my delight, agreed to my launching a course on banking law. This enabled me to drop some tutorials in the introductory course.

On the negative side, Sheridan did not nominate a successor. In those days, the appointment of a dean was still in the hands of the faculty. The main contenders were Leslie Green (the Professor of Public International Law) and Harry Groves. This placed me in a difficult situation. I was friendly with both and keen to hurt neither.

In the event, a third name was mentioned, namely that of F., a senior lecturer who did not aspire for promotion to a professorship. Initially, F. was reluctant to stand. He knew that his reputation in the faculty was benign rather than outstanding. He was the sort of chap whom everybody liked but did not take too seriously. All of us, though, regarded him a fair and open-minded person. His term as sub-dean also established his sound administrative capacity.

Initially, F. had some doubts about his suitability for the deanship. However, Leslie, who realised that the odds were against him, insulted F., who thereupon decided to stand. Leslie simply dropped out. Harry remained in the ring. Following a close vote, F. won.

I have a vivid recollection of the party F. threw shortly thereafter. F's wife, D., who was usually stern, mellowed and sanctioned 'free' drinking. Before long, most of us were inebriated, including an ageing guest who was in charge of law reporting in Singapore. When he decided to sleep it off at home, we feared he might stumble on his way to the car and fall into a monsoon drain. It seemed best to place him between a two-group phalanx that would lead him to his destination. I was one of the few who thought it best to remain behind.

Unexpectedly, Tommy Koh, who led the procession and who had remained as sober as a judge, burst back into the house roaring with laughter and yelling: "X didn't fall; but T. (one of the guests) did!"

Poor T., who arrived within a few seconds, did indeed look like somebody emerging from a monsoon drain. Bestowing on all of us a look of censure, D. bandaged T.'s bruises, asked him to take a shower and then sent him home in a cab.

F. did not remain dean for long: within a few months, he joined Sheridan in Belfast with the hope of completing his Ph.D. Still, during his short-lived deanship, we managed to revise the syllabus. Under Sheridan's system, students who passed their second-year examination had to select a specialisation, such as property law or constitutional law. Most members of the faculty felt that such a specialisation came too early. We replaced Sheridan's system with a proper four-year course. Once a candidate passed the requisite core subjects by the third year, he was free to choose a prescribed number of electives.

F.'s departure was followed by yet another election. This time, Harry was elected by a clear majority. For me, the result was satisfactory. I trusted Harry and was convinced that Leslie's only aim was to promote his own cause. Regrettably, (for reasons not clear to me) Harry lost his trust in me. In a sense, I lost two friends.

By and large, the faculty continued to function smoothly. I sensed that, although Leslie resented Harry's administration, he knew that he had no cause for complaint. Harry was careful not to antagonise Leslie and actually helped him to broaden the scope of courses offered in international law. I, too, was able to promote courses in commercial law. One of them was insurance law. I had to teach the course but did not really enjoy doing it.

Before the end of the year, LKY made us aware of another aspect of his policy. Up to this time, admissions were left entirely in the hands of the university. To the surprise of all of us, LKY decreed that in addition to satisfying the university's admission board on his (or her) scholastic calibre, a candidate would have to present a certificate of eligibility — issued by the police — confirming that the holder was not a communist or a member of a subversive organisation. The senate — a university body dominated by expatriate professors — took exception to the decree and the vice-chancellor, Dr. Sreenivasan, refused to adopt it. In response, LKY threatened to withhold all staff salaries. To avoid turmoil, 'Sreeni' resigned. His successor, Professor Lim Tay Boh, accepted the decree.

I found myself in a quandary. My academic training advocated that I join the protesters. My worldly wisdom suggested that this was not my business. It seemed best to discuss the issue with friends. Lalith advised that I turn a blind eye. My doctoral thesis was still incomplete. A mere qualification from Jerusalem might not enable me to get another job as law teacher. He also pointed out that my marriage to a local girl dictated caution. Pat would have to accompany me if I sought promotion overseas but would not wish to see me assuming the role of a pariah. Lu Sinclair, the Assistant Registrar, advocated caution on the very same grounds. So did Harry.

Maurice Baker supported LKY's move. His view was that whilst the university should retain the assessment of a candidate's scholastic calibre, an institute of learning ought not to become the breeding ground of subversives. He was satisfied that the communist threat remained very much alive and that the Internal Security Department and the police were in a better position to tackle it than an academic body. "We better leave politics to the politicians," he told me.

After a brief discussion with Pat, I decided that I was really out of my depth. On the one hand, I recalled that in the Hebrew University, we often mellowed dogmatic thinkers. I recall one occasion in which an avowed Marxist became a pragmatic economist, imbued with capitalist ideas. I also remembered how a liberally minded girl turned an ultra-orthodox thinker into a hedonist. I was still inclined to think that the best way to meet a challenge was to persuade the protagonist to rethink matters.

On the other hand, I realised that my experience was confined to dealings with Jews, who deep at heart were pragmatists. I was not certain that the same truisms would be applicable in other societies. I concluded that I did not fully understand the East. In the event, I kept my silence. So did most expatriates, including all who were married to local girls. Further, after careful consideration, I concluded that Maurice was right.

At the end of the term, I took my sabbatical leave. Pat and I sub-let our house to a visiting fellow and then flew to Rome, where we met my parents. Pat, alas, did not get on with my mother. I sensed that the two women were not going to develop a cordial relationship.

Mother came with us (and Father) to Vienna. Pat enjoyed the sights, especially the ferries wheel, but I felt that she was not at home in Europe. To her, the West was even more alien than the East had ever been to me.

It will be recalled that Father had by then acquired a studio flat. It was suitable for a single person but too small for a couple. I was not surprised when Mother told me that after our departure, she was going to fly back to Israel.

After some three weeks, Pat and I left Vienna. We rented a car and had a pleasant drive through Austria, Germany and then on to Belgium and the Netherlands. It was a lovely excursion, and I believe that Pat enjoyed herself. She became particularly fond of Amsterdam. I recall visiting Rembrandt's house and how Pat admired his printing press. After returning the car to the rental company at Ostend, we took the ferry to Dover. We spent a few days in London — where Pat relished Chinatown — and then proceeded to Oxford.

We were lucky to be offered accommodation at Queen Elizabeth House in St. Giles Street. Most residents were postgraduate students, who came to Oxford for further studies. The House was run as a dormitory, serving breakfast, lunch and dinner. There was a comfortable hall-cum-sitting room with a television set. I recall watching the historic boxing match between Sonny Liston and Cassius Clay.

Queen Elizabeth House had the further advantage of being close to the new Bodleian Law Library, which had acquired a building of its own near the banks of the Cherwell River. As I already had all the published materials, I did not have to spend more than half a day in the library (mainly to check the accuracy of my existing notes). In the afternoons, I worked the chapters of the thesis into their final version. Pat helped me to read the proofs.

As Treitel was spending a few months in Chicago, the Board of Legal Studies appointed a replacement supervisor. Tony Guest read all my chapters patiently, made excellent points on both substance and style and returned the chapters to me within a fortnight. Tony Guest's meticulous comments and my meetings with him were also of benefit as regards my English style. Whilst Treitel enlightened me on all points of grammar and vocabulary, Guest taught me how to write fluently, with a view to enhancing readability. By the time he had completed the perusal of my draft chapters, I had mastered the finer points of writing both simply and grammatically. Under his influence, I made my final transition from Hebrew and German to literary English.

As I was making good progress, we were able to accept Sheridan's invitation to spend a week in Belfast. It was an instructive trip. By the time we returned to Oxford, I had learnt a great deal about the politics of Northern Ireland. It was also clear to me that as a cultural centre, Belfast lagged far behind London, Oxford and Singapore. It was a dull and uninspiring town.

Back at Oxford, I arranged for the final typing and binding of my thesis. I recall how Pat waited outside in the cold whilst I was having the *viva voce* session with the two examiners. In point of fact, I had an easy time. One examiner asked all the questions; the other gave all the answers. All I had to do was to nod sagely. A few weeks later, when Pat and I were already back in Singapore, the examiners submitted their positive report.

We were glad to move back into our house in College Green. When I reported for work, I was surprised to discover that Harry was annoyed with me. The colleague to whom I had delegated my duties as editor of our Law Review had taken a long time over one submission. The author had sent a poisonous letter, addressed to "The Dean", and complained about the delay.

It took me some time to convince Harry that I had not even seen the article. All the same, I defended my colleague, pointing out that a submission had to be considered by a referee and that, on occasions, one had to wait for up to three months for replies from the editorial team. Harry accepted the argument, but I could sense that he remained unsatisfied. It seemed best to resign from my post as editor of the Review.

Shortly after our return to Singapore, the Jewish community celebrated the high holidays. When I returned home after the morning service of the Day of Atonement, B. asked me to give her the usual pocket money.

"I can't go to the bank today. Our religion forbids us to conduct business on this day. I'll get it for you tomorrow."

"What a strange religion," she observed.

I was about to retort when Pat stepped in. She gave B. some money and asked me to repay her on the next day. To avoid contention, I kept silent and nodded my consent. Deep inside, though, I felt anger. B. was a guest in our house. She had no right to criticise her host's religion.

Some two weeks later, matters came to a head, when one evening B. tried to proselytise to me and urged me to convert. I retorted angrily and, rather than listen to further arguments, grabbed a manuscript I had been working on and left the house. For a while I worked on it in the office but actually was unable to concentrate. In the end, I went over to the staff cafeteria.

To my pleasant surprise, David R. was there. His girlfriend, he explained, had gone out with her old group. We had a drink and then went to our favourite restaurant. David's face brightened when I told him, "This is my treat; come have a steak!"

"Why not a chateaubriand for two?"

I knew that David, who was a gourmand-cum-glutton, would devour most of it. In truth, though, I had no appetite. "OK. And have a glass of wine," I told him.

During our dinner, I told David what had happened. For a while, he kept his silence. I knew that, fundamentally, he was reserved and reticent. He expressed his view only after I prodded him. In his opinion, I was making much ado about nothing. Knowing that I was an agnostic, he could not understand why I preferred to remain a Jewish sceptic rather than a Christian one. As far as he was concerned, religion was no more than a façade. I realised that the ethnic and sociological issue was far beyond him. It also dawned on me that both David's girlfriend and Geoff's wife were English-educated. I alone had been captivated by a Chinese-educated girl.

To further calm me down, David suggested we go to a cinema. I agreed and, in consequence, returned to my home in a mellowed mood. As anticipated, Pat and B. looked at me anxiously. Having reiterated what I had said before my departure, I retired.

The matter, which did not come up again at home, kept gnawing at me. In a sense, David R.'s words made sense. Did it really matter which religion you doubted? I knew at the same time that quite regardless of the tacit promise I had made to my mother, conversion was out of the question.

After some two weeks, I assumed the courage to discuss the issue with the only person whose advice I wanted, namely, Harry Groves. Initially, Harry was surprised when I made an appointment to see him in the office. He knew that I was satisfied with my teaching courses and my very light administrative duties. His face brightened when I assured him I had not called on him to seek promotion. He listened, imperturbably, to my account of the events that had taken place. To my surprise, he assured me that he would have taken the same stand as I did although, in all probability, without feeling angry.

"You see, Peter. Your Judaism is not just an adherence to a religion. It is an ethnic affiliation. I am in a similar position. Everyone who sees me knows I am a Black. Some people try to change the colour of their skin. Others adhere to their heritage. I do; and, I think, so do you. So stick to your point but without fuss."

I knew that Harry had hit the nail on its head. To my delight, I saw more of him after this heart-to-heart conversation. On one occasion, he invited me to the American Club. On another, Pat and I were invited to his house. To my utter surprise, he had an air conditioning unit in the kitchen. Bearing in mind that such devices were still rare, I raised my eyebrows. Harry then told us that his wife, Evelyn, liked to cook; the kitchen was unbearably hot and so an air conditioner was needed.

All in all, life in Singapore was peaceful when we came back from Europe. LKY had by then released some of the detainees, including James and his brother, and life went on smoothly. LKY's PAP did well in the general elections and came in with an absolute majority. I recall that David Marshall made a last-ditch attempt to win a seat. I knew that he was an excellent court room advocate but sensed that he lacked political acumen and, in my opinion, was politically naïve. I was relieved when he was overwhelmingly defeated.

LKY kept his election promises. HDB blocks were rising in many parts of the town, and the transport system was much improved. I sensed that, for the time being, the PAP was bound to remain in power. LKY had a fine economist — Dr. Goh Keng Swee — in his team. Goh's contribution to the Lion City's success was substantial.

The next development was the finalisation of the merger. As from 16 September 1963, Singapore, the Federation of Malaya and Sabah and Sarawak (in Borneo) became the Federation of Malaysia. As anticipated, the Malayan Government guarded its flanks. Singapore was allocated only a given number of seats in the Malaysian Parliament. In this way, the Malay leaders obviated the danger of Singapore politicians, together with those in Sabah and Sarawak, dominating Parliament.

Regrettably, the Malaysian Prime Minister, Tunku (Prince) Abdul Rahman, and LKY did not get on. I suspect that the special privileges conferred by the Constitution of Malaysia on ethnic Malays (Bumiputras) irked the Chinese in Singapore. Before long, pamphlets published in Kuala Lumpur denigrated Singapore and vice versa. I recall reading some of them and must confess that I found them ominous.

Another regional problem was the confrontation (Konfrontasi) declared by Indonesia's President Sukarno. Thereafter, Indonesian armed personnel infiltrated West Malaysia and Singapore to cause mayhem. Whilst they did not cause much harm, they were feared. Singapore was one of their prime targets. I believe that Sukarno hoped to rebel-rouse the Malay community and subdue the Chinese community. His efforts remained futile, although he managed to create a tense atmosphere.

My personal life was not affected by these developments. I continued to concentrate on my teaching courses and on the writing of articles submitted to prestigious foreign law reviews. I also published a number of papers locally. Before long, Harry sent me a note suggesting I apply for a senior lectureship. I did and was promoted. For the first time in my life, I felt wealthy.

Interestingly, by securing my academic credentials I became well established in the eyes of the local Bar. Quite a number of lawyers, including prominent David Marshall, sent me briefs. This opinion work augmented my income.

In addition, I was invited to conduct a number of extramural courses. One was on aspects of banking law, in which bills of exchange and cheques still played a prominent role. Another dealt with aspects of company law.

These courses were well attended and provided yet further income. I believe that I earned as much as a junior partner in an established law firm. The future appeared rosy, and I was looking forward to it. I was actually contemplating buying a house with a view to settling down in Singapore. However, a hidden hand — or perhaps my Goddess Fortuna — had made other plans for me.

At the time of writing — when I have reached the advanced age of 89 — I frequently think about the twists of fate in my life. I do believe that, in most cases, I made the correct decisions. However, if fate had not been kind to me, I would not have been given the chances that came my way and the option of grabbing them. I often think about my first few years in Singapore. They were years of trials, tribulations and also of achievements. It was during this fine period that I believe I became an established member of the academic community.

I shall tell you more about the end of this first spell in the City of the Lion in my next letter.

In the meantime, I wish all of you the very best.

With kind regards,
Peter

Letter 16: Plans to Leave Singapore

20 January 2018
Singapore

Dear Friends,

During the ensuing two years, my life ran on an even keel. At Pat's suggestion, I applied for a house in Kheam Hock Road. It had large grounds and a garage but one room fewer than the terrace house in College Green. As B. occupied one of our two rooms, I had no study at home. Still, B. did not make any further attempts to convert me. Life, accordingly, was peaceful and harmonious.

In the evenings, we often went for a meal either to Koek (pronounced Cook) Lane (which has long ago disappeared under the Centrepoint) or to Albert Street, which in those days was a pleasant lane with excellent food stalls. I recall that on one occasion I had been told that in Albert Street you could get a fine oyster omelette. As hawkers were not able to direct me to the stall involved, I went into premises which appeared less crowded than the stalls. A well-groomed Chinese gentleman asked what I wanted. Having advised me that an oyster omelette was unavailable in Albert Street, he recommended a curry puff stall. When I returned to our table, Pat was frightened. She explained I had entered the headquarters of the 'secret society' which was in control in that area. She thought I had had a narrow escape.

Another pleasant pastime was visiting the night market ('*pasar malam*' in Malay), which stretched along Tanglin Road right to the corner of Orchard and Paterson Roads. Both of us bought many attractive knickknacks as we followed the crowd. In addition, local artists exhibited their works there. Over the years, I acquired a few fine pieces.

Things fared less well at the faculty. Harry Groves took four months' leave, to which he was entitled. He had intended to return to Singapore and resume the deanship. Regrettably, for purely technical reasons, Harry had to go through the formality of swapping appointments. To my dismay, Leslie convinced the vice-chancellor that as a consequence the deanship was vacated. Harry took this development as a slight and resigned from his position. I sent him a lengthy letter, asking him to reconsider and expressing the hope he would return to us as dean. To my surprise, I received no reply. Initially, I thought that Harry had decided not to answer. Nowadays, I suspect Harry might not have received my entreaty. Be this as it may, he did not return to Singapore.

Leslie was now the only full professor. He was appointed as dean without any opposition. He did not hold the reins for long. He was offered a post at the University of Alberta in Edmonton and left us.

Before his departure, Leslie made one remarkable appointment. A legal practitioner from a town in Johor was constituted a lecturer on the understanding that he would prove his academic calibre during his three years of probation. As the appointee had no qualification except of having passed English Bar examinations and his having entertained Leslie and his wife royally, many eyebrows were raised.

After Leslie departed, we decided to appoint a visiting professor from Belfast, J.L. Montrose (Jimmy), as our dean. The then deputy vice-chancellor invited me to assume the role of acting head of the department. I was surprised but took his point when he explained that a department had to be run by a permanent staff member. Being the only senior lecturer, the vice-chancellor's choice fell on me. The administration hoped that the dean and I would work harmoniously.

I knew the vice-chancellor, Professor Lim Tay Boh, quite well. We often met at the petrol station. It turned out that originally his family came from the same area in China as Pat's. He and his wife conversed with Pat in Hokkien; I tried to look wise. It pleased me to think that this indirect link may have been instrumental in my being accepted as an honorary local.

Jimmy and I worked in harmony. My main task was to assign teaching duties. Jimmy usually endorsed my proposed schedules. By and large, we followed the schedules previously composed by Harry Groves.

Another duty which I had as Acting Head of the Department was to get the examination papers printed. In those days, we still depended on typewriters and on traditional printing. Stencils were not used in the university and the only photocopying machine was in the vice-chancellor's office. It was not made available to other university departments.

Examination papers had to be written out in long hand and then typed by the dean's secretary. The transcripts were then taken to a trusted printer, who delivered the printed forms to the faculty in sealed envelopes. Sheridan had delegated the supervision of this printing process to our chief clerk. The deputy vice-chancellor considered the arrangement insecure. The result was that I had to personally deliver papers to the printers and, in effect, oversee the printing process. The task was time-consuming. Today, I am satisfied that this precaution was a sheer waste of time.

An amusing incident took place during Sheridan's days. One year, after the papers had been printed, Sheridan received an anonymous letter. The writer alleged that the dean's secretary had shown the relevant papers to her boyfriend, who was a law student. None of us believed this to be true. Still, for the sake of certainty, we were asked to reset our questions. The typing was entrusted to an outsider. The relevant student's scripts disclosed no shock or disbelief when he wrote his exams. I am confident that the dean's secretary, who was a singularly good-looking girl, had many suitors. The letter must have been composed by one she had spurned.

My most important task as Acting Head of the Department was to consider applications for appointments and promotions. Here, too, Jimmy and I usually saw eye to eye. I recall one difficult case of a candidate whose LL.B. results left much to be desired. However, he sent us a dissertation he had written on a topic in jurisprudence. Jimmy read it, lauded it and the candidate was appointed. Today, he is a well-known scholar in an Australian university. I am glad I followed Jimmy's lead.

Another matter that was settled satisfactorily was the appointment of a new external examiner. In those days, the university's examination scripts were scrutinised not only by the teacher-in-charge of the course but also by an external examiner. Originally, Sheridan appointed two external examiners. After one of them resigned, I managed to replace him with Tony Guest. I am pleased to say that Tony was an outstanding choice.

The only problem that arose concerned the practitioner who had been appointed by Leslie. To my utter surprise, the vice-chancellor asked me to attend a meeting of the University Promotions Board. Usually, the members included only the deans of faculties (or their delegates), who came to the meeting with information pertaining to the promotions requested by their respective departments.

Unexpectedly, Jimmy proposed that our probationer be promoted to a senior lectureship. He explained the matter had just arisen so that he did not have the time to consult the Acting Head of the Department but trusted I would give him my support. Before I could reply, the Dean of Medicine requested details of the applicant's performance since his appointment. Jimmy explained that the candidate had discussed interesting ideas with him and that he was a fine teacher.

As everyone was looking at me, I explained that the candidate had not published any work and that I was unaware of the excellence of his teaching performance. To my relief, the Dean of Arts stepped in. He took the view that, in the circumstance, a promotion was premature. Jimmy, however, persisted. I then recalled that the candidate's wife was friendly with the Jimmy's wife. Presumably, Jimmy had promised to deliver the goods. The matter was put to vote. The motion that the candidate be promoted was not seconded. The vice-chancellor then turned to the next item on the agenda.

For a while, Pat and I saw little of Jimmy and his wife. To my surprise, there was a sequel. Leslie wrote from Edmonton, copying the letter to me. The gist of it was that, although Leslie did not intend to tell our vice-chancellor how to run our university, he thought he should express his firm support for Jimmy's recommendation concerning the probationary lecturer and added that, in his view, the person in question would know how to run a department. I knew Leslie had never forgiven my having supported Harry Groves but was surprised that he manifested such indiscreet behaviour. The matter was no longer any of his business and his advice had not been solicited. The deputy vice-chancellor's telephone call assured me that Leslie's tirade had had no effect on the university's authorities. In point of fact, they were irked.

Shortly thereafter, I discovered that Jimmy was a very sick man. As the acting head of the department, I had to attend meetings of the senate. On one occasion, I sat next to one of the medical professors. In a sheer breach of confidentiality, he told me that Jimmy suffered from bone cancer. His prognosis of Jimmy's life span was negative.

"[J.] is a brave man," he told me, "but some cases are hopeless."

"Why do you say he is brave?" I wanted to know.

"He must be experiencing extreme pain but manages to ignore it. I wish he had consulted us at least three months ago."

A few weeks later, Jimmy moved on to Auckland, where he was to hold yet another visiting chair. His stay with us was too short to enable him to make any significant contribution. Still, many of us benefitted from his searching comments on our writings. I attended his farewell party with a heavy heart. I did not realise at that time that I was going to see him again before long.

Jimmy's departure left a void. Our faculty no longer had a full professor and none of the sub-professorial staff was prepared to stand for the deanship. Fortunately, the vice-chancellor met Geoff Bartholomew in Melbourne and convinced him to come back to us. I was delighted: Geoff was an outstanding lecturer, had the makings of an excellent dean and was fondly remembered by his former students. I recall ringing him in order to convince him to secure the best terms. To my dismay, it turned out that the original offer made to him was lower than the salary which had been paid to Leslie.

Initially, my suggestion that Geoff ask for an extra S$300 a month led to a negative reaction. Geoff wondered whether I had, surreptitiously, discussed the matter with his wife. She too had urged him to demand a higher pay. He then added that his name was 'Bartholomew' and not 'Shylock'.

"An extra pay will enable you to buy a better car, Geoff. And if Winnie and you are going to settle here you ought to buy a house! Staying in subsidised university accommodation would be stupid. You may not be able to buy a good house with your superannuation after retirement. I am sure prices will go up!"

"Are you buying a house?"

"I may, that is, if we decide to settle here."

In the event, Geoff took my advice regarding his remuneration and was, indeed, offered a higher salary. I fear that initially he had failed to realise that under the new management bargaining was legitimate.

I recall Geoff's arrival in Singapore. To my delight, the university agreed to accommodate him for a week in the upmarket Goodwood Park Hotel. From there, he moved to a luxury bungalow offered by the university. I kept urging him to give it up and buy a house of his own. Geoff, though, decided to stay put.

Within two weeks of Geoff's arrival, the faculty, by a unanimous vote, appointed him as dean. He was also made the head of the department. I was glad to see that his former students invited him out frequently. All of us regarded him as having returned to base.

Geoff was an excellent leader. Under his guidance, our Law Review was reinforced, an excellent mooting system was restored, and the syllabus was revised and much improved. Geoff also dealt effectively with our probationary colleague, who left us shortly after Geoff's arrival. I felt vindicated. I further benefitted directly from Geoff's leadership.

Within a few months of his arrival, he launched a series of Singapore legal monographs. My Oxford doctorate was accepted for publication.

I believe that Geoff was a worthy successor to both Lee Sheridan and Harry Groves. Like them, he was good with our students, regarded the faculty's welfare as paramount and did not try to further his personal interests. In my opinion, he brought with him a breath of fresh air. The future looked rosy.

My only concern respected Geoff's tendency to be blunt. The father of a first-year student, who had been failed by the board of examiners, tried to persuade us to overturn their decision and pass his son. Both Jimmy and I had refused to hear about this. The father, though, had made substantial donations to the university's charity funds. The deputy vice-chancellor asked us, accordingly, to handle the matter gently. In the event, Jimmy agreed to reread some of the boy's papers and came up with a brief memorandum endorsing the board's decision. We remained firm but handled the disappointed father with delicacy. When Geoff arrived in Singapore, the disappointed father approached him. Geoff handled him curtly. The deputy vice-chancellor was not pleased but endorsed Geoff's decision. All the same, I realised that the deputy vice-chancellor was no longer a reliable supporter.

Then, to my dismay, Geoff made a blatant error. He was asked to assume the chairmanship of the Expatriate Staff Association. When he told me about the offer, I did my best to persuade him to turn it down. He had come back to Singapore with a view to settling down here; he was no bird of passage. Accordingly, the interests of the purely expatriate staff did not coincide with his own. The appointment would not enhance his standing and might be counterproductive.

Geoff did not listen to me. At the behest of the deputy vice-chancellor, who had become a good friend of mine, I made another effort to reason with Geoff. Regrettably, he had by then accepted the appointment.

I believe that, notwithstanding this incident, Geoff would have continued to go from strength to strength under the existing university administration. Both the vice-chancellor and his deputy continued to regard Geoff as an honorary, even if somewhat blunt, local. His acceptance of the chairmanship of the Expatriate Staff Association was regarded as an aberration. Regrettably, the pendulum swung when the vice-chancellor, who suffered from high blood pressure, died from a stroke.

By then, I had, however, left Singapore for New Zealand. Shortly after his return to Singapore, Geoff encouraged me to apply for a full professorship. I knew that I had the requisite number of publications, that my thesis was just about to be published as a book and that my teaching record was sound. The only negative factor was my age and my having been in academia for just five years.

After careful consideration, I lodged my application. When it was turned down, I felt it was time for me to change venue. Further, many expatriates had left, and I feared that if I stayed behind, the authorities might conclude that I had nowhere to go. I would then remain a senior lecturer for the rest of my life.

Yet another ground for moving away was the hope that Pat would get closer to me if we went overseas. I did realise — with some disappointment — that she had remained closer to her family than to me. Naively, I thought this could be altered. It took me years to realise that I was hoping for a miracle, and that it was most unlikely to happen.

I discussed my prospect for promotion overseas with Tony Guest when he came over as external examiner. Tony told me that my chances for an appointment to a chair in an English university were dim. He thought it would be more realistic to apply for such a position in New Zealand. Shortly after his return to Oxford, Tony sent me advertisements for chairs in Wellington and in Auckland. Within a few weeks, I applied.

I did so with misgivings. My life during the entire period was actually comfortable and smooth. Every Sunday, Pat went to her church service by taxi and took B. with her. I remained behind and awaited the arrival of our bridge players. I recall, in particular, one occasion in which an international award was conferred on our Professor of Mathematics, who was one of the players. Knowing he would come sharp on time, we gathered some twenty minutes before his arrival. We greeted him enthusiastically with a 'for he's a jolly good fellow' welcome and formally moved to elect him as the honorary chairman of our unincorporated bridge club. Many players had brought cakes and drinks and Pat, who rang me shortly after lunch, hurried back with a celebration cake. All of us were happy. From a purely social point of view, things could not have been better.

However, politics in Singapore were strained at that time. The PAP and the leading Malaysian party — the United Malays National Organisation (UMNO) — were at loggerheads. The tone of the salvos exchanged between LKY and Kuala Lumpur became vitriolic. Furthermore, *Konfrontasi*, that is, the Indonesian Confrontation, started to leave its mark. I believe that the objective of the saboteurs was to incite racial feelings and that UMNO fed the fire. On 21 July 1964, the local Malay daily, *Utusan Melayu*, published articles inciting riots, by advising the Singapore Malays that they were being poorly treated by the PAP. On that very day — the anniversary of Prophet Muhammad's birthday — the procession in honour of the Prophet turned into an anti-Chinese riot, claiming the lives of some 23 people. LKY imposed a three-day curfew and made firm promises to the representatives of the Malay community. For the time being, order was restored.

Pat and I were only marginally affected. We had to use the hours in which curfew was lifted to restock our larder. I was amused to note that when we arrived in the nearest Cold Storage supermarket, the counters were manned by the British management staff. The local staff lived too far away to brave the journey there and back. To my delight, the store gave us a 10% discount on our purchases. So, in a way, Pat and I benefitted from the security measures imposed by the government.

A second set of riots broke out on 2 September. It was clear that they were provoked by the assassination of a Malay trishaw (Betsa) driver. My belief is that this particular riot was occasioned by *Konfrontasi* activists, who came over from Johor. In any event, peace was restored on the very same day.

There is no doubt that tensions were experienced both in Singapore and in Kuala Lumpur. The Tunku and UMNO feared that LKY would be able to make headway in Malaysia through cooperation with the Chinese and non-Malay populations. They were also perturbed by LKY's refusal to recognise in Singapore the special rights conferred on indigenous Malays (later, expanded to Bumiputras) in Kuala Lumpur (Selangor) and in other states of the Federation.

LKY, in turn, was opposed to the granting of special rights, such as quotas in the legal service, to Malays in Singapore. Guided by a drive for meritocracy, he expected the Malay community to rise by pulling up its own boot strings. The two policies were inconsistent with each other. LKY's advocacy for a Malaysian Malaysia led to acrimony with UMNO leaders. I am still not certain about the indirect role played by Indonesian activists. However, I knew that Singapore was easily accessed from the Riau Islands. All in all, I am inclined to think that saboteurs posed a real threat and that they contributed to the tension between the Tunku and LKY.

Their worst atrocity was the bombing of MacDonald House in Orchard Road on 10 March 1965. Three people were killed. The perpetrators were apprehended, tried for murder and convicted. Although confrontation drew to a close shortly thereafter, when President Sukarno was ousted by Suharto, LKY refused to grant pardons. To Suharto's chagrin, the culprits were hanged.

Before the end of the year, Singapore was expelled from Malaysia (9 August 1965). LKY wept on television. In contrast, the merchants in Chinatown fired crackers. They now had an independent city-state of their own. The quest for an independent Singapore, which Britain had rejected in 1956, was now a political reality. I recall the Tunku's letter, in which he ordered the commander of the forces in Singapore to take all new orders from LKY. I admire the Tunku for obviating bloodshed.

Economically, Singapore had to tackle the vacuum left by the withdrawal of the British Army. As in Palestine prior to 1948, the British army base was a major work provider in Singapore. To a point, the British ameliorated the ensuing economic problems by giving most employees the choice of moving to Britain. However, many merchants lost their British customers. Fortunately, LKY had an excellent economic adviser. Goh Keng Swee helped LKY to steer Singapore in the right direction. Between them, they mastered the economic problems the city-state was facing. Still, in 1965, there was a cloud on the horizon.

The uncertain outlook respecting Singapore's future encouraged me to consider making a move. Notably, during this entire period, my applications for a Chair of Law in New Zealand were pending. Shortly after Singapore's expulsion from Malaysia, I was invited to fly over to both Wellington and Auckland for job interviews. I recall my trepidation as I packed my suitcase.

On the way to New Zealand, I made a stop in Sydney in order to meet Auntie Ida. She and her second son took me for a tour of Sydney, which I admired. I also met my first cousin Ted — Auntie Ida's oldest — who was a successful solicitor. To my surprise, he spoke good German. Apparently, the old milieu had not been uprooted in toto.

I spent two days with Auntie Ida. On the first of them, she viewed my slip-on shoes critically. She decided I was not properly dressed for the occasion, took me to David Jones and made me buy an elegant pair with laces. To my surprise, she offered to pay for them.

On the second day, we went to Australia Square — a high-rise building topped with a rotating restaurant. The view was staggering. I realised that Sydney was a growing metropolis with fine architecture. Initially, Auntie Ida had doubts about having a meal at the restaurant. She thought it was singularly expensive. She accepted my invitation only when I explained that I had just submitted two opinions to lawyers in Singapore. In the course of our lunch, she asked me why I had not brought Pat with me. Pat should see the place before we decided to move to it.

"What will you do if she does not like it?"

"I really don't know. I hope she will."

"Make sure she meets people from her own community. She may find it difficult to adjust to an unfamiliar environment. And does she know how to cook Viennese food?"

"She taught herself," I replied proudly.

"That is good," she observed. "I still cook Viennese food at home. And I taught Erica (Ted's wife)."

"Is Erica Jewish?" I wanted to know.

"Of course; and I'll do my best to find a girl from a Jewish home for Henry (her second son). Marrying out can be risky."

Auntie Ida's observations gave me food for thought. Was Pat going to mix well in New Zealand? In any event, my first task was to secure a chair.

My meetings in Wellington went well. I was offered the post although my hosts suggested that it would be good if I delayed my acceptance until after my trip to Auckland. There, the dean advised me that he would not support my application. In consequence, I decided to accept the post offered to me in Wellington.

Whilst in Auckland, I met Jimmy. He had lost weight and looked haggard. Recalling the words of the medical man in Singapore, I realised that our Jimmy was sick beyond redemption.

He encouraged me to opt for the chair in Wellington. He thought the dean in Auckland and I would not get on.

"He expects his staff to toe the line. You are not particularly good at that. You like to have your own way or to be consulted!"

"True. He has already told me he would not support me."

"That's that, then," concluded Jimmy. Then, after a short pause, he asked me to do him a favour. He was undergoing radiation treatment, his only hope in the circumstance. He let his disgust show, when I told him that I was familiar with his condition following my conversation in Singapore. He thought the physician had been indiscreet and in breach of the relationship of patient and doctor. He then told me that he was keeping details of his treatment from his wife. He had told her that he was spending the evening with me and asked me to cover up for him if she rang.

"Come on, Jimmy. You are asking me to be a cad!"

"Not really, Peter. I ask you to help me. The decision to keep M. in the dark is personal. I don't want her to fuss over me. You come from a background similar to mine. So you must understand and help."

Although I hated the idea of being involved, I gave way. When M. rang me, I told her that Jimmy was in the bathroom and promised to let him know she called.

"Is he really with you, Peter? I want to have the truth!"

"I'll get him to ring you as soon as possible," I assured her lamely, sensing that in all probability she did not believe me. A few minutes later, Jimmy rang me from the hospital. He promised to ring his wife promptly but said he needed to rest in my hotel room for a while.

"This treatment takes a lot out of you, Peter. I need a respite!"

"But what will you tell her next time, when I am no longer here?"

"I'll improvise," he assured me.

"Are you trying to protect her or yourself?"

"That is my business, Peter," he replied spiritedly.

I returned to Wellington with a heavy heart. It is possible that M. had forgiven me. All the same, I continued to feel guilty and ashamed. Jimmy passed away a few weeks later. His wife took his body back to Belfast. Both Auckland and Singapore held memorial services. I have never attempted to contact M. thereafter.

Whilst in Wellington, we finalised the paperwork. I undertook to take up the post some six months later. When all was done, I sent a telegram to Geoff, asking him to advise Pat that I had accepted the chair.

When I was back in Singapore, Geoff castigated me for reaching a decision without consulting Pat. At the very least, I should have given her a formal right of veto. I knew he was right and that I had acted unfeelingly and, in all probability, selfishly. Still, Pat knew that I had flown over in order to secure a professorship. She was bound to support me.

By the end of the term in Singapore, I was entitled to a sabbatical leave of six months. I treated it as a bonus and took it willingly. I had worked extremely hard during my six years in Singapore and felt the right to take every privilege to which I was entitled.

My first stop was once again Belfast. I had not expected to visit the town again, but Sheridan's kind offer was irresistible. I flew over before Pat and conducted a number of staff seminars. My parents came to see me, and we had a pleasant reunion.

I then proceeded to London where Pat joined me. After a few weeks, we returned for a final spell in Singapore. Both of us felt sad when we vacated the house in Kheam Hock Road. My friends in the faculty gave me a pleasant farewell lunch a few days before we took our flight to my new posting.

When I think about my first spell in Singapore in hindsight, I feel that this first job shaped my entire academic life. When I went to Oxford, in 1960, I was a young legal practitioner. Oxford made me contemplate a switch to academia. My first spell in Singapore convinced me that law teaching was my vocation. To date, I believe I made the correct choice. Much later in my life, after I had become a specialist in my chosen field, I engaged regularly in consulting work and became a practitioner. My real home, though, was in the ivory tower.

My next few letters will deal with our life in New Zealand. I loved the country but, alas, Pat never settled down.

In the meantime, I wish all of you the very best.

With kind regards,
Peter

Part III

THE WANDERER'S STAFF

20 February 2018
Singapore

Dear Friends,

Letter 17: Our Early Years in Wellington

On our way to New Zealand, Pat and I stopped in Perth and then continued to Sydney, where we spent a few days with Auntie Ida. Pat liked Sydney and, I believe, enjoyed Ida's company.

In Wellington, we were met by the dean, Colin Aikman, and by Ivor Richardson, who was appointed at the same time as I and who was keen to be made the head of the department. Pat and I were taken to the Midland Hotel, an old and well-thought-of establishment. We had two weeks to find accommodation. I recall one amusing event. The mustard served at dinner was in powder form; the diner was supposed to mix it with water. I was unaware of this time-honoured New Zealand custom and simply tried to spray the powder over the meat. One of the waitresses looked at me with concern, stepped over and mixed the mustard for us.

Pat and I spent the best part of the two weeks looking for accommodation. In the end, we rented a unit owned by one of my colleagues. It was a flat in a two-apartment block, down the slope of hilly Wadestown. The owner lived in a house at the bottom of the section, accessible by a lift van. I soon discovered that Wellington spread over a number of hills and that many houses were located at the bottom of slopes. In my long life, I have visited quite a number of countries. None had a city as picturesque as Wellington.

Right from the date of our arrival, I felt at home. My colleagues were a pleasant lot. Most of them were tolerant, cheerful and easygoing, and our students were keen and amiable. Many of them were more outgoing than my students in Singapore, were eager to participate in class discussions and frequently came up with new ideas. I enjoyed myself.

We were invited to the homes of many colleagues. Before long, I came to know most of them well and formed some lasting friendships. Ivor, in particular, helped me a great deal as we searched for a house to buy. He was familiar with the property market and stopped me from making a number of mistakes. He and his wife lived in a pleasant house in one of the better suburbs in town. Another colleague, George Barton (who became a close friend), lived in the same district.

Colin Aikman, the dean, lived in another part of town, right at the top of a splendid hill. I recall one cute incident. Once, when we were invited by the Aikmans for coffee, Colin — who was an odd-job man — greeted us whilst dressed as a plumber. Pat failed to recognise him and asked for 'Professor Aikman'. Colin was highly amused.

My office was in an old block known as the Hunter Building, within the library precinct. It had a stunning view over the harbour and some of the nearby isles. I enjoyed it and often relaxed near the window and took in the sight.

Shortly after our arrival, Pat decided we should travel around during weekends. On the first occasion, we drove to the nearby coastal villages, which were lovely. We found an excellent and modestly priced restaurant and a nice coffee house. I did not have a map but simply drove straight ahead and, in the afternoon, proceeded back on the basis that all roads lead to... our dwelling. To my relief, I arrived in Wadestown without losing my way.

About two months after our arrival, the Reserve Bank devalued the currency. On the one hand, this meant that my professorial salary in New Zealand was lower than my take-home package as a senior lecturer in Singapore. On the other hand, it meant that my savings, which I had kept with our bank in Singapore in the local currency, soared in value. This enabled me to put down a deposit on a house in a fine inner district of Wellington. It had three bedrooms, a dining room and the usual amenities. To my delight, it had a roomy garage. Further, it was close to the university.

Pat enjoyed being the owner of such a splendid house. She started to return our colleagues' invitations. I do believe they enjoyed her first-rate cooking and liked coming to our home. In effect, we had a pleasant and rewarding social life.

We discovered some additional ways and means to overcome the effect of the depreciation of our currency. For instance, we found a chicken farm situated on our town's outskirts. Naturally, the main product — chicken — was sold at a much lower price than in the shops in town. On top of this, we discovered that chicken livers and fat were sold for a token. New Zealanders did not use these in their cooking and so the farmer was happy to sell them at any price. Pat, who had mastered Jewish recipes, prepared excellent chopped liver and pâtés, relished by me and many of our occasional guests.

Frequently, I took lunch in a small cafeteria near the campus. Usually, though, I took my midday meal in the university, walking from the Hunter Building to the cafeteria in the adjacent Rankine Brown

Building. The snacks were good and the coffee strongly brewed. At least two tables were occupied by our bridge players. Invariably, I joined and, in this way, met scholars from other faculties, such as Arts and Science, and some Administrators. A number of them became family friends and, before too long, they came to our house, and Pat and I were invited to theirs.

From my personal point of view, things could not have been better. Being the capital of New Zealand, Wellington had a cosmopolitan ambience. We were often invited for dinner at the Singapore High Commission and Pat became a regular participant in the activities of the spouses of foreign diplomats stationed in New Zealand. In an attempt to perfect Pat's spoken English, one of my colleagues' wives came to our place in order to teach her. In my view, both of us were treated extremely well.

My only personal problem related to the climate. The pollens during Wellington's summer triggered off asthma attacks and hay fever. These, however, were readily controlled by an inhaler. I got used to carrying one with me regularly. In a way, this solved the only handicap faced by me.

Regrettably, another problem surfaced in respect of my wife. It was a matter of genuine regret to me that despite the welcoming approaches of colleagues and neighbours, Pat did not settle down comfortably. She longed for her environment in Singapore and felt alien. She kept complaining that New Zealand was a dead end and that Wellington was a very small town. Letters received from family members in Singapore exacerbated the problem. They, too, felt that Wellington lacked 'life'.

For a while, I tried to ignore the issue and escaped into books. To compensate for its remoteness from Europe and North America, Wellington sponsored cultural and scholarly events. For instance,

Wellington had two theatres, a sound — even if not brilliant — philharmonic orchestra and, most importantly, excellent bookshops. Suffice it to say that my autodidactic work on the *Dead Sea Scrolls* commenced during my days in New Zealand. One of the bookshops boasted comprehensive catalogues and reference manuals. The owner was proud to identify and order the books I required. I believe he really enjoyed tracing books for me. In addition, a professor of religion gave me access to his comprehensive library, which covered books on bible critique. When read together with some of the texts from the *Dead Sea Scrolls*, they opened a window into a lost world.

Regrettably, my enthusiasm was not shared by my wife. In the end, I felt the need to discuss the situation openly with Pat. Having sung Wellington's praises to her, I wanted to know what was remiss. She conceded that our town had good amenities and that people were nice to her. Still, she missed Singapore's night markets, food stalls and the Asian ambience. She then asked me a pertinent question:

"Yes, everybody treats me well. But do they like Patricia or Mrs. Berger?"

"What do you mean?"

"Suppose I was here on my own, without you. Wouldn't they simply ignore me?"

I could not find an answer. I realised that, in truth, Pat craved to be back in her own environment. I had taken her away from it and did not provide an adequate substitute. Unlike me, Pat was not adaptable. Our conversation highlighted the point.

A few weeks after my chat with Pat, I ran into Colin Aikman's wife during the lunch break. Bettie had sensed what I had on my mind and before long raised the issue. After listening to my domestic problem, she suggested that, at least twice a week, I ought to take Pat for lunch.

"She must feel very lonely at home, and she does not ring anybody. You must try to fill in the void in her life. Why don't you take her to meet members of the Chinese community?"

"They are Cantonese; Pat is Hokkien, and so they don't really click."

"Then, try to take her to functions of the Jewish set up. The main thing is to get her involved in some social activities. In the past, we lost two staff members whose wives wanted to 'go back home'. We don't want to lose you this way."

"You know: Aislie Campbell comes over to our place once a week to teach Pat English. Everybody is good to her."

"All of us try. But in a way, she always ends up feeling left out. You must help her get over this."

Bettie's advice appeared sound. I began to ask Pat at least once a week to take the bus from our place to the university. Usually, we went downtown by the municipal cable car. There were good eateries and sandwich bars on Lambton Quay. On other days I picked Pat up at home, and we drove downtown. Usually, I would work at home after these outings.

I recall one memorable outing. We went to the only sophisticated delicatessen shop in town, entitled Fullerfullton. I was looking covetously at a tin of braised pheasants. It was expensive, and so I was going to give it a miss. Then, unexpectedly, we experienced a tremor, that is, a mild earthquake. The local shoppers, who had become accustomed to such events, remained calm and composed as if nothing had happened. I was startled and then saw, to my surprise, that the desired tin simply flew into my shopping trolley. As the whole shelf collapsed, I thought it best to return the tin to the cashier at the counter.

"Have it on the house," she smiled and handled the next item I had decided to buy. In the event, Pat and I had a free, outlandish dish.

For a while, Pat appeared less gloomy. In my heart of hearts, though, I knew this was but a temporary solution. Pat had to find a focus, and none appeared on the horizon. She started to look for a job. I too searched and found her an opening in a bank. To my disappointment, she refused to give it a try.

My next attempt was to get her enrolled in a course of studies at the university. With the aid of one of my bridge partners, she was admitted but, after a while, dropped out.

Once again, I turned to Bettie Aikman for advice. I recall how I hurried and arrived for lunch just in time. Having muttered my profuse apologies for being covered in sweat, Bettie observed, with a smile, that animals sweat, men perspire and women glow. Everyone at the table grinned. When all others left, I asked Bettie what else she would recommend.

"You better have children, Peter," she told me. "Pat needs at least one."

"Wouldn't Pat want to take our child back to Singapore?"

"This is a possibility. But let us hope she wants her child to grow up as a Kiwi (New Zealander)."

Bettie's advice was sound. Regrettably, Pat did not conceive. The specialist we consulted concluded that it was a problem of seminal incompatibility. I pause to add that nowadays — in the 21st century — such an issue could be readily resolved. In New Zealand of the sixties, it presented a stumbling block.

Initially, Pat suggested we adopt a child. The social worker recommended that we take on a boy parented by a Singaporean male Chinese and a New Zealand girl. In the end, though, Pat was deterred when she discovered that an adoptee had to be told the identity of his or her physical parents. She also concluded that she would adopt only a girl. This, alas, was the end of the matter.

Pat's constant complaints worried me. I felt fulfilled at work but had to face unhappiness at home. For a while, though, I had respite. B. flew over from Singapore, bringing with her a Thai man she wanted to marry. I knew that, in one regard, B. lagged far behind Pat. My wife was a beautiful woman, who could hold her own in any society. Socially, she was self-assured. B. was a plain Jane and, in consequence, lacked self-confidence.

Pat and I drove B. and her friend through the beautiful South Island of New Zealand. I recall the exciting ferry passage from Wellington to Picton (on the tip of the South Island). We drove through the West Coast down the Haast Pass, one of the enchanting routes to Queenstown — the pearl of New Zealand — and to the Lake District. We proceeded to Mount Cooke and flew by helicopter up to the Tasman Glacier. Regrettably, I suffered from airsickness and so did not enjoy the view as much as the others. We then returned by ferry from Christchurch to Wellington. All in all, the trip took about two weeks and I know that Pat enjoyed herself.

B. left shortly thereafter. To my surprise, she was prepared to migrate to Thailand to marry. I considered that to be an unsound decision as it would interrupt her course of studies. In the event, the boy's family took exception to the marriage and B. remained in Singapore.

Shortly after B.'s departure, I experienced an extremely busy spell involving the drafting of a report on reforming the New Zealand Moneylenders Act. The work had to be carried out for the Contracts and Commercial Law Reform Committee, a government body to which I was appointed on Colin Aikman's recommendation shortly after I took up my chair. The work of the committee was interesting. We constituted a committee of troubleshooters, to whom the Justice Department referred shortcomings in private law that emerged from time to time. Usually, we met four times a year: twice in Wellington and twice in Auckland.

When my report respecting the Moneylenders Act was in progress, we scheduled a meeting in Auckland. I used the occasion to drive all the way up north to the Bay of Plenty — the first spot on which a European ship had landed. We visited Waitangi, where the Europeans (*Pakeha* in Maori) and the Maori chiefs had signed a treaty that neither party observed. We then drove down to Auckland via Tauranga — a delightful town — only to find, on arrival, that the meeting had been cancelled.

After a few days in Auckland — which I did not like — we drove to the fascinating geyser land of Rotorua. I enjoyed every moment and, I believe, so did Pat. I was particularly impressed by the clear streams in which trout (a protected species) swam merrily. We then visited stormy Lake Waikaremoana and proceeded to Lake Taupo and the allegedly extinct volcano, Mount Ruapehu, towering over it. Notably, the trip was free: the generous government compensated me royally for time spent on travelling to attend a meeting that was cancelled! In effect, we toured the North Island at the taxpayers' expense!

Shortly after our return to base, my parents flew over to visit us. I knew that the expense created a hole in their pockets. I made them comfortable in our spacious house and was glad to introduce them to some local Jewish friends. I had met these people because one couple were our neighbours in Wadestown. Through them, I met other Holocaust victims, who had fled Europe at about the same time as my parents. I believe all of them spoke good German and, like my parents, liked to play cards.

My parents felt at home with them. Regrettably, Patricia was not in a welcoming mood. From the very day of my parents' arrival, she kept nagging me and was inhospitable to them. It is possible she was driven by envy. She sensed that, culturally, I had remained closer to mid-European Jews than to her.

In an attempt to lighten the atmosphere, I took my parents for a drive through the North Island and intended to follow it up with a tour of the South Island. My hope was that Pat would enjoy acting as guide. Today, I know that I had misjudged the situation. I overlooked Pat's insecurity. I suspect she considered my parents' visit a threat. Be this as it may, Patricia and my father had a shouting match in Taupo. Although matters were smoothed over, my parents left prematurely. From the day my parents departed, I ceased to take Pat out for lunch and spent most of my time at work.

Whilst work went smoothly in my new university, my former colleagues in Singapore were experiencing tribulations. The new vice-chancellor, Dr. Toh Chin Chye — a founding member of the PAP — was sent to the university to persuade it to toe the line. He was an authoritarian individual. His main contribution to the university was the building of a new campus in Kent Ridge.

Toh and Geoff did not get on. In due course, Geoff gave up the deanship. The next dean served for a term and then took up a partnership in a law firm. She was succeeded Tommy Koh, who had returned to Singapore after finishing a three-year term as Singapore's Ambassador to the United Nations. Tommy, who was a born diplomat, managed to handle Toh. Still, by the time Tommy took over, many expatriate and local staff had resigned. The faculty was decimated.

I was disturbed by rumours that Geoff had turned to drinking. In the old days, Geoff could always hold his liquor. Invariably, he had remained stone sober. It grieved me to hear that this was no longer the case.

News from Israel was also disturbing. The six-day war broke out on 5 June 1967. In effect, it concerned the right of passage of Israeli ships through the Straits of Tiran. These had been closed to Israeli ships from 1948 to 1950, although ships often sailed to Eilat under foreign flags. The right of passage was guaranteed after the Suez Crisis of 1956, and a United Nations emergency force was deployed on the borders to safeguard access. In 1967, Nasser ordered the United Nations forces to leave the Sinai Peninsula, threatened to close the Straits and was getting ready to wage war. To a point, he relied on the fact that the United Arab Republic ensured solidarity between Syria and Egypt. He overlooked the fact that there was no military union or joint command.

On 5 June, Israel's Air Force made a pre-emptive strike, which destroyed most of Egypt's warplanes on the ground. Far from admitting these losses, Nasser bragged about the success of his war. An Egyptian diplomat in Wellington, whom I knew well, appeared confident and self-assured. For two days, I sat glued to our television set and hoped for the best.

As has become well known, Israel's military vanquished its opponents. It conquered the Gaza Strip and the Sinai Peninsula (from Egypt), the West Bank (including East Jerusalem; from Transjordan) and the Golan Heights (from Syria). Undoubtedly, the victory was largely due to the excellence of the Israeli Army. However, Nasser aggravated the situation by broadcasting misleading information about Egyptian victories. These spurred his allies into actions leading to losses.

In a sense, the Arab military was defeated in this war in a manner reminiscent of Napoleon's Victory at Austerlitz. The disunity and lack of coordination of the Arab forces enabled the Israeli army to eliminate them one after the other.

I was relieved when it became evident that Israel would be victorious. The episode made me realise that although I was living far away from the scene, the welfare of Israel remained close to my heart. Whilst the war was raging, I even thought of giving up my post and returning to Tel Aviv. I could, in the very least, undertake some administrative task. The issue did not arise once the outcome was clear.

When the war was over in the Middle East, I took stock of my personal situation. I was committed to my marriage but was loath to leave New Zealand. I loved the country. All the same, I had to find some way to make Pat's lot easier. I suspected that the chance of her settling down comfortably was remote.

To ease the situation, I applied for a short period of sabbatical leave. I was going to spend part of it in Singapore and kept hoping that a spell in the City of the Lion would convince Pat that Wellington was acceptable after all.

Colin Aikman granted me the leave willingly. Ivor expressed the hope that an overseas trip would clear the air.

I shall tell you all about that trip in my next letter.

Till then, all the best to all of you,
Peter

28 February 2018
Singapore

Dear Friends,

Letter 18: Sabbatical and Tragedy

On our way to Singapore, we stopped in Medan (in Sumatra). It was Pat's birthplace, and one of her sisters, May, was still living there. May's husband, Poh Cheng, drove us around. Pat retained a soft spot for her hometown but, in my eyes, it was an unattractive third-world country town.

Over the weekend, Poh Cheng drove us to hilly Brastagi, with its cool climate and pleasant ambience. After that, members of the family drove us to Lake Toba in the centre of Sumatra. It had been nicely developed by the Dutch and had remained a pleasant resort. I realised, however, that the entire area was prone to earthquakes. Lake Toba itself was the crater of an extinct volcano.

On our return from the trip late in the evening, Poh Cheng had to remove the barricades from his entrance door. Throughout the proceedings, he felt the need to stand sentry with a gun in his hand. Housebreakings and sheer vandalism remained as real threats.

From Medan, we proceeded to Singapore. The then dean, Tommy Koh, had arranged a teaching assignment for me. This entitled us to university accommodation, which was a saving.

On the very day of our arrival, I looked up Geoff. He was downing one pint of beer after the other in our staff house and, in addition, was chain smoking. As he spotted me, he suggested we do some 'real drinking'.

"Why don't you simply concentrate on some new projects, Geoff? You are killing yourself."

"More easily said than done," he muttered.

"Then leave Singapore. It should not be too difficult for you to find a new job in an Australian university."

"I'll think about it. But come, have another drink."

It seemed best to leave. I realised that Geoff had passed the point of no return. He had simply decided to let things ride.

Before I left, Geoff told me that B. had to repeat her final year because her results were adversely affected by health factors. I was prepared to support her for another year. However, she advised us that one of her lecturers had decided to see her through. As my own financial position was tight, I felt relieved.

To my surprise, Tommy came forward with a suggestion that I return to Singapore. I was intrigued. Accordingly, Tommy arranged an interview with the vice-chancellor. On the face of it, the interview went smoothly. Nonetheless, I sensed that working with Toh would be difficult. He appeared to me a man who would refuse to reconsider issues on which he had already made up his mind. To my relief, Pat understood my misgiving. Her brothers, too, thought it would be a mistake to return to Singapore at that time.

Despite my decision that the time was not right for a return to Singapore on a permanent basis, I did enjoy the three weeks I spent there. Orchard Road, which used to be a two-way street, had become the artery for downtown traffic. Orchard Boulevard — which had just been opened — was a one-way street running up town. The old-fashioned circuses which slowed down traffic had been largely replaced by efficient light signals.

I was also impressed by the land reclamation that had taken place during the three years following my departure. I sensed that LKY had mastered the problems arising from the British Army's departure and from Singapore's expulsion from Malaysia. His team was in the process of developing Singapore into an international hub of commercial activity. My assessment was confirmed when a colleague told me that work had started on the first highway, namely the Pan Island Expressway ("PIE").

In retrospect, I conclude that during this short period of less than one month I became committed to Singapore. I was, of course, aware that New Zealand was, in many ways, superior. Nature had been kind to this lovely country, and I have continued to admire it. In sheer contrast, Singapore was not well endowed by nature. But its engineered progress gave me a sense of pride: It was as if, in some inexplicable way, I had contributed to it. I also sensed that, one day, I might return to it.

From Singapore, I flew on my own to Belfast. To my delight, Lee Sheridan had come up with another fine package. I accepted and arranged for my parents to fly over for a reunion. Pat was to join me later, in London.

I was delighted to see my parents again. Then, I received disappointing news. One day, when Father had a nap after lunch, Mother asked me to take her for coffee. I sensed that she had something on her mind. After we had ordered our coffees and scones, Mother told me she had decided to join Father in Vienna.

"I am delighted, Mama. It is a pity you didn't join him earlier. Now you can sell his studio flat and move into your apartment in

Döbling (a fashionable district on Vienna's outskirts). It is roomy and you will feel at home."

"It isn't that simple, Peter'le."

"What do you mean?" I asked with a sense of foreboding.

"I am not leaving Tel Aviv because I want to return to Vienna, Peter'le. They had sent me to wash the pavements; I have not forgotten! But I must come back. You see, when Papa was last in Israel, he went for a checkup. Bobbie (our family physician) tells me that Papa has cancer. I am coming over to see him through."

Suddenly, the scones were stale and the coffee bitter. Bobbie was an excellent diagnostician; he would not raise a false alarm.

"Is it curable?"

"Time will tell. You know your Papa. He is a stubborn old man and has simply ignored the matter. Bobbie says it's urinary. So an operation will be unavoidable!"

"Have you taken him to a specialist in Vienna?"

"He refuses to go!"

"Oh God," I muttered in a shaky voice. When I recovered and looked up, Mother smiled sadly. She told me she knew I had always loved Father more than her. He always humoured me whilst she had to bring me up.

"It's a bad business, Mama. But if you settle in Vienna, you simply must move to Döbling. You must have your own room and Papa may need a sick room!"

"He won't hear of it. He says Döbling is too far out. He wants to remain near his business premises. And I think he still expects me to fly back to Israel."

I had nothing to add. Back in the hotel, Father was still asleep. I looked at him with a heavy heart and a deep feeling of guilt. Mother, who took in my expression, told me to pull myself together. Father should not find out she had talked to me.

My parents left after a few days. I flew to London, where Pat was already waiting for me. We were going to stay for a few days with Robert Goh, Pat's brother who was working in London and had taken up British citizenship. Robert had spent a few years in Australia but returned to Singapore without a degree. When Robert declined to marry a girl he was dating, it was felt that he ought to migrate. With some difficulties, my father managed to secure him a job in London. Robert had since switched jobs, married a very pleasant Swedish girl, who presented him with two children, and decided to settle in the United Kingdom.

I spent two days in the Middle Temple Library and renewed my contacts in the banking world. In addition, I recall our visit to Kew Gardens and to Hampton Court. I am pleased to confirm that I did not try my luck in the famed maze. Instead, I spent most of the time looking at the splendid portraits on the palace's walls.

Pat was looking forward to a short sojourn in Halifax, where the Faculty of Law of the University of Nova Scotia had offered me a post. Initially, Pat refused to build in a stop in West Lafayette, where I wanted to stay for a few days with my uncle Henry. She took the view that, as I had been admitted to her family, I should not contact my own family members. To my delight, Robert — who had come to understand European mores — objected to my turning down my Uncle Henry's invitation. In point of fact, I was irked by Pat's reaction and went so far as to tell her that, if she refused to accompany me, she could proceed to Singapore on her own. In the event, she gave way.

Both of us disliked Halifax. Pat pointed out that it would be a bad mistake to change it for Wellington. Apologetically, I turned down the offer. We then spent two days in Chicago. An acquaintance drove us around. It struck me as a dreary town with some depressing slums. Still, I enjoyed visiting Al Capone's erstwhile headquarters. It occurred to me that the city had little else to boast of.

Uncle Henry was glad to see us. Pat, I am glad to say, became friendly with Henry's wife, Paula, who was also a university teacher. Paula's skills did not include cooking. Pat had to prepare the Wiener schnitzel; and she enjoyed herself.

After three days in Salt Lake City — which struck me as well organised and safe — we proceeded to San Francisco. We had a delightful week in the charming town and — in sheer disregard of conventional wisdom — went for pleasant walks in the evenings. I was amazed by the sharp contrast between miserable Chicago and sparkling 'Frisco.

Whilst in San Francisco, I visited Stefan (Steve) A. Riesenfeld, a well-known scholar working in my field. I had met him in a conference and was pleased to persuade him to come over to Wellington as a visiting professor. I also managed to get his comments on the draft of a paper I was working on. His observations were helpful.

Hawaii, too, was a pleasant place to visit. My only problem arose as we traversed Waikiki Beach. Pat looked annoyed as I glanced at the scenery. It appeared best to fix my eyes on the shiny sand.

The flight from Hawaii straight to Wellington took some nine hours. When I think about this stretched sabbatical, hopping onto and out of planes, I wonder if, from an academic point of view, it served any purpose. True, I had renewed contacts and established new ones. But a lengthy spell in a library, like the Bodleian, would have been more productive. Today — at the ripe age of 89 — I begin to question the usefulness of sabbatical leave. A sound working programme should be a prerequisite to it being granted.

Back in Wellington, we had to house-hunt once again. We had sold our first house before our departure and now had to start afresh. Again, we rented a flat. We then purchased a plot of land and built a house. Pat drew the basic plan.

Having the house erected was a challenge. The plan had to be modified several times so as to give effect to Pat's dream. The end result, though, was good. The sitting room was spacious and the attached dining room comfortable. Further, our new house, in a district called Wilton, was near the university. We had a bus stop nearby, which meant that Pat could easily go to town. However, I acquired a car and, after a while, drove home for lunch and then took Pat to town.

The faculty in Wellington had undergone some changes. Colin Aikman had left and became the vice-chancellor of the new University of the South Pacific established in Fiji. Another senior professor was elevated to the post of deputy vice-chancellor. He continued to teach one course in the faculty but kept aloof of our administration. Ivor Richardson agreed to stand for the post of dean but hinted that he might leave and return to private practice.

When he left, two colleagues vied for the post. The successful candidate — a sub-professorial employee called John Thomas — turned out to be an excellent dean. Before long, I delegated to John the responsibilities imposed on me as the head of the department. Grudgingly, he took over.

Just before the end of the year, B. advised us that she had passed her examinations and was now a qualified biochemist. She obtained a part-time posting at the university but, before long, met a fellow from mainland China, who graduated from Singapore's Bible College. In her next letter, she told us she had married him and asked whether I could help her migrate to New Zealand. They needed a change of scenery. She also needed a job. Accommodating her was time-consuming. Still, with the help of one of my colleagues, I managed to get her an entry permit and, with the help of another, found her a job in a laboratory.

B. and her newlywed husband came to stay with us. To my dismay, I had to vacate my study so as to make room for them. In consequence, I had to spend longer hours in the university, coming home late in the evening. Pat was not pleased.

Sad to relate, B. and her husband did not get on. In a sense, I was surprised. In her letter to us, B. had lauded her husband, who — at least in my eyes — was a singularly pleasant and decent man. He had a smattering of Biblical Hebrew and I enjoyed traversing with him difficult passages in books such as *Job*. I was further impressed by his aptitude to adapt to changed circumstances. Once he realised that he had to look for an opening other than a religious calling, he passed a course in computer science and secured a fine post. I was impressed.

Regrettably, Pat did not like him. I suspect that in the eyes of both sisters, he did not come up to their expectations and lacked social graces. Before long, Pat became a party to what ought to have been domestic scenes. In the end, we had to ask B.'s pastor to come over to our place. He concluded that the only way out was to take the poor husband over to his own house. The pastor, so B. told me subsequently, regarded her as being a most unreasonable woman.

As B. was also disappointed with her new job, she decided to flee to Sydney. Although my finances were, once again, tight, I had to give her some money. I also introduced her to Auntie Ida so as to provide shelter.

B.'s letters to us alleged that Ida thought B. a god-sent relief from Ida's own unsatisfactory relationship with Ted. Father, though, sent me letters, indicating that Ida was counting the days to B.'s move to a dormitory for foreign students. In due course, B. did shift and was admitted to a Masters course. She then filed for a divorce. I never met her estranged husband again. I hope he remarried and found happiness. He deserved it.

At the end of this sad saga, I was hoping to regain my study at home. Pat, though, developed an interest in pottery and needed a room for her work and a potting wheel. I continued to do my research in my university room. In reality, the outcome suited me: the faculty and my bridge game were warm and welcoming; my home was becoming dreary and depressing.

Then, in quick succession, there were two further developments. First, Father wrote to tell me he was suffering from cancer. He still thought the operation would be of a minor nature and, despite my entreaties, refused to move to Döbling. Mother, too, was inclined to remain in the studio flat. I could not understand how they were going to manage in the miniscule dwelling but realised that I was unable to influence them.

The other development was a formal approach by New Zealand's Foreign Office, instructing me to make proposals for a reform of Tonga's commercial law. I gathered that Ivor Richardson had already made proposals for the regional tax law reform and that he had induced the authorities to refer the commercial law reform to me. It was a somewhat tricky project and took up much of my time. I prepared the basic report in the university's library and was getting ready to fly over to Tonga to finalise things. I did not like the idea of taking Pat with me. All the same, I realised that it would be difficult to leave her in Wellington on her own. She was far too dependent on me.

Unexpectedly, a reprieve came from my in-laws in Singapore. They suggested that my mother-in-law stay with us for a while. B. was to fly over to Singapore and accompany her to New Zealand. The only hitch was that they booked her on a flight to Auckland. They thought I should not mind driving up the North Island to pick her up after she landed. They ruled out a flight to Wellington as it would have entailed a change of planes in Sydney. Reluctantly, I accepted the tedious itinerary proposed by them.

The drive to Auckland was tiresome. One of my tyres burst on the way. In the event, we had to spend a night in Taupo. Fortunately, a workshop run by two Maoris changed all my tyres late in the evening. We continued to Auckland early in the morning, arriving in the airport just before B. and my mother-in-law went through customs. On the way back, I stopped in the lovely Coromandel Peninsula and then drove leisurely back to Wellington.

It now appeared sound to proceed to Tonga. By the end of the week, I took a flight to Fiji, expecting to transit to Tonga. Regrettably, the roads in Tonga were flooded by heavy rainfall so, unexpectedly, I had to spend two days in Fiji.

I enjoyed myself. On the first day, I took a cruise and on the second went to see Colin and Bettie Aikman. Colin had metamorphosed into a *Pukka Sahib* whilst Bettie retained her '*grande dame*' ambience. When Colin excused himself to take some urgent telephone calls, Bettie asked me, directly, whether or not my home life had improved. She listened sadly to my account and made but one observation: "You have to stick it out, Peter. Pat is insecure, and she depends on you. I know that a divorce is one way out. Still, I cannot see you splitting. You need one another; and you, Peter, need something to complain about."

The next day, the airport in Tonga reopened. I had a lovely time on this pleasant island, although I have some doubts about the implementations of the reforms proposed in my report. On the way back to Wellington, I had to stop in Samoa — a charming underdeveloped island — and in Western Samoa, which had turned itself into a hectic and semi-efficient American suzerainty.

A few days after my return, B. departed. My mother-in-law stayed with us for a few weeks. I treated her well and willingly drove her to coastal towns in our area and also to Napier and Hastings. I knew it would be inappropriate to treat her as unkindly as Pat had been to my parents. All the same, I refused to take one week off and drive her through the South Island.

One disturbing incident that took place during this period concerned the wedding of a colleague, my friend Tony Angelo, who asked me to be his best man. I felt honoured and, of course, gladly accepted. To my utter surprise, Pat took exception. She refused to attend the wedding and tried to prevent me from carrying out my function. To this very day, I do not know what had possessed her. Be this as it may, she remained at home with her mother and I proceeded to the celebration. My mother-in-law calmed Pat down so that when I came back there was no quarrel.

Shortly thereafter, B. came over again from Sydney so as to take her mother back to Singapore. Pat, alas, was unable to chaperon her mother and I was not prepared to drive her on to Auckland. I could not spare the time and, in any event, felt that my in-laws did not have the right to make such demands on me.

A few days after my mother-in-law's departure, I received a tragic letter from Mother. Father had required a second operation. He was resting and, hopefully, recovering in the polyclinic. A move to Döbling was now out of the question. They had to fit a sickbed into the studio flat. I wondered how they would manage and, despite my attempt to forget the past, felt bitter about Pat's treatment of my parents. I knew Father would never live to see the magnificent South Island.

Two weeks later, my mother rang from Vienna. International telephone calls were still rare in those remote days and so I gleaned the news before Mother elaborated. Father had passed away at home. He had been in a cheerful mood that morning, enjoyed a cup of warm chocolate, insisted on having a nip of rum with it and then lapsed into a coma. He died without regaining consciousness.

Mother asked me not to attend the funeral. In truth, I could have easily dropped Pat in Singapore and proceeded to Vienna. But I was not ready to bid 'goodbye' to him. In the event, and bearing in mind Mother's words, I stayed put. Nowadays — when I live in retirement on Singapore's East Coast — I often think about the event and feel deeply ashamed.

Later that day, in the early evening, I walked with Pat along the strand in Lower Hutt, a town adjacent to Wellington. Feeling depressed and ashamed, I walked gloomily in silence. Then, out of the blue, Pat turned to me: "One Ellinger less; what is the big deal?"

It took me some time to recover from the shock. I knew that my only dignified response was to demand a divorce. I was too cowardly and simply continued to stride. It was, however, a moment I was not going to forget. It kept gnawing at me for years. From then on, my only task was to be a dutiful husband. Love and affection were gone.

I spent the remaining months of our session on finalising chapters for a new book on the law of sale of goods. Tony Guest had invited me to contribute them. I was determined to adhere to the proposed deadlines but regret to have to admit that my progress was slow. In a way, Tony was a martinet. His own work was excellent — the fruit of meticulous research and painstaking accuracy. I knew I had to keep up with him. His regard was important to me. He might turn a blind eye to minor errors but would be critical if he detected serious errors or omissions.

As our typing pool was poor, it seemed best to type the chapters on my own. This I did and, in consequence, felt exhausted most of the time. In the end, Pat insisted that we take a holiday. With a typewriter and my notes in the boot, we drove for a fortnight to Napier, a fine coastal town renowned for its excellent climate.

Before long, I finished my work. A kindly stationer packed the manuscript meticulously and, on the very same day, I posted it to London.

A few days later, we returned to Wellington.

I shall tell you all about my remaining years in Wellington in my next letter.

In the meantime, all the best to you,
Peter

7 March 2018
Singapore

Dear Friends,

Letter 19: Wellington — Later Years

From a professional viewpoint, matters were running smoothly during my next few years in Wellington. My list of publications was growing steadily. I sensed that I was becoming known in my field of banking law.

The faculty was efficiently run by our dean. I was able to concentrate on my writings and on my autodidactic biblical studies. George Barton was most helpful. Though an avid believer in his own brand of Christianity, he was interested in the Hebrew texts. I recall with pleasure our discussions of *Jeremiah* and of *Isaiah*. George was displeased with my dislike of the *Psalms* but took my tirades against them in good spirit. Neither of us convinced the other.

Quite apart from his standing as an academic, George was also a fine and popular counsel. He had all the attributes of an accomplished litigator: a fine grasp of the facts of each case; an outstanding analytical ability, which meant that his arguments were invariably sound and convincing; an excellent command of cross-examination techniques, including the knowledge as to when to pull his punches; and a commanding presence. Over the years, I had attended quite a number of his cases. I was impressed by his timing. He never missed the opportunity to rise to his feet and make a sharp comment or raise an objection when needed.

It grieved most of us in the faculty when George decided to give up his chair and dedicate himself to his practice. All attempts to persuade him to stay were fruitless. He took the view that his role as an academic and his commitments in town often clashed. We gave him a fine farewell party. To my delight, George remained in close contact with all his friends in the faculty.

In an indirect way, George's departure had an adverse effect on me. To my dismay, I inherited his mantle of being the faculty's wise old man. Problems that would have usually been referred to him were discussed with me. Whilst he would have handled them in his stride, I agonised over many of them. My existence in the ivory tower ceased to be carefree. Occasionally, I even had to miss my beloved bridge luncheons.

A pleasant reprieve was an unexpected visit paid to me by Lalith Athulathmudali, with whom I had remained in close contact over the years. I recall with fondness our exchange of Christmas cards. He normally wrote: "to celebrate the birth of one of your people" or "from a Buddhist to a Jew, to celebrate a Christian festival". I usually wrote back: "with all best wishes sent by one disbeliever to his fellow sceptic".

On this specific occasion, he advised that following a convention to be held in Auckland, he planned to tour our fair country. Would I be able to take him for a drive through the South Island? I was keen and Pat approved.

I enjoyed our break. Once again, we proceeded via Picton, down the West Coast and onwards to the Haast Pass. The trip took a few days. To my relief, Lalith offered to share the driving. Usually, I took the wheel in the morning and Lalith relieved me in the afternoon.

I recall with a smile a trick I played on my friend. On the morning of our third day, when we were about to cross the Haast Pass, which I was keen to absorb, I explained that this span could be traversed only by a skilled driver. Grinning from ear to ear, Lalith volunteered to take command. By the middle of the way, I felt remorse and offered to take over.

"Nonsense," retorted Lalith, "just continue to take in the scenery. I can drive and enjoy the sights in full."

Two days later, when we took rooms in a motel near Queenstown, Lalith and Pat were keen to take a speedboat down a ravine. I was afraid of catching a cold and so stayed behind and awaited their return.

"So our hypochondriac is still well and kicking," observed Lalith.

"He is," I said, feeling deeply ashamed.

The only ugly event took place in a restaurant on the slopes of Mount Cook. Lalith invited us for lunch in a posh restaurant. The food was good but, to my dismay, the waitress treated Lalith with condescension. I was about to summon the chief waiter and protest, when Lalith stopped me. Explaining that this type of behaviour was a product of the girl's insecurity, he pointed out that a complaint would only exacerbate the situation.

"She would have never dared to behave like that if I were the host," I told him.

"True; she is disturbed when she sees a well-off coloured man. I have learnt to ignore this sort of thing."

Lalith returned to Sri Lanka a few days after we were back in Wellington. He had enjoyed his break and invited us to visit him when we were next on our way to Europe. Before his departure, he observed that from what he saw and sensed, New Zealand was not the haven I had been hoping for. It was a beautiful country, and the majority of the people were fair-minded and tolerant. Pat, though, was unable to settle there, which meant that my home life was bound to remain difficult. He also feared that, unless I went elsewhere, my research might become narrow and stale.

A few days later I had a telephone call from a former student of Singapore. He and his wife, who had also been enrolled in one of my classes, were touring New Zealand. I was delighted to meet them. The two had not been sweethearts during their days of studies but actually met whilst both were pupils in well-known law firms. By the time they married, both became salaried partners in their respective firms, had bought a house and were getting ready to start a family.

Over a pleasant lunch, they gossiped about many of my former students. One had become a highly regarded member of the Attorney-General's Chambers; another had joined a leading law firm, was happily married and had a son; and yet another had become a successful litigator, dealing mainly with white-collar crime. There were also sad developments. One of my students had committed suicide; another had been found guilty of criminal breach of trust, involving the misappropriation of clients' funds; and a third had died from a heart attack.

"I only hope we're not boring you. You never fraternised with us," observed my fair guest.

"I accepted many of you as friends after graduation," I defended myself lamely.

"True," replied her husband, "but you know, some of our lecturers — like Bartho — mixed with us even during our student days."

"I wasn't as secure as he was," I explained with conviction.

We had coffee in a nearby coastal town. I felt at home with them and knew they would welcome me back. I also realised that time was not standing still for any of us. Most of my former students would have had the time to launch their careers and embark on their home life.

The couple's visit made me reflect on the relationship of teacher and student. During my days as fellow of KE.VII in Singapore, I had played *mahjong* and other games with our medical students. With my law students, who were frequently only a few years younger than I, keeping my distance was a natural precaution; and students felt comfortable this way.

In Wellington, in contrast, the students took the initiative. I recalled how, shortly after the beginning of my first academic term, Ivor and I received the Law Students Club's invitation to attend a 'Stein Evening'. Expecting it to be a cultural event, entailing intellectual discussions, both of us appeared in suit and tie.

To our surprise, the occasion was a merry party of Stein beer drinking. Our hosts were dressed in rags and consumed one mug of beer after the other. Before long, Ivor and I took off our jackets and ties. I managed to excuse myself from heavy drinking on the pretext of an allergy to hops. Ivor had to partake. The episode did not affect the discipline in our teaching classes.

At present, when I compose my memoirs, I sense that the issue involved is, in all probability, one of culture and background. A predominantly Chinese society, as in Singapore, emphasises hierarchy. In contrast, the less structured environments — like Australia and New Zealand — thrive on bringing equality to the forefront. An educator active in Singapore had to protect his hierarchical standing. In

Australasia, hierarchy lost its importance once the educator was outside the classroom.

Naturally, some law teachers in Singapore, such as Geoff, felt secure enough to relax outside the lecture room. In most cases of this type, though, the informal teacher's status was guarded by the age gap between him and the students.

Turning back to my years in Wellington, I was pleased to find that a number of my students had their own autodidactic interest in biblical studies. I often argued points with them and, on two occasions, volunteered to teach them biblical Hebrew. Occasionally, students from other faculties attended our informal discussion groups. In a way, the pursuit of this interest brought me greater satisfaction than my legal studies.

Pat, too, had every reason to be pleased. She became a skilled potter and many local experts gave her full support. Our plot of land was too small for a kiln, but friends enabled her to use theirs. I still have some of the pieces she fired. I like them.

All the same, Pat did not feel fulfilled. She wanted to change scene and occasionally complained that her pottery was nothing but an escape. Having decided to ignore her unkind remark respecting my father's death, I made an effort to cheer her up and to make her feel needed.

Usually, I would be home early in the afternoon and then take her to town. Before long, I became an expert on pottery clay, discovered all relevant shops, drove her to her sessions and, on some occasions, watched her placing her items in a kiln.

I also discovered the pleasure of bottling fruit, like blackboy peaches, pears and plums. It became a ritual. Pat boiled the fruit in water with sugar and when ready, dished the appropriate quantity into a bottle. I ladled in the syrup and fixed the cover. We had quite a stock of preserved fruit and often consumed them with sugar-free whipped cream. Our guests approved. Nowadays, such delicacies are proscribed on medical advice given to me because of my diabetes.

Another source of pleasure was the numerous invitations I kept receiving from law societies and real estate institutes. I usually travelled to the respective destination and took Pat with me. We were always treated hospitably, with Pat being invited to special functions organised for the speakers' spouses.

One such seminar took us to Rotorua. By then both of us had developed a passion for Maori concerts and for all other attractions of this unique geyser land, especially for the thermal water pools. We stayed on for an extra three days.

Nowadays, when I go down memory lane in my old age, I believe I did my best to make Pat feel at home. My success, though, was limited. It is possible that if we had had children, my wife would have settled down. Regrettably, we failed in this regard. Further, I was unable to make her feel wanted. All I can say in my defence is that I tried my best.

During the second term, I managed to invite Steve Riesenfeld to spend a few months with us. It will be recalled that I had met him during my sabbatical leave.

Right from the start, there was an empathy between Steve and me, based on our sharing a similar background, namely mid-European secular Judaism. An additional factor, though, was our approach to research. Both of us knew that the law was but one facet of the order to be maintained by a society. It was as fluid, and as changeable, as the social or political structure prevailing from time to time. In a sense, both of us had a commitment to the history of law and therefore often saw eye to eye on issues. I pause to add that I was aware of Steve's orientation from reading some of his works.

Steve was an accomplished teacher and a brilliant researcher. Like our students, I too learned a lot from his analytical skills. His classes were well attended and he was held in high regard. Like me, he did not fraternise with students but willingly accepted invitations to their functions. I had an additional benefit from his visit. Steve introduced me to Ernst von Caemmerer, a leading German scholar working in my field.

Shortly after Steve's departure, our dean, John, stepped down from his administrative position and took a year of sabbatical leave. He spent most of it in Canada. The new dean appointed by the faculty was Geoffrey Palmer, the future Prime Minister of New Zealand.

Geoffrey was a good administrator. He was careful when colleagues competed for promotions and tended to err on the side of caution. On the academic plane, he appointed a committee charged with the revision of our syllabus. I have to admit that frequently the discussions produced more heat than light. All the same, under his guidance, the courses became less parochial. The emphasis shifted from a purely disciplinary orientation — or black letter law — to a comparative approach. I noticed with delight that during his term our reading lists for basic courses often included American materials. We were no longer confined to English and Australasian authorities.

When our previous dean, John, returned from Canada, he started to needle Palmer in faculty meetings. To my surprise, Palmer frequently swallowed the bait. It amuses me to think that the future leader of New Zealand often took a beating in academic debates. I have to confess that I usually enjoyed the proceedings. To hide my schadenfreude, I immersed myself in the papers in front of me and refrained from voting.

On one occasion, John told me (after a meeting) that I should change my surname to Ostrich. Geoffrey Palmer grinned supportively.

On the domestic front, things remained difficult despite the efforts I have mentioned. Although I never referred to Pat's behaviour following my father's death, it kept gnawing at me. My spells of sullen demeanour, to which I succumbed from time to time, kept disturbing her. In the end, Pat decided to spend some time in Singapore, pointing out that our marriage lacked harmony. She wanted me to tell her frankly how I was going to feel after some time. I agreed.

I accompanied Pat to the airport. Socially, my next few weeks were pleasant. Once it became known that I was on my own, my colleagues invited me to their homes for dinner. In addition, I had to master the culinary arts. Before long, I became an amateur chef, often inviting my colleagues to meals. I do believe they enjoyed themselves and so did I. To my pleasant surprise, I discovered a German cooking book and soon mastered some dishes unknown in New Zealand. Later on, I managed to acquire a Jewish cooking book, which Pat had also used, and after a while, taught myself the art of preparing chopped liver and Jewish desserts. In due course, I acquired the reputation of an imaginative host.

The difficulty, though, arose in the later hours of the evening. I was not used to living on my own and frequently felt abandoned. At the beginning, I got over it by immersing myself in work. But after a while, I started to experience difficulties in falling asleep. In the event, and notwithstanding the feeling of freedom, I tired of my lonesome existence. I kept hesitating about the best course to adopt when an unexpected letter from one of Pat's siblings told me she appeared forlorn and out of place in her old hometown. I ended up by asking her to return. Within a few days, she booked her flight and I picked her up at Wellington's airport.

In hindsight, I know I acted hastily. My marriage was not working. The sensible thing to do was to suggest that we divorce and start afresh. I had no doubt that Pat would have been able to remarry. She was no longer a beautiful young woman but as a sensible divorcee, weary of her battle scars, would have been in a position to contract a second, satisfactory, marriage. She would no longer have expected a romantic marriage — which I had failed to give her — but would have set out to build up a harmonious home. I am equally confident that I was in a position to find a suitable partner, especially from amongst my own people. This would have been preferable to trying to remedy a marriage gone stale. Wisdom, though, often comes too late.

Be this as it may, upon Pat's return, we tried to remedy our relationship. Today I know this was a futile exercise. All I can say in my defence is that I acted impulsively rather than rationally. My hope was that in the future we would have more mutual respect than we had had in the past.

I tried my best to encourage Pat to gain success in her pottery venture. She had the necessary talent, ability and commitment. I also went out with her more often than previously. The local Jewish community was actually forthcoming. Some of its members had married out so mixed marriages did not run against their grain. Up to a point my efforts were successful. Pat mixed reasonably well with mid-European Jews who had settled in New Zealand. All the same, I realised that Pat needed a change of scene.

For a while, I was occupied by another development. On 6 October 1973, on the Day of Atonement, Egypt and Syria led a coalition and started a war against Israel. Their surprise attack on the holiest day of the Jewish calendar enabled them to have some initial success. Thus, they pushed Israel back from the banks of the Suez Canal. At first, they also made some gains in the Golan Heights. The Soviet Union armed and supported the Arabs; the United States came to Israel's aid. At that time, many political commentators thought that the end result might be a conflict between the superpowers. Fortunately, this did not happen.

The final outcome was an Israeli victory, albeit achieved at the cost of substantial casualties. A particularly brilliant move was the encirclement of the advancing Egyptian Army by the Israeli Defense Forces. To my way of thinking, the conflict involved a confrontation of Soviet arms with those of the United States. The latter were, I believe, superior. Further, the Israeli soldier was better trained and more highly motivated than his Arab counterpart.

Living at the time in Wellington, I was, of course, not an eyewitness. Unlike in the case of the previous war, I had no wish to give up my job and go as a volunteer to Israel. But like all Jews in town, I was deeply concerned and worried. I felt as if the attack was against my family.

All members of the local community made donations to the Israeli cause but, of course, we were too small to make a substantial contribution. Notably, most New Zealanders I met were pro-Israeli. In their eyes, Israel was the underdog. I believe that many of them contributed generously when requested.

On this occasion, Pat was supportive. Like many Christians, she felt empathy for the Jewish state. She went willingly to gatherings made to show support to Israel. I sensed that on this occasion she was an ally.

A few weeks after this war, I received an invitation from the German Humboldt Foundation. I was offered a one-year fellowship to be spent in the Institute of Comparative Commercial Law in Freiburg. The honorarium was fair and, in addition, I was entitled to six months of sabbatical leave. The combined income was on the high side. Pat encouraged me to accept.

We had no difficulty in finding a good tenant for our house and left some stuff in a closet in the garage of friends. The university approved my sabbatical willingly and, as an add on, granted me six months of leave without pay. Our last task was to sell our car. Thereafter, we were ready to embark on one year of leave.

For the time being, our personal problems ceased to be mentioned. Undoubtedly, they were there and had remained unsolved. Both of us were, however, too busy to dwell on them. We were looking forward to a year in Europe and to a stopover in Singapore.

I shall have a great deal to tell you about that splendid year. Despite my mid-European upbringing, I went to Germany full of suspicions. The memory of the Holocaust had remained fresh in my mind. Naturally, I was aware that most of the perpetrators of the war crimes had been punished or had simply died of old age. All the same, I kept wondering whether the brutalities then committed had become part and parcel of modern German culture. The year in Freiburg wiped these misgivings away. It turned me from a suspicious explorer into an admirer and friend.

I hope to explain the metamorphosis I experienced in my next letter. Further, I hope that you will find it interesting even if controversial.

In the meantime, I remain yours as ever,

Peter

15 March 2018
Singapore

Dear Friends,

Letter 20: A Humboldt Fellow

Our first stop was in Bali. We rented a room in Kuta Beach but, of course, toured the entire island. On this occasion, I found the persons who bathed in the nude repulsive. Bali struck me as a touristy and highly artificial environment. Lake Toba and Brastagi, which I had visited in the past, appeared more indigenous.

We proceeded to Singapore, where I hired a room in a flat adjacent to my in-laws' dwellings. It did not take me long to realise that Singapore was going from strength to strength. Additional land had been reclaimed, new parts of town were developed and the PIE was nearing completion. Further, Singapore had become an oil refining centre. Its future appeared bright. LKY's PAP was in full control and, I sensed, was using its powers wisely.

The faculty had undergone changes. Geoff had left to take up the Foundation Chair of Law in Sydney's Technology University. I was pleased for him and hoped he would do well.

Tommy Koh had given up the deanship. The new dean, S. Jayakumar, was a former student of mine. I was certain that his move into politics was only a question of time. The vice-dean was Tan Sook Yee. She was the Attorney-General's wife and had all the attributes of an upper-class lady. Originally, she was appointed by Harry Groves as an assistant lecturer but rose quickly through the ranks. She was a fine leader, being endowed with a cool disposition, an excellent grasp of situations, the ability to make decisions and the gift of determining a course for the faculty's redevelopment. I was impressed.

Pat decided to spend a few weeks with her family. My first stop on the way to Freiburg was in Vienna. Mother had lost weight and looked frail. Regrettably, I was unable to convince her to return to Tel Aviv. She had decided to stay put in the studio flat in the 9th District — the very flat in which Father had died.

Before Father's demise, they had sold his business to their apprentice, who retained Mother as consultant. She explained to me that if she returned to Tel Aviv, people would consider her a deserter who was unable to integrate in her original environment. They would treat her with disdain.

"But, Mama," I pleaded, "surely this is unimportant. You have a nice big flat in Tel Aviv, a good circle of friends and enough money. You needn't give a damn about what people say. They ought to mind their own business."

"Perhaps," she replied, "but I am going to stay put. I don't want to lose face all over again. And don't you argue with me!"

Two days later, I flew to Frankfurt and then took the train to Freiburg. My hosts — the Humboldt Foundation — put me up in a hotel. With the help of junior assistants at the Institute of Comparative Commercial Law I found a suitable flat in a nearby village. To get to town, I had to acquire a car.

Up to a point, I felt lonely. I did travel around and enjoyed the sights. But I was loath to go out on my own. I was no longer used to that. To a certain extent, I enjoyed the excellent television programmes. In this regard, my knowledge of German became a major asset. All the same, I felt depressed when I took my lonely evening meal.

Fortunately, I discovered an author I had not come across before. Heinrich Böll gave me new insights into WWII. For once, I grasped the hardship of the ordinary man at the front, the sufferings of civilian populations and the moral dilemmas faced by common German people. As I kept reading his works, I realised that the average German was not evil. He was simply a family man caught in a war. I also realised that if I had been an ordinary German citizen, I might have joined what we now consider a 'mob'. In an extraordinary situation — and Hitler's ascent was exactly that — an individual's behaviour is unpredictable.

The discovery of Böll's work provided good reading for lonely nights. I further started to reread Bertolt Brecht and after a while turned to Gerhart Hauptmann. In addition, I often brought with me legal texts which I did not have the time to digest in the institute.

Indeed, the work in the institute was demanding. I started to study the German law of obligations and of property. I then turned to the materials respecting the promulgation of the Civil Law Code. Before long, I realised that code had borrowed heavily from the law that preceded it. I concluded that I had to study the materials in detail. I sensed that in this instance legal history and comparative study complemented each other. My orientation resembled Steve Riesenfeld's.

My host, Von Caemmerer, was idolised in Freiburg's university. His severe Prussian manner, which did not fully camouflage his warm heart and kindly disposition, suited the ambience of Freiburg. Outwardly, people appeared cold and distant. In reality, most were benevolent and, in their own way, welcoming. I often had pleasant chats with people in pubs and coffee houses.

By the time Pat flew over to join me, I had come to like Germany. I even played card games in the pubs. I am aware that all this was superficial. However, the deeply ingrained hatred — preached during my schooldays — struck me as misguided. I felt confident that atrocities could be committed by any person if steered into such behaviour by charismatic demagogues who harped on the economic reverses and the sufferings they were going through.

Pat flew to Zürich — the airport nearest to Freiburg. I left my flat in the morning and arrived in the airport well before her flight landed. We drove back through Constance [Konstanz], which is partly in Switzerland and partly in Germany, and then wound our way through the Black Forest. It was a fine trip. To my utter surprise, many villagers were monolingual.

Pat did not like our landlady and within a few days of her arrival found fault in our lodgings. Fortunately, we soon embarked on the Humboldt tour of Germany, to which we had been invited.

It was an excellent tour. The Humboldt Foundation hired a bus driven by a skilled driver accompanied by an accomplished guide. I was impressed with the sights and the state of the country. No WWII scars were left in Western Germany. The entire country had been rebuilt; and it was thriving.

In Munich, one of our fellows took us to the art gallery. We spent a morning there. In the evening, we were taken to a performance of *The Magic Flute* by the local opera. Later in the week, we were driven to Garmisch-Partenkirchen in Bavaria and on to Germany's highest peak, the Zugspitze. I was amused to see *Lederhosen*-wearing tourist guides, who tried to direct our feet to local taverns. The area was cute but highly commercialised.

I had one notable experience. It was cold and so I took Pat to a boutique and bought her a loden coat. When we climbed aboard the bus, everybody was clapping. Pat blushed but, I believe, was pleased.

The most interesting occurrence, though, was during the drive through East Germany (the German Democratic Republic, or DDR) to West Berlin. Our bus had to stick to a prescribed route and, for about three hours, we were not allowed to leave it. When we arrived at a stopover, everybody rushed to the toilets. One chap, who had not vacated his bladder before stepping into the bus, emerged from the commodious chamber with patent relief.

The same person, who was a German language teacher in America, experienced an unpleasant encounter. When he tried to jump the queue, the bartender told him, "*Warten Sie doch, sie Schwein* (wait your turn, you swine)."

Without replying, he left the place, fuming. Back in the bus, he conceded that he should not have tried to jump the queue. But, in his opinion, the sharp, highly uncivil affront was disproportionate. I had my doubts about the validity of his conclusion. Most of us were equally tired but waited for our turn to order a drink. Why had he been so impatient? It seemed to me that the blame ought not to be treated as one-sided.

We arrived in West Berlin late in the afternoon. All of us were fatigued. Still, before we drove to the hotel, we visited the Jewish Museum. It was impressive and I sensed that West Germany's Government did its best to display the contributions made by German Jews to the development of the nation. It dawned on me, however, that the very existence of such a museum suggested that, even after the

Holocaust, the Jews remained a group apart in the eyes of German society.

The next day, we had a tour of the palace and an adjacent museum in Charlottenburg (an affluent part of West Berlin). We then visited a number of other museums. I found them exciting. It was clear to me that Frederic the Great did his best to turn Berlin — the then capital of Prussia — into a world metropolis. In the evening, we enjoyed a performance of the Berlin Orchestra. I recall that one of the pieces was Beethoven's Fourth Piano Concerto.

The next morning, I went to the Egyptian Museum. To my pleasant surprise, Pat offered to come with me. I was so engrossed in the exhibits in general and on the head of Nefertiti in particular that I hardly noticed the surroundings. Then, in a kindly way, Pat nudged me back into the present.

"To you, all this is alive, Peter?"

"Quite so. I am back in the remote past. I love it!"

"You never looked like this before. Not even in the museums in Vienna."

"I know. You see, Susu, this is special. Have a good look at Nefertiti. She wasn't Egyptian. Some scholars aver she was a Mitannian princess. Her husband, Akhenaton, was the first man to proclaim the existence of just one god."

"Not Moses?"

"You know many have doubts about his existence; and Akhenaton's period is far earlier."

We had lunch in a nearby cafeteria. Sensing that I was keen to go back to the museum, Pat volunteered to wait for me. When I returned after an hour and a half, Pat looked at me thoughtfully.

"You should have never married, Peter."

"Why?"

"You live in the remote past. Most women live in the present. When the pastor tells me Moses proclaimed the existence of a single god, I accept his word. You go on researching and doubting."

"True," I conceded. "What do you want to do now?"

"Go back to town and do some shopping. I saw a lovely boutique not far from the hotel. And you must not be bored! There is a nice coffee house next to the shop. We can go there after I have finished."

The next morning, we crossed over to East Berlin. My main objective was to see the Middle East Division of the Pergamon Museum. I admired it, especially the Victory Stele of Esarhaddon — the Assyrian Monarch who succeeded Sannecherib. He had ruled his empire with an iron fist and expanded it. I then noticed a group of schoolchildren, who were guided through the exhibition. To my dismay, propaganda was broadcast by a loudspeaker. It told viewers that the monarchs of old had no scruples in relying on forced labour. No reference was made to their glorious attainments.

My deepest impressions, though, respected the differences between West Berlin and East Berlin. The former was a large, modern Western town. The latter evidenced its being ruled by a dictatorial regime. Policemen armed with light machine guns paraded the streets, the people were plainly dressed and the atmosphere projected regimentation.

We had lunch in a cafeteria in the museum. The food was typically German: sausages with *sauerkraut* and a cake. A conservatively dressed man, who must have been an employee, joined our table. Before long, I noticed that his German was exactly the same as in West Berlin, namely *Hochdeutsch* (BBC German). Having noted that I had Jewish features, he mentioned that in his eyes all people were equal. He then wanted to know whether I was traditional or secular. When I referred to my interest in bible critique, he came up with an impressive analysis of the writings of Julius Wellhausen, the leading 19th century expert on the subject. Later on, he gave us detailed instructions of the shortest way to the Brecht House. He was glad when I told him that I wanted to visit it.

Pat and I had to take a bus to our destination and, as we disembarked, were guided by kindly people and by a uniformed policeman, who was actually very friendly. I went through the rooms once occupied by Bertolt Brecht. I had read him with admiration in my teens and considered it a privilege to walk through his dwelling. I recalled how a group of amateur actors performed *The Good Soul (Woman) of Szechwan* (albeit in Hebrew translation) in Tichon. I believe they captured the spirit.

I kept reflecting on our experience after we arrived back in our hotel in West Berlin. It seemed clear that most people would fall in line with the regime that governed their life. I appreciated the difference between the East German totalitarian government and the liberal, democratic system of West Berlin. All the same, I realised that most people who grew up in East Berlin would rearrange their way of living if transplanted to the Western part. I did not see a core distinction between the segments of the population.

Nowadays, when I write my memoirs, I am satisfied that the position might have changed permanently if the two parts of Germany had been kept apart for about three generations. The two separate countries would by then have developed different dialects and normative patterns. The two populations might in that case have become more difficult to unify and individuals might have found it hard to relocate. Thus, the

Bosnians and Croats came, originally, from the same stock. Over the generations, though, they became distinct ethnic groups. To harmonise them became problematic. I fear that the same might have happened if Western Germany and the DDR had been kept apart for a lengthy time.

One further thought comes to my mind. In general, most of us have two images. One is the face and demeanour we adopt when we are with others. This is our public image. A separate façade surfaces when we converse with ourselves. Robert Louis Stevenson discussed the subject in *Dr. Jekyll and Mr Hyde*. Gerhart Hauptmann dealt with the problem in *Fuhrmann Henschel*.

Our external image frequently follows the crowd. Our internal image may subsequently be ashamed. The visit to East Berlin brought the issue to the surface. I knew that the policeman, with his threatening machine gun, could be a kindly and accommodating individual when he dropped the masquerade. The dangerous individual is the man or woman whose internal image is in full accord with its public image. I suspect that Adolf Hitler and Joseph Stalin fell into this category.

To me, the rest of our trip was an anticlimax. I did enjoy visiting Cologne and the drive to and the sojourn in Trier. But they did not leave as deep an impression on me as Berlin. Before the trip ended, our group gave a party to the driver and guide. I delivered our speech of thanks; my fluent German stood me in good stead.

Back in Freiburg, I spent as much time as I could in the institute. In the evenings, I usually read Böll and some DDR authors I had discovered. My own life was satisfactory. In more than one way, I felt fulfilled.

Regrettably, Pat was restless and developed a real aversion towards our landlady. The only solution was to take Pat with me in the morning, let her do her shopping or plain walks in Freiburg and then take her for lunch. Fortunately, she made some friends during our Humboldt trip. Occasionally, we visited them and went together for lunch or afternoon coffee.

During weekends, we often drove to the picturesque villages of the Kaiserstuhl. I recall with pleasure the vineyards and the orchards. In one establishment, we became well known and were occasionally treated to a bottle of wine. After a while, both of us developed a penchant for the local rosé, that was best when drunk on the premises. As it did not travel well, I had to forego all thoughts of sending a few cartons to New Zealand.

On one long weekend, we crossed to Colmar in France. I parked our car on the outskirts of the town and had real difficulties finding it when it was time to go back. Oddly, the food in this part of France was similar to the food in Freiburg. From Colmar, we proceeded to Strasbourg: a lovely drive and an impressive town. However, our stay there was too short to form any reliable impression. The one point which I noted was the similarity of the features of many French and German people. It dawned on me that Central Europe was a melting pot. Purity of race was sheer nonsense.

Basel and Zürich were also within a comfortable weekend tour. Visiting them was a pleasure, especially the walks in the latter's Old Town. On one occasion, I managed to acquire a nice watch for Pat at a bargain price. She loved to wear it and it is still stored in my safe at home.

For a few weeks, I stayed put. The tension between Pat and the landlady was, unfortunately, getting worse. I too became difficult. Annoyed when the landlady switched the heating off on 1 May, which was actually a chilly day, I made a real fuss. I had my way, but the landlady became antagonistic.

As Pat kept remonstrating with me about the situation, we quarreled incessantly. The few hours I spent on my own in the institute were a reprieve. Then, one bright day, Pat said she wanted to see Venice. Initially, I suggested we join a tour but, in the end, agreed to drive us there and back.

We proceeded through the Black Forest, where we spent a night, and onwards to Bolzano. I loved the Dolomites and suggested we spend some time there. In the event, we opted for a one-day rest in Cortina and from there drove all the way to Venice.

Pat was impressed by Venice, the gondolas and the fine restaurants. My reaction differed. It is summarised in one word: vainglory. I knew that Venice had had its own empire and an impressive history. The city we visited was, however, living on tourism attracted by its glorious past. I found the canals unhygienic and evil-smelling. It did not surprise me to learn that most of the shopkeepers and restaurant owners lived in modern houses on the shore.

On the way back, we spent a night in the Dolomites. To my pleasant surprise, I received, a few days after our return, an invitation to visit the Institute of Banking Law in Cologne. Von Caemmerer, who I believe arranged the visit, strongly advised me against driving up. Pat, too, felt we had had too many trips by car. An express train took us to our destination. After the delivery of my paper, the head of the institute, Professor Plyer, invited me to have coffee with him and a friend from a leading bank. I had observed that Plyer, who used orthopaedic shoes, was unsteady on his feet. I suspected that his toes had been amputated. His guest had lost an arm.

For a while, we talked shop, that is, about credit facilities used in trade financing. I soon noted that Plyer and his guest were addressing one another informally and by the use of proper names. Noticing my perplexed glances, the banker explained the position. I do recall the conversation verbatim. It opened my eyes to a sad and unpleasant truth.

"Today, Klemens Plyer and I are good friends," said the banker, who spoke with a heavy Slavic accent. "A few years ago, both of us were soldiers; we could have clashed."

"Please explain," I replied, although the facts spoke for themselves.

"I was in the Red Army. Plyer was with the Wehrmacht. Our units never engaged each other. But suppose they had?"

The image of two civilised men, like Plyer and his guest, rushing at each other with pointed bayonets was appalling. Plyer, who nodded sadly, added: "In the words of Heinrich Böll: 'Every killing at war is murder.' But a soldier has to obey orders. It is a matter of life and death."

Clearly, the two were close. Was it possible that, in a sense, their having earlier on fought on different sides brought them closer together? After all, the two had shared the misery experienced by men on the front. Was it, further, possible that when either of them advanced with a pointing bayonet, he was a mere savage?

I spent three days visiting the legal departments of international banks. I soon realised that despite insurmountable differences between our common law and the civil law, bankers used a unified terminology in international transactions. In effect, commerce had breached the gap between the two legal systems.

Plyer and I remained in touch. On two occasions, we collaborated on a project. He did visit me in Wellington a few years later. Still, we continued to address one another formally.

On the last day of our trip, Pat wanted to do some shopping and also see the famed cathedral. I too wanted to visit it, but my first priority was the Roman-Germanic Museum. We compromised. Pat went on her shopping spree, and I went to the museum. We agreed to meet at the cathedral's entrance.

The museum was outstanding. I would have willingly spent a week there. The one item I recall clearly was an Egyptian scarab. Its owner must have been a Roman trooper who served both in the Levant and in 'Germania'. He would have acquired the scarab in Egypt and lost it in Cologne, where it was eventually dug up, put in the museum and catalogued. In all probability, the trooper reached Cologne by ship. I knew the Romans had mastered the art of moving regiments by sea.

Pat was waiting for me in the cathedral. I liked it but, after the exhilarating museum, it was an anticlimax. The same afternoon we went by boat up the Rhine to Koblenz and from there took a train back to Freiburg.

My sabbatical was now drawing to its end. I had to index my materials and arrange to ship them back to New Zealand. We went a few times to the Kaiserstuhl and, just before our departure, went by car to Vienna. It was a lovely trip. We spent a night in Landeck and then proceeded over the Arlberg to Salzburg, where we had lunch, and on to Vienna. Mother was glad to see us. I sensed that she was recovering from the ordeal she had undergone during Father's final struggle.

Mother came with us to the popular opera (Volksoper), which performed *The Gypsy Baron*. She managed to get excellent seats, and we enjoyed the evening. The next day, Pat and I went to Gounod's *Faust* at the State Opera. I suspect Pat enjoyed only the famous waltz. I admired Mephisto's solo. I knew, of course, that Gounod's opera did not come to grips with the complexity of Goethe's magnum opus. All the same, the solo touched on the main theme of the masterpiece. Mephisto clarifies that he does not instill evil. His role is to bring out the darker side of a human's psyche. This is, indeed, one way of looking at evils such as war and mayhem, which form part and parcel of human nature. Even without Mephisto's aid, a skilled demagogue knows how to bring out the worst impulses already present in his audience's makeup.

The next day, we departed, proceeding via Munich. As soon as we were back in Freiburg, I had to unwind our affairs. We then took a train to Zürich's airport. Early the next day we were back in Singapore.

For Pat, the three weeks spent in Singapore were a homecoming. For me, it was a breather: a period of leisure without deadlines. I used the time so as to catch up with former students. I was pleased to hear the numerous success stories; and was saddened by a few failures.

I also looked up the developments in Israeli politics. Golda Meir, who had been the Prime Minister when the Yom Kippur War broke out, resigned and was succeeded by Yitzchak Rabin, who had led the Israeli Army to victory. I knew that under his leadership there was a chance for peace in the region. Regrettably, years later, he was assassinated by a religious maniac. I appreciate that the murderer is regarded a hero by hardline fanatics. They think that his hand was guided by providence. In my opinion, his aspiration came from a different source.

From Singapore, we took a direct flight back to Wellington. For me, it was a return to base. Pat's view differed.

Some forty-five years have passed since our year with the Humboldt Foundation. I do believe that it left a profound effect on both of us.

First, it gave both Pat and me firsthand knowledge of West Germany. The Humboldt trip with the expert guide opened our eyes to the beauties of the country. So did our numerous trips to towns and villages adjacent to Freiburg, the excellent sojourn in Cologne and the cruise up the Rhine.

Second, it brought me even closer to the understanding of the German society. I felt comfortable with it. Pat lagged behind but, at the very least, she acquired a basic knowledge of spoken German.

Third, I read widely and filled gaps in my knowledge of German literature and culture. It dawned on me that, by and large, the Germans were a tolerant people. I am not certain that Pat would have agreed. In her eyes, the structure was too rigid and the need to conform paramount. Today, as an aged widower, I have to concede that both views are tenable. The German hierarchy was rather stiff and unbending.

Fourth, I became a better lawyer. Under von Caemmerer's influence, I had a further look at the comparison of laws. Still, I adhered to the historical approach postulated by Steve Riesenfeld.

Finally, the days spent in East Germany and in Cologne made me reflect a great deal about human nature.

In my last letters, I may come back to some of the points raised. Currently, I have to turn to our remaining years in Wellington and our spell in Melbourne.

In the meantime, I wish you all the very best.

Yours as ever,
Peter

19 March 2018
Singapore

Dear Friends,

Letter 21: From Wellington to Melbourne

Professionally, my remaining years in Wellington were peaceful. My academic position was secure. I had no administrative chores, and my list of publications was growing steadily. In particular, I had to work hard on polishing up my chapters in *Benjamin's Sale of Goods* and in *Chitty on Contracts*. The finished product was good.

My home life, alas, lacked harmony. Pat was open about her ever-growing dislike for our windy city. In an attempt to help, I spent a great deal of time with her; took her out regularly and assisted her as much as I could in her pottery.

Then, I made a major blunder. We had saved sufficient money for the acquisition of a second house. We let out our first dwelling and moved to our new townhouse, which was in a suburb on the outskirts. Public transport was good, and we had a bus stop nearby; but Pat did not like to commute. By the time she completed the decoration of our new home, she was once again feeling bored and isolated. It seemed best to do as much of my writings as I could at home. After a while, I went to the faculty only every second day. In due course, I started to feel frustrated.

One particular pastime which relaxed both of us was eeling. The streams just outside Wellington were the habitat of black eels. They swallowed baits only at dusk and so you had to wait patiently for a 'bite'. You then had to pull the eel out of the water. If it bit the bait 'correctly', you were considered a good fisherman. I am not certain the eels relished this sport.

In a way, our existence was enlivened by three visits. Shortly after our return, our faculty invited von Caemmerer to spend a term with us as visiting professor. He and his wife stayed three months in Wellington. Pat was keen to shower hospitality on them. My colleagues were supportive: they invited the von Caemmerers to dinners and some took them for drives.

Von Caemmerer enhanced our comparative law courses. These were conducted by my friend, Tony Angelo. Our syllabuses benefitted greatly from the new Continental influence. A further advantage was triggered off because von Caemmerer was close to the leading scholars in Hamburg's Institute of Comparative Law, which was in charge of the *Encyclopedia of Comparative Law*. To my delight, Tony Angelo and I were invited to contribute chapters. I was asked to take over the discussion of Bills of Exchange, to be included in Volume 9. Tony took charge of the chapter on Fiduciary Obligations. Both saw light in due course.

A few months later, Plyer paid us a visit. He and his wife had decided to take a world tour and spent a few days in Wellington. Plyer took over some classes in my course on banking law but, to my regret, the students did not like him. His lectures were above their heads.

Later on, we were visited by Lu Sinclair, who had by then risen to the post of Registrar. Lu stayed with us. We took her for a tour of our coastal towns. As she had to leave after that weekend, we were unable to take her to see Taupo and Rotorua.

Lu thought I should consider a return to Singapore. She promised to see if there was any a suitable opening for me in a bank. She understood only too well my unease of returning to the University of Singapore at this point of time.

Lu's visit opened my eyes to the enormous progress being made by Singapore. She told me that the PAP was doing a fine job and, further, indicated that the university was likely to be high on the list of priorities of development projects. Later on, she wrote to tell me that banks considered me 'overqualified' (a cordial 'no'); but she encouraged me to think of a return to the faculty. She whetted my appetite, especially as it was becoming clear that Pat was keen.

Then, unexpectedly, Pat discovered an advertisement of a new Chair of Law established by Monash University in Melbourne. Initially, I was loath to apply. I knew that Monash had two excellent scholars. Both were readers (effectively, associate professors) and chair-worthy. I did not want to risk a failing application. It would stain my sound academic record. Pat, though, stood her ground. Despite my misgivings, I went ahead.

As expected, I was shortlisted together with three other applicants. I was invited to fly over for an interview with the Board of Selection, which comprised the dean, the existing Professors of Law, two judges, representatives of the local Bar and two members of the sub-professorial staff.

The four applicants shortlisted were the two readers, a well-known local Queen's Counsel who wanted to give up his practice and become an academic and I. A former colleague from Wellington, who had moved to Monash, advised me that I was not the favourite. He explained that the staff members would support the appointment of an internal candidate. He further thought that the Q.C. would have the support of the Bar and the Bench.

I recall the paper — or 'job talk' — I delivered on this occasion. It dealt with the collapse of a merchant bank in New Zealand (entitled 'Securitibank'). My address was well received, especially as I managed to incorporate some puns, making fun of the institution's title. However, I remained pessimistic. In reality, I was the only candidate who was trying to break into Melbourne from outside. I suspected that a straw vote might exclude me from the shortlist.

Fortuna, though, was on my side. The two internal candidates cancelled each other out. The Q.C. had antagonised one of the members of the Board of Selection. In a sense, my being the only 'external applicant' stood me in good stead. I had never had occasion to tread on any toes. In addition, the dean advised me that he was going to support my application. He needed a professor who would take on some of his administrative functions. He thought I was the best candidate for this task. It further turned out that, like me, he was a close friend of Geoffrey Bartholomew, who sang my praises in a confidential telephone conversation.

I had one further stroke of luck. One of the members of the selection board was my predecessor in Wellington. He knew I had adopted his synopsis and that I had followed the pattern of teaching introduced by him. He too made some enquiries and had decided to give me his support.

During the evening of the committee's meeting, my nerves got the better of me. I knew that the outcome of the deliberations of a selection board was unpredictable. I kept thinking of instances in which I had changed my own vote in university committees in reliance on sound arguments of other members.

The next morning, Gerry (the dean) told me the committee had decided to offer me the post. I accepted it there and then. Apparently, the Q.C., who had been shortlisted, was displeased. It struck me that he had been overconfident: a state of mind which often precedes a fall. The two internal candidates shrugged their shoulders. The decision saved each of them the need to comfort the loser.

Back in Wellington, I enjoyed a hero's welcome at home. Pat was delighted. She thought a move to a metropolis such as Melbourne was going to put an end to her disillusionment. B., who had flown over from Sydney so as to chaperon Pat during my absence, took the same view. Notwithstanding their enthusiasm, I started to have doubts. Was Pat really going to feel at home in Melbourne?

"I hope your wife will settle down well in Melbourne," said George Barton when I told him the news.

"I'll miss Wellington," I replied lamely.

"I know."

"I'll come back to visit you whenever I can."

For a while, George kept reflecting. Then he told me firmly: "There is an old saying — 'Never come back to a place in which you were happy.' Bear this in mind. You may build a palace of Wellington in your mind and then discover much of it was a mirage."

"Does this maxim apply to a homecoming?"

"It does. Have you ever been back to your parents' flat after you left Tel Aviv?"

It was my turn to reflect. My parents' flat in Tel Aviv — which appeared grand to me during my youth — looked somewhat plain when I had flown to Tel Aviv to tell Mother about my marriage plans. "I see what you mean," I conceded.

"If I can, I'll come to see you in Melbourne or perhaps in Singapore if you take Pat back to her home."

John Thomas, our one-time dean, was equally candid. He pointed out that I was changing venues for the wrong reason. I had a pleasant professional existence in Wellington, had left an impact on law reform, had managed to escape any involvement with the administration of our law school and, by and large, did as I pleased.

"You are taking a jump into unknown territory. You are going to have a better salary but, when all is said and done, you are doing financially very well with us."

"You know that Pat never settled here. In a way, this is a salvage operation. You know this."

"I do. But you cannot sort out a problem unless you diagnose it. And that's what you fail to do. You see, Pat dislikes our society. Well, why does she?"

"I suppose she continues to miss her own environment."

"Don't you think she'll miss it just as much in Melbourne?"

"I hope she'll fall on her feet in a new place."

"I, too, hope so for your sake. But I have my doubts. Here she can, at the very least, meet with the diplomatic corps. She could have built up a life of her own. In Melbourne, she may have no outlets."

I sensed that John had put his finger on the pulse. All the same, I was going to give Pat this extra chance. Pat's own view — which put the blame on our having remained childless — suggested that John was right. Our youth was over and the chance of her conceiving at this late stage struck me as dim. A new start in Melbourne might only exacerbate the problem. Would she be able to pursue pottery in this new, far more dispersed, locality?

Be this as it may, we had to get ready for our move. Fortunately, I had discarded many unwanted materials when we changed dwellings in Wellington. Even so, much of what we had acquired over the years, including books I no longer needed, had to be dumped.

We also had to sell our houses. Our bungalow, in Wilton, was snapped up within a few days. We asked Tony Angelo's father, an experienced and reliable real estate agent, to sell our townhouse. The last item to dispose of was our car. We sold it just one day prior to our departure.

We spent our last two nights in Wellington in a hotel. Tony Angelo drove us to the airport. By the time we arrived in Melbourne, I had made up my mind not to look back. To my delight, Pat was looking forward to settling down in a town larger than Wellington.

Looking at the adventure in hindsight, I am forced to conclude that the mistake was in our union. Pat and I belonged to different worlds. Pat was a conformist at heart, stuck stubbornly to the mores and ideals of her home and had no intellectual aspiration or curiosity. Her strength was her aesthetic creativity and the need to look for perfection in decorating her home. She was a good potter and actually liked Chinese painting. In contrast, my life was in my work. Further, intellectual curiosity drove me to bible critique, to the *Dead Sea Scrolls* and to the long-gone glory of Egypt and the Levant. My only aesthetic interest was in porcelain, which, however, was difficult to get in Wellington.

Fortunately, we had some common interests, such as travelling and sightseeing. We were also keenly interested in real estate and loved house-hunting. Nonetheless, I fear that these did not constitute an adequate bond. It is of course possible that a child might have filled the void. However, bringing up children can be a problem. In my heart of hearts, I wonder whether Pat and I would have been good parents. We might have pulled children in opposite directions. The original problems would have re-emerged when it was the child's turn to embark on his or her own life.

I am satisfied that the move to Melbourne was an error of judgment. It involved a change of scene but did not tackle the real problem, which was our incompatibility. I suspect the only sound solution would have been a split. It ought to have given each of us the chance to start afresh. Regrettably, neither of us had the courage to pursue this path.

Up to now, I have concentrated on my personal life following our departure from Singapore. It is now time to turn to the political developments that affected us, that is, the shift in policies in New Zealand. When we arrived, the Prime Minister was one Keith Holyoake, pronounced Holy-Oak by admirers or Holy-Yoke by critics. He was ousted by Jack Marshall of his own party (the National Party), who succeeded him. The shots were, however, called by the Treasurer, Robert Muldoon, who — in my opinion — had the attributes of a leader but, alas, was a quarrelsome and impatient person, who had never learned the art of taking fools lightly.

The main issue at that time was of an economic nature. New Zealand had thrived on the export of wool, mutton and dairy products, mainly to the United Kingdom. Indeed, the country was often referred to as 'Britain's Pacific farm'. When England joined the common market, New Zealand's economy was in jeopardy. Whilst Jack Marshall succeeded in obtaining an accord, safeguarding New Zealand's butter exports to Britain for two years, the future was uncertain.

Shortly thereafter, a general election brought the Labour Party, led by Norman Kirk, into office. Up to the present day, I am unable to pinpoint any major differences between the agendas of Labour and the National Party. I suspect that a great deal of harm was done to the National Party by Robert Muldoon's outbursts during the campaign. Be this as it may, the Labour Party was unable to deliver. In the subsequent election of 1975, the National Party, led by Muldoon, swept back into power.

Muldoon was a pragmatist. He had the mentality of an experienced and shrewd financier. Under his prudent leadership, the country changed its economic outlook and regained strength. The New Zealand dollar recovered during his spell in office.

Muldoon's rise to power had one unexpected side effect on our faculty's development. Geoffrey Palmer decided to enter politics on a full-time basis. He joined the ranks of the Labour Party, was elected to Parliament and, in due course, assumed the leadership role. There is no doubt that, as an individual and as professional, he was superior to Muldoon, whom he kept criticising. However, I had little trust in Geoffrey's ability to steer a ship through turbulent waters. I remain convinced that his real place was in academia.

In an indirect manner, the local politics had a bearing on my decision to move to Melbourne. I feared that shortcomings of the local government might lead to further devaluations of New Zealand's currency. Whilst such a turn of events was unlikely to affect our lifestyle in Wellington, it might have proscribed overseas trips. I had greater trust in the Australian dollar. Notably, I left Wellington before Muldoon's wise policies had left their mark.

The only other country on whose development I kept tabs was Israel. As already mentioned, Golda Meir resigned in ignominy after the Yom Kippur War. Her successor — Yitzchak Rabin — was a man of stature and a first-rate politician. Two critical events confirm his acumen as a decisive leader.

The first, which I consider Rabin's most important achievement, was the execution on 4 September 1975 of the Sinai Interim Agreement. In it, Israel and Egypt declared that the conflict between them in the Middle East should be resolved by peaceful means and not by military force. I believe that this agreement prepared the ground for the peace treaty between the two countries signed in 1979.

The second, most dramatic event during Rabin's first spell in power was Operation Entebbe of 1976, in which the Israel Defense Force srescued the passengers of an airliner hijacked by terrorists, who had diverted it to Uganda. The Israeli Air Force made a surprise landing in the respective airport and departed back to Israel with all but one of the abducted passengers. Two of my colleagues at Wellington thought that the operation involved a breach of Uganda's sovereignty and hence of international law. Most people in the world — including Pat and me — applauded the operation. The episode has even been made into a film.

Regrettably, Rabin's first term as Prime Minister came to a sad end. Prior to his term as Prime Minister, Rabin had served as Israel's Ambassador to the United States. When he returned home, Rabin did not close his American bank accounts. Technically, this was a breach of Israel's Exchange Control Law, under which funds kept overseas should have been repatriated when the owner returned home. The scandal following the exposure of these accounts induced Rabin to resign. His next term as Prime Minister took place in 1992. As already mentioned, he was murdered during his second term in office.

I was living in Wellington during Rabin's first term as Prime Minster. Most of the events recounted by me were reported in the media, including Egypt's. In addition, I received letters from Tel Aviv. My source — one of my late friends — reinforced what I had gleaned on my own.

Having covered some world events, I return to my own odyssey. Pat and I were met in the airport by Dean Gerard Nash. He drove us to a comfortable apartment let to us by Monash University for up to three months at a subsidised rent. Our main task for the moment was house-hunting. Gerry told us that this might turn out to be a difficult task. Prices were soaring and good houses were scarce. Emphasising the need to exercise caution, he told us that some of the practices of real estate agents were on the dubious side. He further told us that it would be in our interest to find a dwelling in the vicinity of the university.

After Gerry had left, Pat had a good look at our residence for the time being. To our delight, we discovered that Gerry had stocked our fridge and had prepared a list of nearby shopping centres. Both of us realised that Gerry was a thoughtful and helpful person.

Our house-hunting experience will be discussed in my next letter. I shall also deal in it with my first period at Monash.

I end this letter with all best wishes.

Yours ever,
Peter

25 March 2018
Singapore

Dear Friends,

Letter 22: Monash under Dean Nash

We took Jerry's advice to heart. In the next few days, we contacted car dealers and real estate agents. The acquisition of a vehicle was easy. Finding a good house was problematic. Monash University was in Clayton. The nearest established district was Glen Waverley, where prices were on the high side. Further, few of the houses available in this neighbourhood were up to the mark.

Most Australians expected their house to have a reception or sitting room for entertaining guests as well as a family room used for everyday activities. Most people also wanted to have a master bedroom with an attached bathroom (known as 'en suite') plus another bathroom for the family. Many of the houses shown to us lacked one of these amenities. Others were run-down and we had no wish to commission extensive renovations. Others still had a swimming pool. Neither of us had any use for such a luxury.

I believe we viewed close to one hundred houses. Soon we became known as 'the time-wasters' and were shunned by many agents. In the end, we found a newly built house in Vermont South, the district neighbouring Glen Waverley. It had a spacious garage with a covered walk to the main door. As you entered, the formal lounge and a dining room were to the left. A master bedroom with an en-suite bathroom was to the right and a corridor led to a spare room, to the main bathroom and convenience area and to the family room. The spacious kitchen was attached to this family room, having also a door opening to the dining room. Two further bedrooms opened to the family room. These were meant for children or relatives. As we did not have any, I turned one of them into a study. Another door from the family room led to our large laundry. In addition to a washing machine placed against one wall, it had adequate room for Pat's potting wheel and a table.

The property boasted a substantial plot of land. There was enough space for both a front and a back garden. One part of the grounds — away from the sun — was suitable for camellias. Both of us were keen on them. In the sunny front of the house, we planted some shrubs and small trees. Within a few months, we had a budding garden.

The plot behind the house would have been large enough for a granny flat. We used it for a shack, in which we placed an electric kiln for Pat. She now had a fine pottery workshop. Regrettably, there were no suitable shops in our vicinity, and it was necessary for me to get supplies of clay and pigments from town.

Pat was proud of her new house. The building contractor declared bankruptcy prior to completion of the house. Having bought it with this information at hand, we bargained hard with the creditors. As a direct result, we had a budget which enabled Pat to furbish the house in a grand manner. This kept her well occupied. Within some two months, our new home was complete and ready for occupation. It was the best property we ever owned.

Matters went less smoothly at work. To start with, I knew my blood pressure was high but, foolishly, failed to disclose this when the contract with Monash was negotiated. Under the then university regulations, I was expected to take out an insurance policy so as to secure my retirement. I was loath to go ahead with the medical examination, which was bound to reveal the flaw. I got so worked up about it, that B. had to fly down to Melbourne to give me moral support. The problem was sorted out by my accepting a policy with a loading. Fortunately, a few years later, the university launched its own pension scheme, which I was delighted to join.

A separate issue arose because under the existing system, each professor had a secretary. In an attempt to guide my feet, Gerry assigned to me an experienced employee. To my surprise, she started to intervene in all my affairs. On one occasion, she went so far as to imply that my appointment was probationary. When I told her to mind her own business, she complained to the faculty's administrative clerk, Alan. The ensuing quarrel, when he came to my office to remonstrate, was amicably settled: he conceded that the secretary had stepped out of line. It was, however, a Pyrrhic victory. Alan became an enemy and the secretary remained a problem until her resignation a few years later.

My administrative duties were yet another source of concern. By the end of the year, Gerry had assigned to me the chairmanship of thirteen committees. I tried my best to cope but, all in all, longed for my previous less cumbersome professional life in Wellington.

Soon, I got convinced that Monash's cumbersome administrative machinery was counterproductive. I preferred the code of honour used in Wellington, which sanctioned the arrangement of a matter by a telephone call followed by a brief confirmation in writing, which was just a formality. At Monash, even a simple matter had to go through a committee, and, in most cases, a memorandum had to follow and be submitted to the members for perusal. In consequence, a matter that would be settled in Wellington within a few days could stretch at Monash over weeks or even months. In a sense, the lavish funding of Monash entailed the creation of an administrative machinery which Wellington could not afford and did not require.

At the beginning, I missed my colleagues, who, of course, remained back in Wellington. In due course, however, I met a few colleagues whose interests, like mine, were not purely in the law. One of them — Peter Heffey — became one of my closest friends. Although his main interest was in music, whilst mine remained in bible critique and the Levant, we shared an appreciation of culture in general and literature in particular. Peter was fluent in Latin and French, which I had to read in translation. Hebrew and German, though, were closed books to him. In many conversations, we complemented one another.

Further, conversations with Peter promoted my understanding of music. My good memory enabled me to retain tunes in my mind. The identification of an opus was therefore an easy matter. Peter improved my understanding by showing me the connection between a composer's life and his or her compositions.

Peter also guided Pat and me to Melbourne's art centre, which encompassed a theatre, an auditorium suitable for concerts and smaller chamber music rooms. I recall, in particular, one classical music performance with an admirable violinist and another in which a pianist performed Beethoven's Fourth Piano Concerto.

Another colleague I befriended was Michael Pryles. He came from a mid-European background similar to mine. His father had fled from Austria in 1937 and became a successful businessman in Melbourne.

Michael's discipline was arbitration. When I joined Monash, Michael was a reader but, before long, he was constituted a full professor.

Michael observed our dietary laws. When Pat flew from time to time to Singapore, I went out with him and his wife to Kosher eateries. His bungalow in Toorak was in one of the suburbs dominated by Jews. I spent many pleasant days in their welcoming home and came to know their daughter.

Like me, Michael was interested in antiques. I recall the afternoons in which I went with him to browse in antique shops in Camberwell. Many pieces I acquired in these sojourns continue to grace my porcelain collection.

On one of my strolls with Michael, I spotted an interesting bookshop. I visited it a few days later and discovered that its owner was of the same make as my bookseller in Wellington. Within a few weeks, I became a regular visitor to his shop.

Another staff member I came to know well was J. Initially, she acted as our solicitor for the acquisition of the house. As the property was purchased from the creditors (a bank) which had foreclosed, the transaction was of some complexity. J. was an experienced conveyancer and made certain that we got a clean Torrens title. Further, whilst the creditors insisted that we buy the property 'as is', J. extracted some warranties respecting the built-in floor heating and the fence. Her performance was that of an accomplished solicitor and the creditors' renowned law firm treated her documentation with due respect.

In the process, I was captivated by her effervescent personality, by her penchant of calling a spade a spade, by her gift of repartee and by her down-to-earth mannerism. According to the grapevine, J. was a Roman Catholic girl who rebelled against the traditions preached in the convent in which she had been brought up. Regrettably, she had been unable to walk away from the hearth amicably. Feeling the need to protest, she led an unconventional life, divorced her husband, who was a good-looking fellow and a fitness fan, lived openly as she pleased and became a radical.

J. had one additional virtue. In a sense, she was a kindred spirit, that is, a person you were able to communicate with. She was widely read, although mainly in English. I called on her occasionally in her house in Brighton. I recall in particular a session in which we discussed D.H. Lawrence's *The Fox* and another devoted to Kafka's *Das Schloss* (*The Castle*), which she had read in translation.

A student who lived across the road saw me when I arrived on one occasion. Being a simple soul, he concluded that two and two made five. In reality, though, my friendship with J. had never become an affair. Rumours about us were rife; but it was smoke without fire.

In an attempt to capitalise on her knowledge of jurisprudence, I suggested we work together on a book on legal change. On the face of it, the subject was suitable. Both of us were keen to come to grips with the forces behind the ever-changing principles of our law. Today, I realise that as our philosophies differed, there was in reality no room for collaboration. J. was an ardent believer in 'American realism', which searched for sociological motivations behind abstract legal principles, such as the legislator's or court's prejudices based on race, gender and class. Like Steve Riesenfeld before me, I was searching for the historical origin of principles, for their conceptual basis and for the factor that had led to a change.

Each approach was legitimate and had the support of a respectable school of thought. But they were incompatible. For a while, I worked on the chapters assigned to me but eventually declared defeat. The book was never completed. J. may still have the drafts I handed her.

Thinking about the episode with hindsight, I suspect I confused the scholar with the woman. As a person, J. was fascinating. As a scholar, she was one-eyed. Doubtless, she was encyclopaedic and knowledgeable. Her difficulty was in her approach to given cases, which was often biased. When, for instance, she dealt with a bank that called up a mortgage loan, she was usually on the borrower's side. She closed her eyes to the fact that the bank was not a philanthropist and that it would have refused to grant the loan if it had had any doubts about the customer's ability to repay.

I believe that, in general, my first year in Melbourne was acceptable. My home life, too, was satisfactory. Pat was busy with the decoration of our home and, in her spare time, used her kiln. After a few months, though, we became isolated. In Wellington, Pat had the mystique of the East. The Chinese wife of a European colleague was out of the ordinary. In reality, she was humoured.

The position differed at Monash. It had two Chinese staff members and, of course, Melbourne boasted a substantial Chinese community. It even had a Chinatown. In fact, Pat was nothing extraordinary in Melbourne. People expected us to conform to some basic Australian norms. New Zealanders were more tolerant than Australians in that they did not expect foreigners to toe the line. In many ways, it was easier to be an outsider in Wellington than in Melbourne.

Regrettably, we did not return invitations or, in other words, did not invite guests to our home. This was a major mistake. Further, the Jewish community in Melbourne differed from my compatriots in Wellington. In the latter, there was a substantial mid-European circle. We fitted in. In the former, the community was orthodox. We had no inroads to it.

For a while, we went out with some Chinese couples but over time became homebound. This meant that Pat became even more reliant on me than she had been in Wellington. Although I went out regularly for lunch with colleagues, I had to return home as early as possible. After a while, I felt stifled. Peter Heffey and Michael Pryles were my only real contacts.

A specific problem arose from the law school's architecture. It was so designed that the staff offices were situated around the library, which had many doors. Each staff member had a key. In consequence, some colleagues built up their own holdings from books 'borrowed' from the library without their being checked out in the appropriate manner. I hope the situation has been remedied. During my time, it often meant that books needed by me were effectively untraceable. I have to confess that I, too, was tempted to 'borrow' books but am relieved to affirm that I never stooped to that level.

Quite a few interesting events took place during my first years in my new post. By the end of my first year at Monash, a student wanted me to assist him and his partner to obtain a licence for the establishment of a bank. Being uneasy about handling such a matter on my own, I asked a colleague, Professor Bob Baxt, to attend my meeting with the interested parties. It turned out that they wanted to develop a very large plot of land but were unable to obtain a loan from an existing bank. Thereupon, they came up with the idea of founding a bank of their own, hoping that the block of land would secure the depositors' interest.

It took me a while to explain to them that the Reserve Bank was unlikely to grant a banking licence for the financing of such a venture. A regular cash flow and an experienced directorate would be an additional requisite. Bob, who understood my difficulty in articulating the points made by me, stepped in and advised the two to seek the advice of an established counsel who dealt with matters of this sort. They departed after a short while. To date, I am grateful to Bob for extricating me. I hated to tell the suitors that the Reserve Bank was not going to be satisfied with their credentials.

Another annoying case arose when a student alleged that he had failed an examination because he had just found out that his father was terminally ill. One of the members of our committee suggested that we ask that the doctor, who had conveyed the sad news to student, to ring me (the chairperson) and confirm the facts. I did receive a telephone call, but the alleged doctor's language was too colloquial. When I dialled the telephone number of the doctor, it turned out he had never rung me. The student involved or one of his mates had impersonated the physician. Our disciplinary committee did not expel the student. They simply made him repeat the course.

Gerry and Bob also looked after my interests in an important matter respecting my career. Shortly after the end of my first year at Monash, they suggested that I be constituted a member of the Chief Justice's Law Reform Committee for Victoria. I enjoyed this involvement, although on many occasions the committee spent much of its time on the thorny issue of whether a matter was within the realm of the law of the state of Victoria, which fell within our mandate, or subject to federal law. As New Zealand was not a federated country, these issues never arose there.

For a person working in my field, the split between state and federal law presented a specific obstacle. All matters respecting cheques and other sorts of bills of exchange were governed by federal law. In contrast, all subjects relevant to the granting of loans, such as the regulation of moneylending and the technicalities of mortgages, were a facet of state law. Serious legal problems could arise where a transaction stretched over more than one state.

The differences between the laws of the different states of Australia had to be reflected in our teaching courses and, of course, in books dealing with financial transactions. Whilst one of my professorial colleagues tended to cover meticulously issues arising from this internal conflict of laws, most of us tended to concentrate on the law applicable in Victoria. This was the easy way out! I consider it important to add that my membership of the Chief Justice's Committee furthered my understanding of the legal issues involved.

My membership of this committee had an additional and useful side effect. Legal practitioners who were members introduced me to lawyers in town. As a member of the committee, I met a number of colleagues from our rival institution, the University of Melbourne. Most of them had remunerative consultative practices. Before long, I started to consider passing the required examinations so as to qualify as a barrister. I was confident that, thereupon, opinion work would come my way.

A letter from Tony Guest decided me to put this matter on hold. He suggested that I write a new book on banking law. He thought that the existing texts were out of date and that a new analysis was timely. I was flattered. I knew that Tony would have raised the matter only if he thought I had the required background and zest. He had also prepared the ground for my contacting the publishers. Oxford University Press commissioned the book.

All in all, my academic progress during my first two years at Monash was satisfactory. Whilst I missed my more relaxed existence in Wellington and my regular bridge luncheons, I made good use of my higher income. My library grew and my porcelain collection became substantial. Further, it was useful to have a secretary of my own. I no longer depended on a typing pool.

My home life, though, became a matter of concern. When Pat completed the decoration of our house, she had too much spare time on her hands. For a few months, she continued to throw and fire fine ceramics. She was, however, unable to join a pottery club. To a large extent, this was due to my inability to drive her to classes. Melbourne was a large town and public transport was poor. Pat was unable to use it.

For a while, Pat amused herself by watching television programmes and by joining me when I hunted for antiques. Occasionally, we went to plant nurseries in our vicinity and at other times drove to scenic Olinda, which was nearby.

The situation was exacerbated by a decline in Pat's eyesight. Initially, the specialist in Wellington had thought the deterioration was due to a weakness of her eye muscles. In Melbourne, the ophthalmologist thought it was a congenital problem, involving the gradual loss of sight. The effect on Pat was devastating. In the first place, she lost the art of moulding pieces of ceramics. Secondly, firing her products became risky. She was no longer able to supervise the firing process and, in addition, lost the ability to arrange her wares appropriately in the kiln. In due course, Pat gave up her pottery.

Another problem arose because the magic chemistry of youth was over. By about the middle of our second year in Melbourne, Pat suggested I move to the bedroom next to my study. I agreed.

To my dismay, Pat started to throw tantrums. I knew that these were manifestations of her increasing frustration but was unable to be of assistance. Our family doctor was equally helpless. In the end, Pat had a nervous breakdown. Her older sister, A., flew down from Singapore and took Pat back for a spell at home.

Life on my own in Melbourne was acceptable. Both Peter Heffey and Michael Pryles took me out regularly. In addition, I started to invite colleagues to our house. I recall in particular one party, in which Peter set the tone. It was pleasant and harmonious. Everybody felt at ease. So did my guests in some other parties I threw. I did not realise at that time that I was harming Pat's reputation. People noted that after her return to Melbourne, I ceased to invite colleagues over. They drew their own conclusions.

At the beginning of my solitary existence in Melbourne, I perfected my culinary skills. One of my concoctions was a new version of chopped liver. Another was a sour cream-based salad with a meat loaf. Often, though, I did not feel like cooking and bought snacks from nearby fast-food outlets. Later on, I discovered some good and reasonably priced restaurants in the neighbourhood.

In the evenings, I worked on one of my projects. The chapters of *Legal Change* took up some of my time. Most evenings, though, were devoted to my forthcoming book on banking law or to my autodidactic bible critique. It dawned on me that in order to tackle the latter topic adequately, I had to acquire some additional Semitic languages and, if possible, some Mid-Egyptian. All in all, I was immersed in my work.

Pat returned to Melbourne after some six weeks. She had recovered, appeared cheerful and, I hoped, wanted to start a new chapter. She was accompanied by her mother, who was keen to see some of Australia. Shortly after their arrival, I drove us to Bright (near the border of New South Wales). To me, the excursion was a disappointment. In comparison to the lush habitat of New Zealand, Victoria appeared parched and dry. It was also monotonous. I suspect my mother-in-law agreed. Before long, she returned to Singapore.

Shortly after driving back, I started to feel unwell. For apparently no reason, I broke into profuse sweltering and at times felt dizzy. Initially, I assumed it was flu, triggered off by being overworked. Then, one morning, I had a bad spell on my way to a lecture in town. I had to ask the taxi driver to take me back home. Initially, our family doctor did not take the matter seriously. He assumed it was an instance of speaker's nervousness. Still, he asked me to have a full blood count.

I recall our lunch whilst we waited for the result. Having had a sweet tooth since my youth, I savoured the splendid dessert. It was actually the last crème caramel I ever had. The blood count disclosed that I had succumbed to diabetes.

Having read a great deal about this illness, I am now certain that I must have had early symptoms that ought to have been noted and investigated. I also knew that my maternal grandmother was diabetic. The gene must have been in the family. Still, I was so preoccupied with my fight with high blood pressure and with asthma that I failed to notice my ever-increasing thirst and hunger. Be this as it may, the diagnosis was confirmed by a specialised, unpleasant, glucose sensitivity test.

It was difficult to come to terms with this unpleasant development. I recall with dismay how I had to attend functions without partaking of the very starchy or fatty foods I loved. I felt devastated.

Pat had the wisdom of insisting that I consult a specialist. He made me take very light medication, which worked well. He opined that my disease had been discovered in time. The pancreas had slowed down because it had been overworked. It had not been damaged or destroyed. The tablet he prescribed stimulated the organ but, of course, I had to adhere to a strict diet. I have done so ever since.

The new illness took its toll. Dr. B. insisted that I should never overtire myself physically or mentally. He explained that I had to exercise regularly but ought to take a rest when I felt flat. In consequence, I started to cut corners when it came to my administrative chores. I sped through meetings, became tardy in the preparation of our reports and generally seemed out of humour. Gerry and Bob (the vice-dean) noted this and raised their eyebrows. When I told Gerry openly that I was in dire need of rest, he wondered whether I might want to take a year off.

To our relief, the National University of Singapore ("NUS") was keen to engage me as a visiting professor for two terms. Gerry, a man of understanding and compassion, urged me to accept. On his recommendation, Monash granted me one year of leave without pay.

The preparations went smoothly. We found a good tenant for our house and a colleague volunteered to take care of our car. On our way to Singapore, we stopped in Darwin, in the Northern Territory. I found the city dreary and boring but was concerned to note the large number of aborigines, who had become alcoholics and roamed the streets aimlessly. We then proceeded to Bali, where both of us had a good rest. After some three days, we flew on to Singapore.

Up to this point, I have concentrated on my personal experiences during my first three years at Monash. The world, though, did not stand still. During this period, the Australian party in power was the conservatives. I was impressed with Malcolm Fraser, who was a fine and reliable Prime Minister. I was blissfully ignorant of the state governments, except that Queensland's premier, one Bjelke-Petersen, was always in the news. To date, I am unable to understand what he sought to achieve, except his loud-mouthed talk about ceding from

Australia. Fortunately, this never materialised and, eventually, he was ousted by the electorate.

I have to admit that I never understood the difference between the policies of the Conservatives and those of the Labor Party. In my eyes, Australians voted for a figurehead rather than for a party. I may be wrong on the subject but am certain that I am not the only person to take this view.

In Israel, too, there were developments. The ruling party, Mapai, lost the general elections and Begin, the ex-terrorist, became Prime Minister. In 1979, Anwar Sadat concluded with him the famous Egyptian–Israeli peace treaty. I do believe the real credit goes to Rabin, who had laid the foundation, and to Henry Kissinger, who assumed the role of broker. Sadat and Begin were awarded the Nobel Peace Prize. Israel's one-time Prime Minister, Golda Meir, said that the two should have been awarded the Oscar. As regards Begin, her words made good sense.

As I was no longer living in Israel, I had to form my opinion on the basis of letters received from friends. I believe that Mapai's defeat was primarily due to two reasons. First, as already noted, the mass migration to Israel led to demographic changes. Many of the new migrants did not believe in socialism or welfare. They had a capitalist outlook and did not accept the notions of equality and of sharing. Secondly, Mapai's three decades of rule led to widespread corruption. The population lost its trust in the leaders.

It is possible that another factor contributed to the political change. The prime ministers who succeeded Rabin had little to boast of. In contrast, Begin was a fine orator and had played an important — although to me unacceptable — role in the foundation of Israel. Is it possible that in the country of pale contenders, the man with a memorable past became the best option?

Notwithstanding the fact that my feet were now far from Israel, part of my heart remained with it. Still, I was unable to follow the political developments in the region after Begin's rise to power. I shall, accordingly, refrain from opining about them in detail in my remaining letters.

In my next letter I intend to concentrate on my year as visiting professor in Singapore. I shall also discuss the progress made in some of my projects.

Till then, I wish the very best to all of you.

Yours as ever,
Peter

30 March 2018
Singapore

Dear Friends,

Letter 23: Visiting Professor in Singapore

At the airport, we were met by one of my future colleagues. He took us to the flat allocated to us by the university in a well-established condominium called Pandan Valley. We had three bedrooms, a sitting room and the usual amenities. One disadvantage was that the flat spread over three levels so much space was taken up by staircases.

The next morning, I went over to the faculty. Sook Yee had by then assumed the deanship and was doing a superb job. Her objective was to revive the morale of all staff. I knew that quite a few of them stayed put but wailed and grumbled incessantly.

Under Toh's reign, the faculty had been relocated to the new campus in Kent Ridge. In due course, this new campus became the University's main grounds. Even the administration moved to it. However, when the law school was relocated, the campus was still new. Most faculties had remained in the Bukit Timah Campus.

From a personal point of view, the new campus at Kent Ridge was well situated. Pandan Valley could be easily reached from there by bus.

The faculty was, however, isolated from the main campus. Students who took some Arts courses had to commute from campus to campus.

The teaching duties allocated to me by Sook Yee were light. I taught Commercial Transactions with a younger colleague, Ho Peng Kee, who became a friend, and an LL.M. course in banking law. I enjoyed both. Peng Kee was of great help. Before long, he and his wife became family friends. I recall how, on one occasion, he invited us to spend an evening at his mother's place. On the way, the windscreen of his car was shattered by a stone. We had to remove the remaining glass and then continued. Fortunately, it was not raining.

The batch which I taught in 1982 encompassed some of the leading figures of the future. Davinder Singh became an outstanding litigator and the managing partner of one of Singapore's major law firms. In my eyes, he was as accomplished as the top litigators in London. V.K. Rajah, whose father I had known in the '60s, was another exceptional student. After graduating from our faculty, he went for further studies to Cambridge and came back with first class honours. Thereafter, he developed his father's legal practice, which was at that time relatively small, into one of the largest and most prominent firms in town. He left it and became, in quick succession, a Supreme Court Judge, a Judge of Appeal and thereafter the Attorney-General. The third distinguished student, Andrew Phang, became a Professor of Law in our faculty, then the Dean of the Faculty of Law of the Singapore Management University ("SMU") and thereafter was elevated to the Bench. In due course, he became a member of the Court of Appeal. His book on the local law of contract has remained one of the texts in point.

Teaching a class with students of this calibre was a pleasant experience. I was satisfied that their ability and motivation surpassed that of my students at Monash. Just for once, my objective was not to prepare them for the examination in the subject but to induce them to develop their own reasoning and application skills. I believe I succeeded. The LL.M class, too, was good. It included first-rate students. I have remained proud of them.

One person who enrolled in my LL.M. class was a former LL.B student of my earlier spell in the City of the Lion. Whilst Lim Teck Hwee was not an outstanding practitioner, he was sound and knowledgeable. Two other practitioners enrolled in the course. In a class of this type, the learning process was mutual. Further, this was not an instance in which I had to keep my distance. I was glad to mix with them. Teck Hwee and his family became family friends. Shortly after the examinations were over, we started to go out with them.

My role in Singapore was not confined to teaching. I realised that Sook Yee's objective in inviting me to come over was to help her enhance the standing of our faculty. I sensed that the close ties between the ivory tower and the town were already in place. My assistance was needed in securing Singapore's reputation internationally. To this effect, I recommended the launching of a series of conferences, devoted to different aspects of international banking law.

Sook Yee liked the idea, which, actually, was in line with Harry Groves' vision. Her vice-dean, my friend Philip Pillai, prepared with me the agenda for the first conference, to be held in 1984. We worked well together and, within two months, had finalised the agenda and were working on the list of speakers. I recall how we invited a well-known French scholar only to receive his former secretary's letter, advising that he had passed away.

Our final list encompassed the leading international scholars as well as a number of distinguished local practitioners. I knew most of them and had actually collaborated with some of them. I do believe that our final programme was fine. One person we invited was Sasske (David Sassoon), who had by then left the World Bank and returned to Israel. Even back at home, he specialised in international business transactions and contributed seminal articles to leading journals.

Another source of satisfaction was the matters referred to me by local practitioners for my opinion and the numerous invitations for in-house lectures extended to me by local banks. Of particular interest was a seminar on trade financing conducted for the staff of the Development Bank of Singapore ("DBS"). We had a full house of some one hundred and fifty persons in the bank's auditorium. Other seminars were commissioned by the Association of Banks in Singapore. I believe that, in a small way, these sessions contributed to Singapore's development into a regional banking hub.

At about the very same time, Singapore took the first steps needed for becoming a leading centre for trading in precious metals. The republic made a slow start, but I could see that the cornerstone had been laid soundly. In general, though, the local banks continued to discourage clients from acquiring gold as a backup. Investments in stocks and bonds remained the preferred devices recommended to customers. The argument in their favour was that the holder was guaranteed either interest on bonds or dividends on shares.

Up to now, I have discussed my work. On Sook Yee's advice I did not acquire a car. However, my existence was enhanced by the drives through town with my colleagues. I recall how I went with Peng Kee to a function. He made a detour in which we had to cross the Sheares Bridge. It was built over reclaimed land and connected the city with the East Coast area. I was impressed and noted how Singapore was reclaiming large plots of land. Whilst some of the places, such as eateries along Beach Road, had disappeared under a highway known as the East

Coast Parkway, new hotels and shopping centres took their place. Although I missed the old spots I had loved, I realised that both the town and its population were going from strength to strength.

My professional existence in Singapore was, thus, pleasing. Regrettably, my home life, especially at the weekends, left much to be desired. Pat usually went to church with her siblings. During the first two months, I simply went to the university and worked. Later on, I started to visit local antique shops which were open on weekends. European porcelain was, of course, unavailable. But there were fine shops trading in oriental antiques. I spent a great deal of time browsing through their wares. In the process, I acquired some good ivory and jade pieces. Occasionally, Pat accompanied me on weekdays when I was able to take an afternoon off work.

Pat's problem was how to fill in time during weekdays, when I had to go to the office. Occasionally, she met up with her siblings or with friends but generally she spent her time watching television programmes. I sensed that even in Singapore she had a lonely existence. I fear that this would have been the case even if we had had children, as they would doubtless have had to attend classes at school.

In an attempt to break the monotony, we took a few trips. We spent one week in the Cameron Highlands. Initially, we booked a room in the renowned Smokehouse, which still had the ambience of a colonial resort. As Pat did not like it, we moved further uphill to a resort called Strawberry Park. Here, we had a unit of our own and, of course, local tours picked us up from there. I was amazed to see how the place had grown.

A few weeks later, we took a trip to China. This was an eye-opener. Our initial route was via Hong Kong to Shenzhen, which had by then become a thriving tourist destination. One of its attractions was a small garden assuming the form of a miniature of 'China'. I sensed that the zone was vibrant and bound to develop over the next few years. From Shenzhen, we had to return to Hong Kong in order to take a flight to Shanghai, which was a huge metropolis. The Bund was impressive and, to my surprise, boasted two good Western restaurants. However, the local food was splendid and inexpensive. We stuck to it.

We took a cruise down the river to the Yangtze Delta. The vessel was not too hygienic but, despite the flea-infested seats, both of us enjoyed the cruise. I was particularly impressed by the container port. I had no doubt that Shanghai dwarfed every Western town I had visited. However, the miserable poverty in the outskirts of the town was alarming. I recall in particular how some beggars followed us. I felt deeply disturbed.

We spent the rest of our short trip in Beijing. I shall never forget the town's chaotic traffic. Drivers — including those in charge of buses — simply ignored traffic lights. The only way to cross the street was to join locals, immerse yourself in the group, close your eyes and follow the crowd. One consequence was that invariably we dined either in the hotel or in an eatery on the same side of the street. Still, we managed to see the sights.

On the first day, we went to the Summer Palace. It was impressive but, to my mind, lacking in charm. The next day, we visited Tiananmen Square. Even in comparison to squares in leading European towns, it was vast. The Statue of Mao Zedong was there for all to see, and local tourists were queuing in front of the lane leading to his mausoleum. It dawned on me that the hero cult remained predominant in China. Whilst the country had opened its doors to some foreign influences, the heart — or basic outlook — of the population had not changed. It had remained an oriental nation — the 'Kingdom of Heaven' — even though some capitalist notions had pervaded it.

From the square, we proceeded to the Forbidden City, which used to be the ordinary residence of the emperor. You had to traverse it on foot and, candidly speaking, I did not like it. The rooms open to the public struck me as dire and the architecture as monotonous and dull. It lacked the splendour and sophistication I had noted during earlier years in Western palaces and castles. The saving factor of the tour was a splendid collection of Qing porcelain. It was superior to the collections I had seen in Istanbul and in London. I should have liked to return so as to study them further but, alas, we were short of time.

We spent the next morning on a tour of the Great Wall of China. I managed to climb it but kept thinking about the Maginot Line of France. Truth be told, I was far more impressed by the workmen in a jade workshop, who carved pieces without even wearing goggles to protect their eyes, than by the splendour of a massive construction of days past. I recalled that when Genghis Khan went on his onslaught to conquer North China, the Great Wall failed to stop his advance.

I have no doubt that the erection of the Great Wall was an admirable architectural feat. However, it segregated China from the rest of the world. Its impact was to secure China's isolationist outlook. But did it have any military significance?

All in all, I had been far more impressed by Europe than by the Kingdom of Heaven. Nowadays, I realise that my cultural conditioning may have led to my reaction. Europe and its turbulent history were closer to my heart than the alien culture and history of the Orient.

From Beijing, we managed to get a direct flight back to Singapore. We should have liked to visit Xi'an but I had to resume teaching. On returning to the City of the Lion, I felt I was back at home.

Today — when I am writing my memoirs as a retiree — I begin to understand why I felt a stranger in China but an honorary local in

Singapore. The population of the City of the Lion was mixed. As already mentioned, the inhabitants encompassed a number of different ethnic groups. However, even the dwellers of Singapore's heartland had a smattering of English coupled with the realisation that the Chinese were not a unique and segregated race. I believe that this group of Singaporeans adhered to their mainland mores; but they had come to tolerate others and associated with them. They were not monolithic. In a somewhat similar manner, I, too, was a hybrid, straddling between Judaism and the culture of my place of residence. In this respect I was, in reality, a Diaspora Jew. I was neither a Continental nor a British (or Australasian) individual. Neither was I a typical Israeli, who thought that his country was the centre of the universe. I was — and have remained — a mixed character, who was accepted as such in Singapore. Accordingly, any spell in Singapore was akin to a return to base.

My next few weeks were taken up by my three major projects: (i) *Legal Change* written in collaboration with J.; (ii) the chapter on Bills of Exchange in the *Encyclopedia of Comparative Law* in Hamburg; and (iii) my forthcoming *Modern Banking Law*. In addition, I was asked to contribute a column on Banking Law in a well-known British periodical. I agreed to write some four notes per annum. Then, unexpectedly, I received an invitation to a conference on letters of credit to be held in the University of Bielefeld in Germany. Pat encouraged me to accept, and I did so willingly.

On our way to Bielefeld, we made a stop in Stuttgart. Mother came over from Vienna and spent a weekend with us. She had fully recovered from her ordeal and looked well. Stuttgart struck me as a dull town; one of the many I had no wish to return to.

The conference in Bielefeld was a success. I met the leading German and American scholars working in my field. I also made the acquaintance of one of the legal advisers of the Deutsche Bank. Rolf Ebert and I published together articles on a new banking facility, namely the Standby Letter of Credit.

Before returning to Singapore, we flew over to London. My main objective was to visit Tony Guest in order to discuss with him some difficult points respecting *Modern Banking Law*. One of them related to overlaps between the role of the existing retail banks, such as Barclays Bank, and the powerful and ever-growing building societies. In the event, many of them merged with or even took over some banks. In 1982, the position was dicey. Tony's sound advice was that I concentrate on the specific role played by the clearing banks. Another point arose from the fact that building societies did not have the power to issue cheque books. I wondered whether to cover the means used by building societies so as to have a role in payments respecting retail transactions. Tony thought it might be best to steer clear of the thorny problems involved.

Tony invited Pat and me to stay with him. I remember this week with pleasure and gratitude. I recall in particular one evening in which Tony treated us to a salmon trout. It was excellent.

We visited some of the bankers who had helped me so much with my thesis. As expected, some had retired. Fortunately, I managed to contact most of them. I also managed to acquire new contacts in the banking world and in the Bank of England.

We spent one weekend with Robert Goh, my brother-in-law, and his charming wife, Ing-Britt. On one occasion, Robert took us for a pleasant drive through Middlesex and on another right down to Central London, where, of course, he lost his way. Still, we drove along Bayswater Road, which, I noted, was becoming Middle Eastern. I saw some Britons, but — in this part of London — they were few and far in between. Pat pointed out that London struck her as a cosmopolitan rather than as a British city.

Shortly after our return to Singapore, I was invited, for the first time in my life, to appear as an expert witness in a case involving two banks. The role of an expert witness is, in many ways, ambivalent. The best illustration of his role is the case of medical negligence. Usually in such a matter, the actual facts, for instance the details respecting an operation, are established by the evidence of the surgeon and of the patient. Occasionally, it is claimed that the surgeon had failed to ask for a given test prior to his commencing with the procedure involved. Both parties may call experts to establish whether the taking of the test was, in practice, an essential prerequisite. I recall an interesting case in which an eye surgeon removed the cataracts of a patient, who suffered also from glaucoma. The patient lost his eyesight. The outcome of the case depended to a large extent on the evidence of expert ophthalmologists.

In banking cases, the role of an expert is limited to instances in which the issue arising is whether the handling of a given matter was in line with established banking practice. In the case referred to me, the issue was whether a bank had acted in contravention of established practice when it made payment against a set of documents tendered under a letter of credit. A preliminary issue raised by the opposing party concerned my qualification to give evidence on banking practice. The question arose because, notwithstanding my field research and years of teaching the subject, I had never worked in a bank. Could I, thus, possess the required practical experience to be called as an expert? The point was forcefully argued. To my satisfaction, the court ruled that I had the required expertise. In the event, we won the case on a technical point. Thereafter, my expertise on matters respecting international banking practice was established once and for all. In a sense, it was a victory for university teachers in general. The court held that an academic could acquire the relevant expertise in his field through teaching and research.

My sabbatical year in Singapore was drawing to its close. Before the end of the session, Pat suggested that we invite the class to our flat. We gave them a party, which I believe was successful.

As soon as the examinations were over, when I was getting ready to start packing, two problems emerged. The first of them related to Pat's eyesight. Ever since our last two years in Wellington, her vision had been deteriorating. As already mentioned, in Melbourne the specialist had failed to come up with a clear diagnosis. In Singapore, an ophthalmologist finally discovered the cause. As suspected by the specialist in Melbourne, the condition was congenital and involved macular degeneration. In the opinion of the ophthalmologist in Singapore, the condition was not treatable.

Both of us were dismayed. In Singapore, we were able to employ a maid, who came over three times a week in order to clean the house and wash the clothes. In Melbourne, such help would not have been available. In essence, this unfortunate development suggested that we ought to remain in Singapore. My contract, though, was coming to its end.

The second but unrelated problem related to my post at Monash. Shortly before I took my leave, Gerry Nash resigned and went into private practice. He had a fine reputation, was considered an accomplished and effective litigator and, as expected, left his mark on local law. In no time, he was made a Queen's Counsel. A post in a university was bound to remain far less remunerative and, in reality, less prestigious. Further, any Q.C. had a good chance of being elevated to the Bench. Gerry's prospects were positive.

Gerry's successor to the deanship, Bob Baxt, was not as liberal in outlook as his predecessor. I knew he was likely to drive the faculty even harder than Gerry. The time left for an individual's research projects was bound to be curtailed. From my point of view, the development was undesirable.

To aggravate matters further, Bob wrote to advise me that he had decided to take a year of sabbatical leave. He hoped I would agree to assume the role of acting dean whilst he was away. Bob made it clear that the task was cumbersome. He was, of course, fully aware that I had no stomach for this type of work. Naturally, Bob's acting dean was expected to steer the ship to the destination determined during Bob's year in office. Knowing that I was bound to dislike the assignment, Bob asked whether I should like him to approach another person.

Peng Kee, with whom I discussed the matter, asked: "Why don't you reply: 'approach another person!' This would be a clear answer." Regrettably, I dithered. As such a reply was bound to antagonise Bob, I decided to toe the line and accepted, although I hated the very idea of assuming an administrative chore.

I appreciated that the issue could be sorted out if I were able to remain in Singapore. I did send out feelers and then had to face a third problem. The National University of Singapore would have been able to offer me a three-year appointment. I was assured that the contract could be extended. Still, to take it up, I would have had to resign my tenured Chair of Law at Monash. In a sense, the course involved a jump into a blind alley. I was not ready to go ahead.

To my pleasant surprise, Pat, too, urged me to return to Melbourne. We agreed that, whenever things got too difficult, she would go for a spell to Singapore. I was, further, in a position to assure her that we would have ample opportunities to travel. All in all, it was a compromise acceptable to both of us. In its own way, it was the best option.

I shall have more to tell you about my year as acting dean and about my remaining years at Monash prior to my settling down in Singapore. I propose to do so in my next letter.

Till then, I wish all of you the very best.

Yours as ever,
Peter

2 April 2018
Singapore

Dear Friends,

Letter 24: Monash under Dean Baxt

The direct flight from Singapore to Melbourne took some seven hours. The tenants had arranged for the retransfer of our public services account into our names so that we had electricity and gas. Actually, the tenants had looked after our property well.

Bob transferred the reins to me in an elusive manner. He expected me to steer the ship along the course mapped out by him. I had no difficulty with that. However, I had a feeling of unease when Bob advised me that our administrative clerk ought to be able to assist me on matters of routine. It became clear that, in a sense, Bob had decided to have his own channels of communication. In reality, my hands were effectively tied. I regretted my failure to take Peng Kee's wise advice. It would have been best to ensure that I was not the commander of the ship.

All the same, I managed reasonably well most of the time. The allocation of teaching duties had been largely settled by Bob. Promotions and appointments were handled by a committee. I had no specific problems there.

Only one unpleasant matter cropped up during my period in office. The courses of our faculty were set out in a handbook, from which students could glean the nature of the subjects offered and the identity of the teachers. At the end of each academic year, the Law Students Club published a 'counter-handbook', which included a blunt and often not flattering description of the experience of candidates with courses taken. I recall that one year, the lectures of a colleague were described as fit solely for printing on toilet rolls.

During my year in office, the counter-handbook included statements about a colleague which were defamatory. To my dismay, it turned out that, in compliance with a well-established practice, the counter-handbook had been produced on our premises with the use of our equipment. Accordingly, the Law School was liable for publishing the libel.

I was at a loss as to what to do. I felt certain that the relevant colleague would not sue us. At the same time, I was keen to avoid the unpleasantness involved. In the end I asked one of my colleagues, whom I had known since my Oxford days, for advice. He pointed out that, technically, the counter-handbook in question was our property and suggested I confiscate it. I went ahead. Naturally, the students protested about the denial of 'freedom of speech'. Some of my colleagues supported them. Whilst all this went on, our defamed colleague solicited a favourable review of his lectures by one of the students. With its addition to the text, all was settled.

I was deeply disturbed by the use of university facilities for extra-curricular activities. Our administrative clerk defended the procedure by saying that the printing of the counter-handbook had been sanctioned by previous deans. I told him firmly that I wished to be consulted if any extra-curricular publication required our faculty's participation. He was not pleased but gave way.

After some three months, Bob came back. I was relieved to return the reins to him and suggested that he appoint another person as vice-dean. Fortunately, a number of favour seekers were keen to become members of his inner circle. I was now out of it but, in the process, lost Bob's friendship. In a way, I was aggrieved. During my earlier years at Monash, we had been close. Further, Bob had supported my appointment as a Professor of Law.

Today — as I write my memoirs — I do appreciate what had taken place. Bob was a determined leader. He often came up with fine ideas but also with some unrealistic notions. I suspect he was less secure than Gerry, who actually favoured comments and argumentations against new plans proposed by him. Bob tended to take disagreements with his views as incidents of disloyalty. My having specialised in the same area of law as his created an extra problem. Bob was unable to accept that, from my point of view, my personal commitments, albeit in our field, were my priority. His notions were of lesser importance as far as I was concerned.

Another issue related to one of my own shortcomings: I was not a good team player. I preferred to work on my own and might have easily conveyed the impression of being condescending. In reality, this was not the case. I usually asked for assistance when needed. All in all, though, I was a 'bookworm' and a loner. I preferred the desk in the library to the committee room. Before Bob took up the leadership, he sympathised. When he took over, he resented my failure to follow his lead.

To be fair to Bob, I pause to add that many of his ideas were far-sighted. For instance, he appreciated the need of establishing centres, such as of commercial law, which were to involve the participation of legal practitioners. He also saw the need of bringing together economists and lawyers. My principal reservation was his desire to move ahead on too many fronts. He was not fully aware of the limitations of his sphere of influence.

Whilst I was musing about the situation in the law school, I became involved in another project. A major industrial conglomerate, based in a Continental country, sought to adapt its terms and conditions, which were drafted by civilian lawyers, to the needs and issues arising at common law. The law firm approached by it referred the matter to me. Before accepting the brief, I consulted Bob. He was enthusiastic and encouraged me to go ahead. He even promised me to support the acquisition by our library of any materials needed.

The project kept me going. To start with, I worked together with members of the conglomerate's legal department. In the process, I often used materials I had acquired during the sabbatical I had spent in Freiburg. Further, both von Caemmerer and Plyer replied promptly to questions which I had to refer to them. I spent about three mornings per week on the project for about eight months.

During the later part of the project, the conglomerate flew over a member of the legal department of its home team. Working with him was a pleasure. He had an expert knowledge of the issues arising in civil law systems and was familiar with the fundamentals of the common law in point. On the basis of his comments, we revised a number of our proposals. By the time he had to return to his base, we had completed the first draft of our report and also came up with a set of terms suitable both in civil and in common law systems.

In this instance, my secretary was of great help. Some parts of the report had to be dictated, or submitted in long hand, by my collaborators. She handled the work effectively and, in addition, built up a filing system that facilitated our access to initial drafts and correspondence. The progress made by us filled me with the pride of achievement. Our project involved the cooperation of gown and town. To my satisfaction, Bob remained supportive throughout. This type of project was in line with his wish to bring the ivory tower to the world of practice.

My concentration on this project stopped me from proceeding with my other commitments. My work for the *Encyclopedia* in Hamburg had to be put on the back burner. My principals were perturbed by the slow progress made by me but, regrettably, I had to keep disappointing them. The Oxford University Press, too, was getting impatient. In an attempt to please them, I worked long hours virtually every day. The project on *Legal Change* — my collaboration with J. — came to a standstill. In this instance, though, I was not perturbed. My co-author was even less diligent than I.

Another unfortunate side effect of my concentration on my Continental project was that I neglected Pat and, in addition, stopped my autodidactic work on bible critique. This seminal work (which was close to my heart) had to be ignored for the time being. Pat dealt with her loneliness by flying over to Singapore for a visit to her family.

Shortly after Pat returned from Singapore, B. came over with a fellow she had met in Sydney. He was at that time working on a Ph.D. It was clear that B. and he were contemplating marriage. I liked him, especially as he was well versed in literature and music. We had many a pleasant chat.

I recall in particular one evening we spent in Phillip Island, watching the penguin parade. Despite the bitterly cold wind, I was impressed by the sudden emergence of the penguins out of the sea. Each penguin searched for its own offspring, with a view to feeding it. The penguins managed to proceed despite the unruly behaviour of the spectators. As often before, I wished I were back in New Zealand, where people knew how to behave. Still, I enjoyed this new experience.

A few days later, B. and her friend returned to Sydney. Pat, who saw how haggard I looked, was concerned. She knew I was close to breaking point from overwork. Fortunately, my friend Michael Pryles came up with a sound suggestion. As my previous leave had been on a no-pay basis, I had retained my sabbatical leave entitlement. Having completed six years of service, I was entitled to an entire year of paid leave. Being keen to finish *Modern Banking Law*, I applied. Bob was supportive and, before long, Pat and I were on our way to London. On arrival, we proceeded straight to Oxford.

It was a good year. A friend in Oxford helped us to get accommodation in a building owned by his college. It was within walking distance to the new Bodleian Law Library, on the banks of the Cherwell. It was also close to all amenities. I went to the library daily and was pleased with the progress I was making. I knew for certain that I was back on the right track.

One useful development that took place during this period was the advent of the word processor. The first two dedicated types of word processor — the Wang and the Burroughs — had been commercially available during the year preceding my embarkation on leave. Regrettably, neither was mobile and both had features which made their use cumbersome. Still, I had managed to get a Wang in my office at Monash but found out that my secretary made better use of it than I.

During my spell in Oxford, the home (personal) computer came up with a word processing facility. I acquired one machine and, within a few weeks, used it as effectively as a typewriter. My old skill as a touch typist now stood me in good stead. Looking at the system with hindsight, I have to concede that, in comparison with modern computers and software, the original word processing package was basic. However, it was usable and meant that I no longer required the services of a secretary. I do appreciate that some fussy academics insisted on adhering to the outdated system, which involved the use of typewriters and necessitated the employment of typists. In contrast, I was relieved to be able to do my own thing.

When my first draft of the book on banking law was nearing completion, Pat insisted that we take a trip to Israel and Egypt. I was impressed with the progress of my erstwhile home country. We spent two days in Jerusalem. I had visited the Old City — encompassing such attractions as the Wailing Wall and the Dome of the Rock — before the foundation of Israel. During my years as a student in the Hebrew University, the Old City was part of Transjordan and hence inaccessible to Israelis. In 1982, the entire city — both Old and Modern Jerusalem — was governed by Israel. This has remained the position. I did enjoy traversing the Old City and wandered through the antiquities stores run by Palestinians.

Another place of interest was the Crusaders' underground city near Acre. It was excavated well after the Independence War of 1948. I had not seen it before and found it a revelation. I also spent a morning in the Acre Museum. I was keen to visit old friends but, unfortunately, Pat objected strenuously to my contacting them. I gave way.

From Israel, we proceeded by bus over the Suez Canal to Port Said. The visit to Egypt was an eye-opener. We took an impressive boat cruise on the Nile. Further, I admired the pyramids, Memphis and the Valley of the Kings. As Tutankhamun's burial ground was closed to the public at that time, we went to Horemheb's entombment. I recall it with awe. Later, we returned to Cairo, where I spent two days in the famed museum.

Before returning to Israel, our tour guide took us to an excellent restaurant. As we walked through Cairo's streets, I noted that Egyptian Arabs had different features from the Palestinians. It dawned on me that many of them were scions of their grand ancestors.

The tour of Egypt has remained a highlight of my life. Further, I realised that to be an accomplished biblical critic, one had to master Mid-Egyptian and hieroglyphs. I had been aware for years that Egypt's culture had left an impact on the entire Levant, including the Kingdoms of Juda and of Northern Israel. Later in life, I went ahead with the plan formed by me during our days in Egypt and studied Mid-Egyptian.

Regrettably, the tour did not take us to Amarna, where Akhenaton had built his capital. Still, I had seen many of the 18th Dynasty relics in European museums, especially in the British Museum and in the Egyptian Museum in Berlin.

For a few weeks following our return to England, I tidied up the first draft of *Modern Banking Law.* The work was finicky and, more often than not, quite tedious. A particular source of irritation was the endless need of verifying references. Pat tried to help but she lacked the background.

By mid-July, we had to embark on yet a further trip. As a member of the International Academy of Commercial and Consumer Law, I was invited to attend its biannual conference to be held in 1984 at Castle Hofen in Tyrol. B. and her friend, who were touring Europe at this time, joined us. We decided to drive to our destination in the old Renault sedan I had acquired at the very beginning of my sabbatical leave.

We spent one night in Chantilly. The next morning, B. and her friend decided to have a day off in Paris. Pat joined them. I spent the morning locating the pension (viz. modest hotel) in which my parents had found a haven during our period as refugees. The place which had appeared grand to me forty years earlier looked ramshackle and neglected. It was not the sort of place in which Pat and I would have resided. Despite my apprehension, I had lunch on the premises. The food was excellent.

I felt deep regard for my parents. They braved the Nazi storm and laid the foundation for my future. Would I have attained any professional success and a personal life without their support and guidance? They had made many sacrifices for me and done their best to shelter me. Had I been a dutiful son?

I was depressed that evening. The engaging tales about the trio's adventures in Paris fell on deaf ears. I had difficulties falling asleep. Pat looked at me with concern but kept her peace. I was grateful to her. I felt the need to be left alone with my thoughts.

We spent a few extra days touring the Burgundy region. I recall with amusement our first day in a small village near Dijon. We spent our time in a pension, which bragged that Louis XIV had stayed there one day and night. Pat and I arrived for breakfast early in the morning. When Pat asked the waiter where *Le Roi Soleil* had spent his night, she was assured that His Majesty had used the very room occupied by us. Pat was delighted and tipped the 'informer' handsomely. Shortly thereafter, B. joined us. To my glee, B. was assured by the very same waiter that Louis had resided in the room occupied by her. So were the wives of other guests who came for breakfast. Naturally, all of them loosened their respective purse strings. B.'s friend and I exchanged glances. The thought that the hapless monarch had spent his night wandering from room to room was somewhat perplexing. Presumably, his objective was to secure that men of the future would be properly rewarded.

The next day, we proceeded to Interlaken and from there through an alpine road to Liechtenstein. We had a pleasant stay in this minute principality. B. and her friend proceeded to Vienna, which they wanted to see, and Pat and I went to Castle Hofen.

The conference was an anticlimax except that I met a number of scholars with whom I had corresponded earlier. One evening, we watched a Viennese operetta, displayed in open air. We then drove back to England via Belgium. B. and her friend stayed in Oxford for a number of days. B.'s friend was conversant with computer technology. He helped me to improve my skills with the word processor.

It became time to leave Oxford. Before returning to Singapore, I decided to make a stop in Vienna to visit my mother. She was glad to see us. We spent two days with her. Then, Pat insisted on a sojourn in Baden — a pleasant resort near the capital. Unhappily, I rang Mother from Baden and told her we were just about to board a plane back to Singapore. I still feel ashamed of this chicanery.

Back in Singapore, we were put up by one of Pat's siblings. I proceeded to Melbourne shortly thereafter, whilst Pat decided to stay behind for some three weeks. I returned to my office two days later, actually about one week before the scheduled time. To my dismay, I discovered that my secretary had made my office available to a graduating student. I shooed him out unceremoniously and reprimanded her. When the administrative clerk came over and sought to defend her, I made a fuss. Despite his patent disapproval, I instructed my secretary never to let people use my office without first obtaining my consent.

The relationship with my secretary was now tense. She knew I had lost my trust in her. In consequence, she became uncivil. Further, she often placed documents in unexpected places so that I was unable to locate them. I was irked and often was unpleasant to her. She became uncooperative. I recall in particular a case that cropped up a few weeks after I came back.

The issue arose in respect of an examination in an LL.M. subject conducted by Bob and another colleague. They set a take-home examination, which meant that candidates had to collect the paper from the administrative office and submit their scripts within twenty-four hours. The examiners spotted that two scripts were virtually identical. It was circumstantially clear that one was a copy.

The university authorities prosecuted both candidates. Candidate A failed to defend. Candidate B pleaded as a defence that the answer script was written solely by him. Candidate A picked it up and offered to deliver it. In the process, he was able to open the envelope and copy the submission.

I was appointed as a member of the disciplinary committee. To my dismay, I was unable to discover the papers, which must have been sent to me in a separate envelope. Fortunately, the authorities supplied another copy. Accordingly, I was able to prepare myself.

In the event, Candidate B, who was a qualified accountant and whose integrity was in question, engaged a Queen's Counsel. The main argument for the defence was that B had not 'collaborated' in an illicit breach of the examination procedures but had composed the script on his own. Candidate A had somehow copied the script and submitted it as his own without any alterations. The Q.C. argued that his client's participation in the deception had not been established. After due consideration, we entered a 'not proved' verdict but refused to grant B costs. Candidate A was failed and excluded from the course.

When I returned to my office, I discovered the original papers in my 'hold' tray. My secretary had failed to place them in my 'urgent matters' tray. Had she not misplaced them, I could have prepared myself comfortably in my office prior to the hearing.

About a fortnight later, I found out — to my dismay — that one of the members of the Continental conglomerate's legal department, with whom I had collaborated, had passed away from a tumour. His colleague and I revised the report and submitted it formally. The local office forwarded our recommendations to the head office, which decided not to adopt them. I was paid handsomely and, despite my annoyance with my secretary, saw to it that she too was paid. All the same, I was disappointed. All in all, the conglomerate had spent close to $200,000 on the report. Its summary rejection meant that good money and many hours of hard work had gone down the drain.

One other matter that had to be settled concerned *Legal Change*. A brief discussion with J. disclosed that she had actually made no progress during my sabbatical. Although I continued to find her alluring, I realised that it was time to cut my losses. Notwithstanding my emotive qualms, I handed J. my completed chapters and told her I was unable to spend any more time on the project. I believe she was relieved. I, in turn, felt sad and depressed. Rationally, though, it was the only viable option.

Shortly thereafter, I prompted my secretary into resigning her post. Initially, the administrative clerk recommended a secretary I found unsatisfactory. At that time, it became fashionable for secretaries to develop painful wrists, which entitled them to decline typing. My new secretary used the complaint effectively. When she left, I insisted on interviewing applicants for the post. My choice fell on Jenny Neil, who in due course became a friend and a supporter. Thereafter, my office functioned effectively. Jenny was a perfectionist and I benefitted from her zeal.

A few weeks after Jenny's appointment, Pat and I flew over to Singapore. My objective was to deliver a paper at the very conference I had planned with Philip. I recall in particular my reunion with Sasske (David Sassoon). From an ambitious youngster, he had developed into a mature man of affairs. His searching questions and outstanding comments enlivened the discussions. I also renewed my friendship with many scholars working in my field. One of the speakers was my friend, Peng Kee. He and Sasske got on well. I do believe the conference was a success. The papers delivered were published in a neat volume produced by Butterworths — leading punishers of legal texts.

On my return to Monash, I devoted myself to *Modern Banking Law.* I knew Oxford University Press was getting impatient and felt the need to bring this project to its end. Jenny was of great help. Although I typed sections on my own, I needed her help to organise my various documents. Within about one year, I managed to hammer the draft into shape.

Jenny's appointment helped in yet another matter. In Monash, a professor's secretary occupied a small room next to his. The two offices were connected by an internal door. During the years in which my first secretary had the post, she often entered my office unceremoniously. On one occasion, when I was immersed in a biblical text, she came in and interrupted me with a trivial matter. Thereafter, I thought it best to pursue my bible critique hobby at home. Jenny's appointment made it possible for me to carry on this work in the office. She never broke the concentration which I needed for the textual analysis involved.

My home life during this period continued on an even keel. I believe Pat was beginning to settle. Our blossoming garden and the redecoration of some of the rooms in our house kept her occupied. By and large, all was quiet on this front.

Then, unexpectedly, I was invited to apply for a new Chair of Banking Law created by London University. I flew over for an interview and was offered the post, which I was keen to accept. Initially, Pat was supportive. She realised how much this position meant to me. It would have been the zenith of my career. At that time, London was the centre of banking and banking law. Taking up the post would have meant a drop in my salary. This, however, would be more than compensated by the prestige and by my working in collaboration with one of England's leading scholars. Further, remunerative opinion work was bound to flow in.

My only concern related to England's horrid climate. In itself, this would not have deterred me. I wanted to enjoy my return as hero after having initially come to England for postgraduate studies. Further, it seemed quite likely that, with the benefit of modern medicine, my asthma was not going to create problems.

Regrettably, at that very time, Pat's eyesight deteriorated further. To our dismay, the local specialist told us frankly that the condition could not be stabilised. I realised she would not be able to use London's outdated and hard-to-manage underground system. This meant that she would be practically housebound. Pat suggested that I go ahead and that she remain with her family in Singapore.

Although my feelings for Pat had undergone a change, I was not prepared to break up our family. I rang my sponsor in London and advised that I was unable to come. I fear he never forgave me. I believe that, in his own way, he was in the right. My only feeling was bitterness, remorse and shame.

All the same, my decision led to a pleasant change in my home life. Despite her misgivings about my commitment to her, Pat realised that, when it came to the crunch, I would not forsake her. Much of her bitterness thereupon abated.

During my last two years at Monash, I became reclusive. Usually, I grabbed a sandwich and turned down luncheon invitations. When Pat flew for respite to Singapore, I gave but one party, meant to express my thanks to the colleague who had held my hand whilst I had been the acting dean. Generally, I had a lonely evening meal at home although I went out occasionally with Peter Heffey and with Michael Pryles. I fear that my mannerism antagonised Bob. Although he was supportive when I explained to him my reasons for turning down the chair in London, I sensed that I was losing the remnants of his goodwill. I, in turn, continued to distance myself from the projects he sponsored.

My only consolation during this period was the progress made on two fronts: *Modern Banking Law* and my bible critique hobby. The latter, in particular, pleased me. The bookseller I had discovered managed to get me books and articles in both English and German. I recall that on one occasion, when I left his shop with a neat parcel of reading materials, he told me that he hoped that his 'eccentric German scholar' would come over again soon.

One biblical book on which I concentrated at that time was *Job*. I was satisfied that the 'answers of the Lord … out of the storm wind' (Cap. 38–42:1–5) were later add-ons, composed by a person who had failed to see that the points made in them were expressed earlier on, succinctly, in Cap.4:11–21. The materials acquired by me indicated that this very conclusion had been reached by renowned scholars of the 19th century. In the circumstances, I saw no need to publish my conclusions. It was, however, satisfying to know that mine was not a sole voice crying in the wilderness.

Another pastime I engaged in was the writing of short stories. Most of them were self-published years later, when I was back in Singapore.

Composing them was exhilarating. It did not take me long to make the necessary adjustments of vocabulary and of style. Unlike my texts on aspects of the law, the short stories required a lively rather than a dry style. Further, flights of imagination were not precluded.

As already indicated, my last two years in Monash were banal. On one occasion, Pat and I flew to Sydney in order to attend B.'s marriage ceremony. Hers was a modest function, attended only by the groom's family, by two members of the Goh family who flew down from Singapore and by us.

When we returned to Melbourne, I received a communication from Singapore, manifesting an interest in inviting me to take up a post in the National University of Singapore. The proposal was for a three-year contract at an excellent salary. I was still uneasy about the need to give up a tenured chair at Monash and embarking on a new venture. I was getting on and sensed that, at this stage, my first priority was to secure retirement. I was pleased with the salary but asked for tenure.

For a few weeks, we kept bargaining. Then, a faculty meeting at Monash intensified my wish to depart. The issue concerned a new teaching course proposed by the radical wing of the faculty. Initially, the subject was debated in a committee chaired by me. I felt neutral and abstained. The majority of the committee rejected the proposal.

As anticipated, the matter was raised in a faculty meeting. I had expected this and did not feel the need to intervene. I was, however, shocked when one colleague saw fit to launch a personal attack. I was about to refute him when another colleague, active in the field, complained that he had not been consulted. Many of those present felt embarrassed. Somebody suggested the proposal be sent back to the committee for reconsideration. At this stage, I felt the need to step in. Speaking with unconcealed bitterness, I suggested the issue be discussed by the 'thoughtful' proposers with the neglected colleague and then be referred back to the faculty itself. All agreed. J., who supported the radical faction, glanced at me in surprise. I withdrew to my office shortly thereafter. In reality, I had lost interest in the proceedings.

When I recall the matter today, I realise that the fault was mine. To me, it appeared irrelevant whether or not the subject in question was to be offered. I was tackling, both at home and in my study, some tricky problems respecting Psalm 104. Both in imagery and in metre it struck me as being at odds with the majority of the chapters in the book. Where did it originate?

In comparison with this type of conceptual problem, the issue debated by the faculty appeared a flash in the pan. The faculty, however, expected its senior staff to manifest leadership. From their point of view, I did not make the grade. I had been promoted to my level of incompetence. I felt it was time to withdraw from the scene.

My negotiations with Singapore were completed soon thereafter. I was offered a contract to the age of retirement. Pat flew back to Singapore so as to enable me to decide calmly. Although I kept dithering, I had in reality made up my mind.

Bob granted me one year of no-pay leave, so as to enable me to consider all issues after I had left. It was a generous offer and I accepted it gratefully.

Before I left Melbourne, I had a most pleasant evening with Peter Heffey. Then, to my surprise, J. invited me to come over to her place for dinner. Her spell had actually abated during my two periods of leave. It dawned on me that life was simpler without her. I was, further, disillusioned by her failure to work on *Legal Change*.

"What made you decide to leave?" she asked.

"The hope that Pat will be happier there. And, as you know, I was perturbed by our last faculty meeting."

"I'm sure the meeting was not the major cause. You would normally shrug off such an encounter. And, Peter, I am not sure Pat would be happier there than here. You were wrong for one another from the start. Pat was never able to accept your eccentricities and put up with your daydreaming. Your rift is too deep to heal. I wish you well; but don't kid yourself."

"You are probably right. I wish I knew what really prompted me to resign."

"Your need for a fresh start. You are keen to settle in a place that does not want you to be involved in the administration. I think it is the right decision."

"Have I been a complete failure here?"

"I don't think so. You were all right when you got back into your own project. Your attempt to get into policy-oriented areas was unreal. You are interested in the reasons behind a change but not in policy or law reform as such."

"Is this so because I am a conceptualist, divorced from real life?"

"I don't think so," she replied candidly. "You are pragmatic when you deal with the facts of some sordid dispute. But it does not matter to you whether a party is a poor slob, a racially disadvantaged minority person or a wealthy bank. You want to tackle the concepts and win the case."

"True," I replied, "I work for my client once I agree to accept a brief."

"So policy and welfare are really irrelevant to you. To me, they matter. I like to come to the aid of the underprivileged members of our society."

As J. prepared the meal, I reflected that on all previous occasions we had gone out for lunch or dinner. All in all, J.'s cooking left much to be desired. So did the rosé I had brought with me. Actually, my taste in wines had been defective all along.

During the meal we engaged in small talk. Had I ever managed to kindle some response in her? As often before, the answer eluded me. Perhaps I was no longer interested in the subject. I was relieved when I sensed the time was ready for my departure. As I left, J. gave me a cold goodbye kiss on the cheek. It was a befitting end to a spell in dreamland.

A few days later, Pat returned. The terms offered to me by the National University of Singapore were generous. They enabled me to hire a renowned firm of movers, who packed our belongings into a mini-container.

We left the letting of the house to an agent and took our flight to Singapore.

I shall discuss our lives in the City of the Lion in my next few letters. They will, I hope, convince you that at long last, I had moved to a place in which both Pat and I were able to settle for the rest of our days.

In the meantime, I conclude with my best wishes and kindest regards.

Yours as ever,
Peter

Part IV

THE CITY OF THE LION

10 April 2018
Singapore

Dear Friends,

Letter 25: Settling Down in Singapore

We took a taxi to the hotel in which the university booked us. Within a few days, we moved to a flat in Pandan Valley, which the lodgings department agreed to let us use until we found a suitable place of our own. After a few weeks, I managed to get a good, albeit used, car. A stroke of good luck enabled us to purchase a flat in Eugenia Court, the prime block of Pandan Valley. Unlike the flat let to us by the university, it had only two levels. The dining room, kitchen and an extra room (which I was going to use as my study) were on the upper level. A sitting room and three bedrooms were on the lower one. It was a spacious flat and, in particular, our master bedroom was huge. All bedrooms had an en-suite bathroom.

The only difficulty was that it was a walk-up apartment. The lift went to the eighth floor of the block and two flights of stairs led to our unit on the ninth floor. Later in life, I found out that this was a handicap. In my early fifties, this was, of course, trivial. I loved the flat and enjoyed the walks in the well groomed grounds. A pleasant pool was in the centre. I used to play 'sticks' with a dog, who was delighted to fetch them from the water.

The renovation we commissioned took some five weeks. When it was complete, we asked the movers' Singapore branch to deliver our mini-container. As we had taken with us most of our Melbourne furniture, the move was in reality from one home to another. Shortly after we had moved into our flat, I received Bob Baxt's letter concerning my plans. He wanted to know whether I would remain in Singapore or return to Monash. Having discussed the matter with Pat, I resigned from my chair at Monash.

Actually, even prior to the sending of my resignation letter, my mind had firmed. Right from the beginning, I felt the move to Singapore was a correct step. Sook Yee assigned me a relatively light teaching load and no administrative duties of any importance. This meant that I could devote most of my time to research and publications. The proofs of *Modern Banking Law* arrived in Singapore shortly after my arrival. The book appeared in 1987. I then spent my time on revising my chapters in *Chitty on Contracts* and *Benjamin's Sale of Goods* for new editions. I also wrote papers to be delivered in conferences and, of course, worked on my biblical studies. The generous salary paid to me by the university enabled me to acquire a collection of books dealing with the *Dead Sea Scrolls*. Before long, my holdings on the subject were as good as those of some seminaries.

I recall one pleasant incident that could never have taken place in Australasia. One morning, before I had acquired a car, I walked from the bus stop to the law school. I was sweating profusely and felt forlorn. Then, to my surprise, a car stopped next to me. The driver — a student in her mid-twenties — gave me a lift. I never met her again but sensed that this was an instance of a Good Samaritan's aid. Later in life — when

I had to use a walking cane and became wobbly — invariably a person helped me cross the road or manage a flight of stairs.

Teaching, too, was pleasant. Usually, students came well prepared to class. This, of course, meant that the teacher had to be conscientious. In this regard, the average Singapore student was a cut above those who attended my classes in Monash and in Wellington. Notably, some of them became friends, and many others kept in touch. I believe I was a well-regarded teacher. My evening LL.M. seminars, in particular, were a source of joy. Quite a number of legal practitioners decided to enroll for further studies. My courses suited them because they were practical and pragmatic in outlook. Here, too, I made acquaintances and some friends.

Social events, such as luncheons and dinners, were organised by former students. These were yet another source of joy. As was befitting, we invited our hosts back. In consequence, Pat had a busy time. Often, she went out with me and on other days met up with her siblings. On weekends, she went to their family church. I visited antique or book shops. Two colleagues in the faculty were fellow collectors, and so I often went out together with them. Some of them were interested in carpets, and I simply tagged along.

A few months after our arrival, Lu Sinclair introduced me to Michael Hwang, one of the leading lawyers in town. On his recommendation, I was constituted a consultant of his firm. The university approved my spending half a day per week on this work. It was interesting to advise practitioners on conceptual points relevant to the handling of commercial disputes. I was also consulted on the drafting of specific clauses of standard terms contracts used by banks and other financial conglomerates. In addition, I received interesting opinion work from other law firms and was engaged on a number of occasions as an expert witness in commercial disputes. I thrived on this work.

A particularly interesting experience was my engagement as an expert in a case heard in Perth. The matter was referred to me by a former student from Wellington just before I left Melbourne. It concerned a bank reference rendered by my clients — a well-known bank — to another bank for a third-party recipient. The plaintiff — the recipient — claimed that the reference included misrepresentations and was misleading. I prepared the case in Singapore and then had to fly to Perth to give evidence and submit myself to a cross-examination. It was a close shave, ending with a decision in our bank's favour.

I had a number of appearances as an expert before courts in Hong Kong, in London and in Singapore. All in all, I earned enough money to acquire a fine collection of porcelain and of paintings. I had no reason to regret my departure from Melbourne.

A few weeks after my arrival in Singapore, I had an interview with the vice-chancellor. I found Professor Lim Pin an agreeable administrator. It was clear to me that he would toe the official line. That much was to be expected from any leader of a national university. At the same time, I realised that Lim Pin would always listen to arguments and would convey them, diplomatically, to the authorities. I concluded that he was the right man for the job.

Of particular interest was a discussion which his deputy had with our faculty. One of my colleagues emphasised the importance of freedom of speech. In his opinion, there were too many constraints. I was pleased to step in and say that as long as I could express my views freely to the university's authorities, I saw no need to convey them to the media.

I realise that, in this regard, I was in a fortunate position. My subjects — comprising commercial law topics with an emphasis on banking — were not controversial. I could express any view I wanted in my classes. Life might have been more turbulent had I specialised in constitutional or administrative law. However, even if these fields had been my chosen area, I would have concentrated on subjects unlikely to lead to tumult. It is important for me to concede, in this context, that the only country in which I would have aired my political views was Israel. I grew up there. In other countries, I was — and intended to remain — an acceptable guest. Interference in internal affairs was out of the question. However, in my chosen field, I considered it my task to further the interests of my host countries. Future scholars will assess the value of my contributions.

As could have been expected, the faculty had undergone changes in the years that had elapsed since my year as visiting professor. One colleague, who had helped me a great deal on points of style and readability, had left Singapore and accepted a chair at London University. Two others had joined law firms, and yet others had moved to our rival institution, the Singapore Management University, which launched its own law school. My closest friend in the faculty, Ho Peng Kee, had left academia and became a full-time politician. In due course, he rose to the upper ranks of the system. All the same, the core of the faculty had remained unchanged. It turned itself into the leading law school in our region and became renowned for the excellence of students graduating with a sound degree.

A particular stroke of good luck was that Jayakumar, who had been a student of our law school in the sixties and later on served as dean (before he went into politics), had been appointed the Minister of Home Affairs. At his suggestion, I applied for the status of a Permanent Resident. My application was granted, although for purely personal considerations, I decided to retain my Australian citizenship.

My decision to keep out of all internal affairs was tested during my second year of service. A local politician, J.B. Jeyaretnam, was suspended by the law society. He appealed to the Privy Council, which reversed the disciplinary committee's decision and restored Jeyaretnam's right to practice. One of the issues that arose in the case had a bearing on banking law.

I decided not to comment on the case. All the same, I agreed to assist a local practitioner in the preparation of a case note. The ensuing broadsides respecting the case convinced me that I had reached the correct decision. The case related to local politics and its main points involved questions of administrative law. The banking law matter was a secondary issue. The judgment, as a whole, was to be dealt with by locals and not by an expatriate.

I pause to add that I approved of the end result, which was the abolition of all appeals to the Privy Council. First, I had serious doubts about the competence of the judicial body involved. Most privy counsellors came from the ranks of the British Law Lords, whose expertise related to the law of England. Their grasp of issues arising under alien laws — for instance, the intricacies of foreign land laws like the Australian Torrens System — was poor. Similarly, England did not have a formal constitution. Why then should the Privy Council be regarded an authority on issues respecting formal constitutions applicable in some Commonwealth countries?

Secondly, most Commonwealth countries had gained independence. India, Malaysia, Australia and New Zealand were instances in point. It was not clear to me why the sovereignty of such countries should be impeded by the subjection of their legal systems to an alien body like the Privy Council. I am familiar with arguments to the contrary, which are largely based on the notion of granting the Privy Council the final right of reviewing the impartiality of Commonwealth courts. All I can say is that I am not convinced. A judicial review is poor means for combating structural inadequacies.

Thirdly, appeals to the Privy Council were costly. An appellant had to engage his local law firm, which had to approach a correspondent firm in London, which, in turn, would employ a barrister to appear on the litigant's behalf. As a norm, hearings before the Privy Council were the domain of Queen's Counsels, who would appear with a team of junior barristers. Needless to say, expenses mounted. There was, actually, a way around this hurdle. A local lawyer could get dispensation and appear on behalf of his client before the Council. Frequently, however, his expenses were substantial so that, in reality, the client did not save significantly by flying his local lawyers over to London. It is important to add that in some Commonwealth countries, English ceased to be the official language. An appeal to the Privy Council would, if available, have required the preparation of translations into English. Even where translations were not required, parties often compromised so as to avoid an expensive litigation overseas.

I had my own experiences respecting the standing and impartiality of our courts. One case concerned Lu Sinclair's late husband, Don. He had previously been one of Singapore's leading stockbrokers but, late in life, backed the wrong share. In the event, he became involved in proceedings based on alleged misrepresentations made to him. The trial judge did me the honour of inviting me to sit with him. Don was a friend of mine and, in Singapore's tight-knit society, was known to the judge. On the merits, though, Don's argument had to be dismissed. Judgment was entered against him.

Another case was an action brought by an Indonesian conglomerate to recover amounts paid as 'commission' to one of its officers. The main issues related to the law of restitution. The lengthy judgment delivered in the case was not appealed against. I felt that the litigation was well handled and that the judge took his time to familiarise himself with all relevant authorities. Here, again, I was satisfied that justice had been done.

The third case was more complex. A customer's estate included an account with a local bank. Due to proceedings respecting the estate, the money remained on deposit with the bank for many years. The bank claimed the money was kept in a current account and hence did not earn interest. The estate claimed that the bank had been instructed to place it in a savings account and hence ought to have earned interest at the prevailing rate. The bank — represented by our law firm — lost the case. It was established on the facts that an instruction to convert the current account into a savings account had been given and accepted. The succinct judgment in point was affirmed by our Court of Appeal. Even if there had still been an appeal to the Privy Council, the trial judge's decision was bound to be upheld. Notably, the counsel in the case went from strength to strength. One is currently a judge of the Court of Appeal. The other has become the Minister of Law.

Shortly after my arrival in Singapore, I participated in the establishment of Singapore as an arbitration centre. Initially, at Peng Kee's suggestion, I associated with the Singapore Institute of Arbitrators. That body dealt only in local disputes referred to it by individuals or organisations. In due course, it was superseded by the Singapore International Arbitration Centre, an independent body supported by the government. I was one of its founding members. Unlike the Institute, it aimed at establishing itself as a regional centre. Its efforts were crowned with success, and Singapore became a leading hub of arbitration in Asia. My old friend Michael Pryles was made its Executive Chairman for some seven years.

Personally, I sat only once as arbitrator. The dispute concerned a franchise granted by a Malaysian organisation to a firm in the Philippines. It was a dull dispute concerning breach of the agreement by the party in Manila. I was paid handsomely for my award. The litigation, though, was tedious and uninspiring. I had no wish to enter that arena again.

My ability to concentrate on my career and also on my hobbies was largely due to the fact that Pat had her own life. I no longer needed to take her out daily and to spend much of my time looking after her. Once again, she was Patricia Goh married to an 'ang moh' ('European' or 'red-haired devil') called Ellinger. I sensed that step by step she was getting closer to her siblings and distancing herself from me. Realising that the progression was unavoidable, I immersed myself in my own work and hobbies. Both my library and porcelain collection grew steadily. Two excellent Toulouse-Lautrec prints graced our sitting room.

The financial success of one of Pat's siblings drove me even further away from her family. Until then, the Goh family had treated me with respect. On many occasions, I had had to bail them out. My brother-in-law's meteoric rise meant that I was becoming redundant. To my disappointment, even B. — whom I had seen through her first three years as a student — ceased to treat me as a father figure.

My worst experience took place during a trip down the Yangtze from Chongqing to Yichang organised by my wealthy brother-in-law towards the end of 1987. Pat and I agreed to join but, of course, paid for ourselves. To my surprise, B. referred several times to her brother's generosity in paying all the family's fares.

In itself, the trip was interesting, although the Three Gorges did not strike me as glamorous. However, I recall vividly how our ship had to wait patiently before entering a loch. Other — more elegant and upmarket — ships were given priority. Shortly after we emerged from the loch, our ship stopped in a rundown and dilapidated village. Most passengers went ashore in order to hunt for bargains. I was told that a vast dam, to be constructed in the near future, meant that many villages and townships of this type would be submerged. It dawned on me that such grandiose schemes could be carried out only under the yoke of a totalitarian regime. The Pyramids and the Great Wall of China came to my mind. I also recalled how Joseph Stalin exiled two million Crimean Tartars to Siberia. In democratically governed states, it would be impossible to move segments of the population, or subject them to harsh labour, without their consent. Obviously, the People's Republic of China ("PRC") had not changed its orientation. The mighty dam was completed as planned.

The strong family ties of the Goh family were tested shortly after we disembarked in Yichang. After a meal in a restaurant at Wuhan, Pat succumbed to food poisoning. In consequence, she was unable to continue our trip to the famed Yellow Mountain. I was of course going to remain with her. Shortly before the family's departure, Pat's oldest brother came to impart his advice.

"I didn't know you were a doctor," I told him rudely.

"I only want to help," he muttered.

"If any member of your family was really concerned, he or she could have stayed put. In any event, Pat will recover pretty soon. So go and have your fun!"

"Did you have to be so rude?" asked Pat after they had departed.

"I felt like it," I told my ailing wife.

Pat recovered after two days of fasting. Having already booked flights back to Singapore, we proceeded directly to Shanghai. When the family did not keep our rendezvous, I insisted that we proceed to dinner without waiting for them. As the hotel booked by the organisers did not have an acceptable eating place, I took a taxi to a restaurant on the famed Bund.

When we came back, Pat's sibling were waiting for us. Looking daggers at me, B. wondered why we had not waited for them.

"You said you would arrive in the afternoon. I went for dinner when I was hungry," I told her firmly. "And you should learn to be punctual."

"Wee Shin," she told me, referring to the oldest brother, "forgot his camera in the resort. So we had to drive back. We could not find a public phone and tell you we were going to be late."

"This is as it may be," I retorted.

Pat's siblings proceeded to the airport early in the morning. We took a taxi two hours later. On the way, Pat kept her silence. She had understood that my relationship with her siblings had undergone a change. Until then, it was a remote but cordial co-existence. It had become hostile.

I realised how distant the Goh family had become when, shortly after our return from the cruise, Pat's mother proposed to celebrate her 86th birthday. As the festivities were to be held in their native tongue, Pat suggested I excuse myself. I did it willingly because I had to complete an opinion on a complex legal point. I was deeply immersed in my work when, unexpectedly, Pat returned shortly before lunch. She told me her mother had suffered a stroke and had been taken to the Singapore General Hospital ("SGH"). A leading surgeon had been summoned to attend to her.

"Wouldn't it be best to let nature take its course? Your mother has reached old age and ought not to be forced to continue," I said unthinkingly.

"You can say this to me. But don't you tell them."

A drive to SGH took some fifteen minutes. When I lost my way, a driver — whom I asked for help — suggested I follow his car. One of Pat's siblings, who greeted us on arrival, explained that the surgeon assured him he could operate and save my mother-in-law's life but that she would remain a vegetable. In the circumstance, it was decided not to proceed.

In the event, she passed away before the end of the day. The wealthy sibling was bound to become the new centre point. The family was unlikely to turn to the oldest sibling, who was not rich.

A few months later, my own mother had her ordeal. Notwithstanding my prodding, she had refused to take any medication. Having suffered from high blood pressure for years, she had a stroke. When friends alerted the police, the entrance door was broken down and Mother was moved to the nearby policlinic. To my relief, Mother made a partial recovery. Uncle Henry, Mother's younger brother, flew over from the United States and managed to find her a room in an upmarket nursing home. Having secured compassionate leave, I flew over after two days. Pat did not accompany me and none of her siblings expressed sympathy.

Bedridden, Mother lived in the nursing home for four years. Uncle Henry — who was by then a retiree — cleared her flat and terminated the lease. I had to return to my post in Singapore a few days after Mother had been settled in Sanatorium Rekawinkel. Thereafter, all I could do was to ring her daily. I believe I became her lifeline. The people who looked after her in the nursing home told me later on how Mother looked forward to her daily chat. To my delight, Mother's mind had remained sharp and focused. Occasionally, I discussed investments with her.

Applications such as Skype or WhatsApp had not arrived at that time. So, naturally, my telephone bills soared. To my amazement, one of my in-laws asked me whether these daily calls were needed.

B. resided at that time in Singapore because her husband was posted here by his employers, an international conglomerate of computer technology. He and B. rented a flat in the Tower Block of our condominium. B. did not take up a job, so for their two years in Singapore she became a housewife. We went out with them occasionally but, by and large, did not see much of them. On Sundays, B.'s husband, who had experienced an act of faith, went with B. to an English service in a Methodist Church. I continued to spend my weekends with colleagues, on publications or on my bible critique. The latter was becoming my main route of escape from daily problems and disappointments.

By the end of his two-year term in Singapore, B.'s husband was recalled to Sydney. He gave up the Permanent Residence which had been granted to him by the authorities. He preferred to take out all amounts credited to his CPF account during his two years of employment in our town.

Shortly after B.'s return to Australia, Pat and I flew over. Our objective was to buy an investment property in one of Sydney's established suburbs. After a search, we settled on a townhouse in Mosman. Once again, my friend Michael Pryles assisted by introducing us to an excellent solicitor, who helped us secure a mortgage loan.

We stayed in a pleasant suite downtown. I insisted that we visit Ted Roberts, my first cousin. Both of us liked Sydney and concluded that it was a far more pleasant habitat than Melbourne. I recall that we visited many of Sydney's suburbs by taking ferries from Circular Quay.

Shortly after the end of term in Singapore, we took a trip to Xi'an. My main objective was to see the Terracotta Warriors, dating from the

Qin Dynasty. I was impressed. The main attraction though was a Neolithic village on the outskirts of the town. I was fascinated by the urn burials, by the evidence of worship and by the existence of a close-knit society. I realised that humanity might have had more than a single cradle.

When we returned to Singapore, I had one invitation for a conference in Bielefeld (in Western Germany) and another to deliver the Falconbridge Lecture in Toronto. It was difficult to combine the two. In consequence, we took one trip to Europe and another to North America.

On our trip to Europe, I made a stop in Vienna and went over to Mother's sanatorium. Pat accompanied me on this occasion although she remained heartless towards my mother. For reasons incomprehensible to me, she acted unkindly and unfeelingly. I was amused when, on our last day in Vienna, which was a Sunday, Pat asked me to take her to church. She was deeply moved by the sermon on love to the fallen.

We went to Toronto via Vancouver. The train trip over the Rockies was exciting as indeed was the village of Banff. I was amused when our tour guide told us that he would rather confront ten wolves than a single bear. The wolves, he explained, could be kept at bay provided you marked your 'domain' by urinating around the circle of your tent. I hope that wolves, too, were familiar with this edict. We followed this stop with a trip to the Niagara Falls. They appeared majestic but the landscape was not as beautiful as the falls in scenic New Zealand.

Although I was applauded, I suspect that my lecture in Toronto was on the dull side. Pat, who attended, told me that one of my friends slept soundly throughout. However, my host assured me it had been good. Was he right?

Shortly after we returned to Singapore, I was invited to conduct a course on banking in Stockholm. As we flew over in late spring, it was not cold. I spent most of my free time in the Old City (Gamla stan). To my surprise, I managed to get quite a number of Japanese and Chinese works of art there.

We also managed to spend a few days in Copenhagen and then proceeded to Norway. I was taken aback when a Norwegian scholar argued that banking law was nothing but a special branch of the law of contract. It dawned on me that there was, in reality, a marked difference between the jurisprudential approach to banking law in civil law countries and in common law systems. The former sought to bring every legal subject within the ambit of existing codifications. The latter treated any subject as autonomous once an adequate number of precedents justified its being given a distinct or special treatment. In practice, though, practitioners had to cooperate. They usually came up with a set of standard terms and conditions or a normative code, which suited both worlds. My abortive work, carried out at Monash on behalf of the international conglomerate, was an illustration in point.

Whilst in Norway, we visited Bergen and took a cruise through the fiords. I have to concede that that the Three Gorges in China were more imposing. All the same, a lover of Ibsen and of Grieg (like me) found it easier to relate to the former than to the latter. As we went through the fiords I could visualise the King of the Trolls and hear Solveig lamenting Peer Gynt's absence. No cultural bonds of this type bound me to the culture of the Kingdom of Heaven.

I have now come to regard the first years of my second spell in Singapore as my age of achievement. There were clouds on the horizon but, at this stage, I felt fulfilled. I shall be telling you about the ensuing storm in my next letter.

In the meantime, all the very best to all of you.

Yours as ever,
Peter

20 April 2018
Singapore

Dear Friends,

Letter 26: A Banking Lawyer in Singapore

I have already mentioned there were clouds on the horizon. They did not manifest themselves during Sook Yee's remaining years as dean. Actually, with her support, I was granted a period of study leave, which I spent in Hamburg. I used my time to work on my chapter in the encyclopedia.

The Institute of Comparative Law in Hamburg had an excellent library and so I got most of the materials I needed. Regrettably, one document was available only in Cambridge University. We flew over, and I got photocopies. The librarians in Cambridge were helpful and efficient. On the way back to Hamburg, I made a stopover in Vienna and called on Mother. She had declined, had lost command of her limbs, and I could read the writing on the wall.

Shortly after our return to Hamburg, the Brandenburg Wall tumbled down in Berlin. The momentum was, of course, felt all over Western Germany. A few members of the institute flew over to Berlin to lend moral and, if necessary, physical support. Others took a cruise up the

Elba from Hamburg to Dresden. I was too cowardly to join them but rejoiced with them.

At that time, I saw in the move an end to tyranny. Today — as an ageing retiree — I have come to understand that the step was of even greater importance. During my childhood and up to my middle age, we lived in a *Pax Americana*. This was the outcome of the formation of two major political blocks: the Soviet Union and the Free World, guided by the United States. The fall of the wall was bound to change the order of things. It started a change in international politics.

Pat integrated well in the institute, especially as scholars came from all over the world. We had a unit in the institute's building and so invariably had lunch and dinner together. Pat had acquired a basic knowledge of German during our year in Freiburg. Much of it came back to her in Hamburg. Before long, she was able to go on shopping sprees and, on one occasion, even went to see an English film.

I recall with pleasure the excellent performance of the Philharmonic Orchestra and seeing Brecht and Weil's opera, *The Rise and Fall of the City Mahagonny.* We also went, at Pat's behest, to organ performances in the famed Michaelis Church. They were impressive.

Both of us enjoyed our spell in the ancient Hansa city. One particular treasure I acquired was a collection of Mozart's letters to his father. To my surprise, he continued to address his father formally till the end. The very idea of addressing a family member formally is unacceptable to our contemporaries.

Back in Singapore, clouds darkened the sky. To my disappointment, Sook Yee retired from the deanship. I recall one interdisciplinary function attended by our staff shortly after she ceased to be the dean. Several members of the faculty, who feared her, manifested their glee by sitting together in one row in the hall far away from Sook Yee's seat.

I ignored them and joined her. I pause to add that I worked well with Sook Yee's successors but, to my mind, none of them had her extra zeal and intuition. Still, the faculty had not lost its momentum and continued to prosper.

On the personal front, I encountered a new health calamity. Shortly after our return to Singapore, I noticed that my glucose readings kept rising. In an attempt to avoid the need of putting me on insulin, the endocrinologist prescribed a novel medicine. When it raised my liver enzymes above the acceptable level, I had to undergo some further tests. These revealed that I had succumbed to Hepatitis C, a dangerous liver malady.

I was devastated. I knew that the disease progressed slowly. In consequence, I tried Traditional Chinese Medicine ("TCM"), which turned out to be useless. I then took a trip to Europe, during which I subjected myself to a strenuous and demanding exercise regime and a strict diet. These, too, were a sheer waste of time. Today, I know the ailment is a viral infection. I probably picked it up in an unhygienic hair salon or in a dental clinic.

Whilst I was making up my mind about treatment, I received sad news from Sanatorium Rekawinkel. Mother's health was deteriorating rapidly. Uncle Henry flew over in time to have a last chat with her. I arrived for the funeral.

I recall Mother's burial. She had insisted on being entombed in Father's grave and, to my relief, the Rabbi agreed. The only attendants at the dire occasion were Mother's former boss, Uncle Henry, his wife and me. The compulsory *Minyan* (viz. a congregation of not less than ten adult Jewish males) was made up from personnel of the community.

My function was to say Kaddish (קדיש) [a blessing said at a Jewish funeral by the deceased's next of kin]. I broke down. Mine were not tears of sorrow. I knew that for Mother, culmination was a release. Mine was an expression of guilt, shame and deprivation. I had not been a good son; and I knew this only too well. I also feared that I had lost the only person to whom I could speak regularly and without reserve. Uncle Henry, who read me correctly, assured me that Mother had always been proud of me. He added that from then on, I ought to feel free to talk to him regularly. I did so until his own demise years later on.

Uncle Henry had, indeed, been a pillar of strength. Mother told me that in 1938 he had fled with us to Sicily but then escaped before us to France and onwards to the United States. I recall the day we received the first letter he sent after locating us in Tel Aviv. I had corresponded with him during my days in Tichon, in the Hebrew University and in Oxford. I met him for the first time when both of us visited my parents in Vienna. We remained in close touch ever since. Henry was more resourceful and practical than me. Without his help, I should have been unable to settle my remaining affairs in Vienna following Mother's demise.

When I returned to Singapore, friends and acquaintances, both in the faculty and in the law firm, expressed their condolences. I have no recollection of being shown any sympathy by the Goh family. It dawned on me that, in reality, I had been facing a Hobson's choice. My mother and wife had not got on. To be a good husband, I had to turn myself into a poor son. Being a fine son would have entailed my being a bad husband. My solution was the worst: I became unsatisfactory both as son and as husband. It was the easy way out; and I felt mean and unworthy. I had not done my best.

Shortly after my return home, I consulted a hepatologist in the National University Hospital ("NUH"). He insisted that I undergo an invasive X-ray, which confirmed that the Hep C had entailed some liver cirrhosis but that I had not succumbed to cancer. Imminent treatment was mandatory. It was unpleasant, involving an antiviral drug and regular weekly injections. One of the side effects was a drop in hemoglobin, which required some extra treatment. A strict diet, precluding any alcoholic drinks and fatty substances, was also needed. I was restored to health for the time being but at that time there was no cure. The virus remained dormant in my system. A relapse could not be ruled out.

Another problem related to my diabetes. As the new drug could not be prescribed due to my liver condition, my endocrinologist had to put me on insulin. It was a low dosage but occasional upsurges of the pancreas' own production resulted in fainting spells. On two occasions, I had to be hospitalised.

An unfortunate development was a reversal in my wealthy brother-in-law's fortunes. His initial success was, in my opinion, the outcome of cooperation between himself and his partner. The latter was a shrewd businessman and had a rudimentary command of banking. In contrast, my kinsman was an inventor and an empire builder. His grasp of business affairs was questionable. I recall that on one occasion he invited a famous violinist to perform in our town. This cost my relative a fortune and I could not see the benefit accrued to his firm. Furthermore, when he left his partner, he tried his hand in trades which were not familiar to him. Unsurprisingly, he lost a great deal of money. He was also nepotistic in outlook. In consequence, he engaged two of his siblings, who were not up to the mark.

When his business turned sour, Pat wanted me to grant him a substantial loan. Being unconvinced of his business acumen, I prevaricated. In the event, he received aid from other sources. I was pleased for him but did not feel guilty for my negative response. I concluded that his affairs were not mine.

I have little to add about my personal life during these years. Pat and I travelled a number of times to Sydney, where we purchased two extra investment properties. On these occasions, I managed to get my loans from banks in Singapore. Usually, we rented a suite in a Sydney motel. On two occasions, we were put up by B. She did her best, but we had to follow her routine. On one occasion, for instance, she drove us to see a house advertised for sale. We wasted an entire morning on the drive. On another, she made an offensive remark. In consequence, I insisted that we move to a hotel the very next morning.

We also travelled a number of times to China. Pat liked it and I was keen to begin comprehending it. Today — when I am revising my memoirs — I know I proceeded in the wrong manner. It is difficult to understand a culture unless you have a sound command of the spoken and written language. I had ample opportunities to study Mandarin and Chinese writing but failed to do so.

In this regard, my comprehension of the Levant provides a good comparison. I have come across too many 'experts' who have firm ideas about the Hebrew Bible without being able to read the original. My respect for their views is marginal at best. In point of fact, the more fervent their 'teachings', the less credible they are in my eyes. I treat them the way an English language scholar regards a Frenchman who opines about Shakespeare without having any command of English.

Whilst Pat and I developed a reasonable routine, the world witnessed an interesting international development. I refer to what has become known in the Western Media as the Tiananmen Square Massacre of 1989. We were not in Beijing when it took place, but I have the eyewitness account of my late friend, Lim Teck Hwee. His Mandarin was sound enough to follow the account of the event as stated in the local media and by the people. I accept his views because the accounts in the Western media — to which I was confined — struck me as biased.

According to the Western media, the Chinese government suppressed ferociously a popular demand for a move from a totalitarian regime to a democracy. The PRC Government was accordingly decried as being at odds with the people's will. It was blamed for the murder and persecution of human rights activists.

Teck Hwee's account is far more in line with my understanding of the politics of the region. When Deng Xiaoping opened the gates to Western trade, he did not manifest an intention of changing the political regime. The reins of the Kingdom of Heaven had been in the hands of a ruler — be he a monarch or a dictator — from time immemorial. The notion of democracy, which was adopted by the West in the 19th century, was alien to it. Whilst the Western media was convinced that democracy ought to be accepted all over the world, I fear it made few disciples in the East.

When a group of human rights adherents thought to effect a change by means of demonstrations and a hunger strike, the writing was on the wall. Initially, the Chinese government tried to reach a compromise. The softliners wanted to continue negotiating. They were not keen to settle matters by forceful means. The hardliners took the opposite view: They wanted to suppress what they considered a riot by any means available. In due course, the hardliners prevailed. The army was called in and suppressed the uprising brutally.

In years to come, history will shed more light on the events leading to the uprising and to its suppression. Suffice it to say that at the date of writing, as well as at the date of revision — almost thirty-five years after the episode — the PRC has retained a totalitarian regime. It has also turned itself into a superpower. Its economy is slowly but surely overtaking the West's. Furthermore, the standard of living of the population is improving. It is a slow process, but it is not at all certain that a democratic metamorphosis would have yielded better results.

One reflection which may be relevant concerns a much earlier uprising — in the sixties — by the Hungarian population. Stalin suppressed the rebellion brutally and the West and the Western media, which had encouraged the riots, had a lot to say but did nothing. My own conclusion is that, unless a political power intends to support an uprising, it should not invoke false hopes!

The world events just described did not affect my life. Actually, in 1990, I took another European tour. The objective was to deliver a paper at Bielefeld and also to acquire some materials obtainable only in Cologne. Pat and I flew to Stuttgart and from there went by cab to Bielefeld. After the conference, we took a train to Freiburg, revisited the Kaiserstuhl and proceeded by a car rented in Breisach along the west bank of the Rhine. We made a stop in Bacharach — a lovely town with a colourful medieval ambience — but spent the night in St. Goar, on the bank of the Rhine. We faced the Pfalz — a small fortress amidst the river — from which brigands had in the past extracted a toll from ships traversing the Rhine. At present, it simply remains there as a relic. From St. Goar, we proceeded to Cologne. I lost my way in the metropolis and had to hire a taxi and follow it to our hotel.

What impressed me most during this drive was Lorelei. I was familiar with the folklore respecting it, could visualise the sirens at its top, and realised that to a person like me — imbued in the Western ethos — the trip had a cultural meaning. Pat simply enjoyed the scenery.

Back in Singapore, it was back to work as normal. The only significant personal event was my reunion with Paul (Zvi) Zollman. He had left Tel Aviv about one year before me and joined his mother in Montreal. We kept corresponding sporadically and remained in loose touch. He made a stop in Singapore on his world tour and suggested we lunch together. To my disappointment, Pat refused to join me when I took Paul and his wife out.

I knew that Paul's first wife had taken her life. His second wife was older than he. I sensed that to her, Paul was a husband-cum-son; to him, she assumed the role of mother-cum-wife.

Initially, when we faced one another, both Paul and I were stunned. Paul suddenly remembered he had forgotten to take his umbrella and went to his room to fetch it. As the sun was shining bright, his was a lame excuse. I rushed to the convenience and shed tears in my cubicle. We had parted as teenagers; when our reunion took place, both of us were well into middle age. And both of us wore scars of battles ordained by fate.

Paul had to proceed to the airport in the late afternoon. But we had time for a most pleasant sojourn. Somehow, the years of separation fell away. Although we did not meet again, we remained in close touch until Paul's demise in 2018.

Apart from my reunion with Paul, the years passed without any major commotions. Life in the university, as well as my consultancy in town, kept me going. In these years, we often went out with Teck Hwee as well as with Peng Koon, both of whom I had known from my first spell in Singapore.

One interesting development was the invention of the mobile phone. I recall how Pat and I went to a technology exhibition. Out of sheer conservatism, I did not seek to acquire any phone. However, Pat persuaded me and, before we left, I purchased a Motorola. I have changed the unit many times but have kept the very number I opted for on that initial occasion. Today — in 2022 — I would find it difficult to manage my everyday affairs without having the use of a mobile phone. I have to concede that occasionally, I forget my home number. In contrast, I can invariably recall my cell's.

Another important innovation that came onto the market at about that time was the email. Initially, I subscribed to the local system. In due course, I switched to Gmail and have retained the very same account all these years.

Pat and I kept travelling. During one trip to Europe, the media reported that the Soviet Union collapsed. Today, when I revise my memoirs in 2022, I have come to realise that the unification of Eastern and Western Germany, which had taken place during my sojourn in Hamburg, was the first step in that direction. The immediate effect of the collapse was that a number of countries governed by puppet regimes installed by Russia threw off the yoke. Some joined NATO and others declared neutrality. I recall how a former student I met in Vienna told me with glee that Latvia, where he had family connection, was finally free.

At that time, the collapse of the Soviet Union had no direct bearing on my life. About once or twice a year, we travelled to Sydney. On other occasions, we travelled to Bielefeld. In addition, I was invited to the annual festivity of a firm of accountants in Hong Kong. They also organised for me day trips to Macau or to some of the adjacent islands. I very much doubt if my contribution — namely, the papers I delivered on these occasions — were heavyweights. Still, they served their purpose and, in the course of these annual trips, I familiarised myself with Hong Kong and Kowloon. On one such trip, I met Bob Baxt, who was also invited to deliver a paper. It was a pleasant reunion.

By and large, the years went by peacefully. Then, in 1994, we had a test case respecting freedom of speech. A research fellow in political science at NUS, Lingle, published an article in the *International Herald Tribune*, in which he alleged that certain intolerant Asian regimes relied on a "compliant judiciary". The then Attorney-General, whom I have always held in high esteem, concluded that the reference was contextually to Singapore and instituted against Lingle a contempt of court action. Lingle fled from Singapore and did not appear in court to face the charges. A highly regarded judge convicted him in absentia.

I must confess that I had not even heard about the 'article' before the institution of the proceedings. I have no doubt that, contextually, the publication slighted our judiciary. All the same, my own inclination would have been to ignore it altogether. My main reason would have been my disregard for the American media. I had for long formed the impression that it was prepared to 'call wolf', provided the contributor's style and view were acceptable to the 'learned' editor. In particular, I was furious with the American Press for all the nonsense they published about topics such as 'the flood'.

I could, however, understand the arguments opposed to my 'good dog' attitude. It may very well be best to nip slander or contempt of court in the bud. I am aware how the old Jewish tendency to ignore anti-Semitic statements eventually led to persecution and to pogroms.

The action taken against Lingle did not cause me any concern. I am aware that some staff members took a view opposite to mine. They thought that that prosecution was an interference with freedom of speech. Well, I am unaware of the existence of any person 'of principle' who threw a resignation on the table.

My remaining years — up to my emeritation — went smoothly. Naturally, I remained in touch with my friends in Wellington (George Barton and Ivor Richardson) and in Melbourne (Peter Heffey, Michael Pryles and Jenny Neil, who had changed her surname to Laurant). In addition, I had a lively correspondence with Paul (Zvi). Occasionally, I also communicated with boyhood friends in Israel.

Shortly after my break in Hamburg, I completed my chapter on bills of exchange for the encyclopedia. Seeing the finished product brought me satisfaction. I also recall two pleasant trips to Shanghai and one to Taiwan.

Another significant development in those days was the appointment of Catherine Zuzak to an associate professorship in our faculty. She was selected on the strength of a positive reference of a specialist in the law of aviation. Shortly after her arrival, I invited her to a luncheon party. She handled herself well during the occasion and impressed all in attendance. From that time on, we became friendly, often went together for lunch and from time to time discussed both research and political issues.

Before long, Catherine told me that she had a personal commitment in Canada. I gathered that my friendship with her was to be platonic and that she would stay with us for just three years. During that period, she built up our library's holdings in aviation law, developed a course on the subject, conducted excellent sessions on the Law of Contract and on Evidence and distinguished herself both as a colleague and as a teacher. Occasionally, I took her out for lunch on Sunday, when Pat attended her church sessions.

The period in which Catherine was in residence coincided with my own imminent retirement from my chair. I was pleasantly surprised when the then Dean of Law advised me that the university had decided to confer on me an Emeritus Professorship.

It was a strange experience to have this new title conferred on me at the very convocation of the undergraduate and graduate students. I recall the kind words of the orator, who narrated my attainment, and the warm smile on the face of Pat, who was seated in the hall beside the two friends I had invited to the ceremony. I was aware that she savoured the honourable status conferred on me. To me, it came as a wake-up call. In reality, I was not ready to be passed over and felt that my ability to contribute had not come to its end. All in all, it was a bittersweet experience.

My retirement from full-time employment with the university entailed an event which, in the long run, was of genuine benefit to me. I was asked to accept payment of the amount standing to my credit with the university's superannuation scheme. Initially, I was bewildered by my having a substantial amount in my bank account. After a lengthy consultation with Pat, I decided to use it together with our savings to acquire a second property. After a hunt for a suitable holiday or second home, we purchased the flat in Mandarin Gardens Condominium — the very top floor flat (penthouse) in which I live at the time of writing. We had a lucky break in the negotiations. I was able to use some of the remaining surplus to renovate our new flat, which was in a rundown condition.

In the meantime, Catherine had flown to Canada. When she came back, she brought me a gift of two decorative tiles depicting a drake. The lovely hanging continues to adorn my room to the present day. In addition, I have many books that Catherine has sent me over the years, which reflect our shared love for art and literature.

Initially, Pat and I used our second property as a holiday home. We spent our weekends in it and enjoyed the wholesome East Coast breeze. Then, my Hep C took a turn for the worse. For a few months, I was too emaciated to enjoy our weekend sojourns and stayed put in Pandan Valley. The flat in Mandarin Gardens was not in use.

Another significant change resulting from my retirement was my move to full-time practice. Initially, I was keen to remain with the firm that had appointed me as a consultant. When I mentioned my interest to the managing partner, he asked me to discuss the matter with his designated successor. He suggested that his successor and I go out for lunch, and I thought that he was going to brief the fellow involved. Regrettably, the successor did not take up my hint respecting my desire to devote myself to full-time practice in their firm. Years later, I discovered that he had not been prepared.

In the meantime, VK Rajah — who had been my student in 1982 and who turned his father's modest firm to a major enterprise — offered me a post. I accepted and do believe this was one of the best career decisions in my life. To secure continuity of my relationship with the university, I accepted, in addition, an appointment to an adjunct position. In this way, I retained one foot in the academic door.

I look forward to telling you — my friends — about the period commencing with my move to Rajah & Tann. As often before, I had a break of good luck. VK assigned me an experienced and extremely capable secretary. Zalina Badrom, who worked for me during my years at the firm, became a friend and often prevented me from taking the wrong step.

It should not take me too long to complete my next letter. It will deal with my experience as a legal practitioner in Singapore. Based on it, my general feeling is that on many occasions, the winner of complex legal proceeding is not necessarily the most worthy party but, alas, the litigant with the deepest pocket, who can loosen his purse strings when he takes a case to court. Often, he achieves his desired result by insisting on his full protection even before he enters into any transaction.

However, once again, I am jumping the gun. I shall discuss my experiences in practice in my next letter.

Till then, all the best to all of you.

Yours as ever,
Peter

12 July 2018
Singapore

Dear Friends,

Letter 27: Practice and the Ivory Tower

It will be recalled that shortly after my retirement from my chair, I joined Rajah & Tann. Originally, I had a small office in their premises in the Straits Trading Building in Battery Road. Later on, I moved to a large office in their new venue: the refurbished Bank of China building across the street.

Work at Rajah & Tann was interesting. I dealt with many cases and drafted numerous clauses for banking documents. Four cases deserve to be mentioned specifically. One arose from the Malaysian Government's decision to prohibit all remittances denominated in ringgit. In consequence, the free movement of the Malaysian currency was proscribed. A Singapore committee thereupon resolved to 'mature' all obligations to be satisfied by payment in ringgit and to substitute payment in USD at a rate of exchange fixed by it. The parties most badly hit were investors who had sought to make an arbitrage gain from trading in ringgit. One such investor brought an action claiming the physical delivery of ringgit. On the basis of expert evidence and a careful analysis of the wording of the legislation in a fine judgment, the investor lost his case. The trial judge's decision was affirmed by a unanimous judgment of the Court of Appeal. I was impressed by the fine research and argumentation of both parties.

A particularly interesting aspect of this case was a mediation session in which we tried to resolve the matter. The investor involved had originally indicated a willingness to settle at a moderate amount. At the mediation session, he insisted on being paid 90% of the sum involved. He became aggressive when we, in turn, reduced the amount offered to him. He handled the negotiations in person so his lawyer, a well-established litigator, said little.

The second case involved a complex question concerning a letter of credit case. Here, too, the outcome was dubious. I was relieved when, after the second day in court, the parties decided to settle. I am not certain we would have won the case. Our expert tried to be too clever by half. Being an American attorney, he thought he could never be wrong.

The third case arose from a fraud committed by an employee of a business firm. He borrowed money in the name of the company, remitted it to his own account and then gambled it away in Australian casinos. The question was whether the loss was to be borne by the crook's employers or by the hapless lenders. Quite a number of cases were settled. Notably, the fraudster presented to the banks all the documents required for the extension of a loan. The banks could have protected themselves by contacting the Chairman of the firm's Board of Directors but were too reticent to do so. In the event, most cases were settled. In my opinion, the employers should have investigated the rogue more carefully before they appointed him.

The last matter, which never went to court, arose from an ingenious fraud perpetrated in the PRC. An American lawyer, who travelled to the PRC, was shown 'in confidence' a bundle hidden in the ceiling. It contained what purported to be a deposit receipt issued by an international bank in Singapore and attesting the deposit with it of a very large amount of money to the credit of an account purportedly opened by a famous politician. Our task was to affirm that the 'deposit receipt' was genuine. Regrettably, our investigation confirmed that the bank in question did not have an office in Singapore at the relevant time and that such a large deposit would have figured in Singapore's annual budget statement. By the time we concluded our investigation, it became clear that the American lawyer had been duped. The document in question was a clever fake.

Initially, I was inclined to see in it a case arising from a European's inability to read the oriental mind. On further reflection, I suspect that the answer is more complex. Many an Oriental is duped by smart American or European conmen. I am inclined to think that persons are more easily cheated when they spend little time in an alien environment and consider themselves to be superior.

A matter I had handled a few years earlier, before joining VK's firm, demonstrates that even sophisticated professionals can be deceived. A Moroccan businessmen, who wanted to develop an entire district in Singapore, obtained loans from respectable banks by inducing a foreign bank in a Scandinavian country to issue standby credits (which serve, effectively, as guarantees) to secure the borrowings. In reality, the branch of the foreign bank, which opened the credits, did not have the authority to issue them. However, the lenders were keen to extend the loans and make a profit. Many facilities were granted before the irregularity came to light. Eventually, the matter was settled. To my mind, it suggests that businessmen are easily duped when they hope to make a gain.

It is important for me to emphasise that most of my work at Rajah & Tann concerned the preparation of documents rather than litigation. In many ways, the effort involved in preparing foolproof documents is just as fatiguing as the research of issues arising in litigation. Indeed, when a lawyer is instructed to prepare documents respecting a transaction, his main task is to ensure that the bargain involved is valid and enforceable. He must, for instance, take care that all formalities, such as registration, are complied with. By way of illustration, take a charge or a mortgage drafted by a law firm. The lawyers in charge have to secure not just the clarity and accuracy of the documents involved but also that the registration or witnessing is valid. Both in litigation and in documentation, the lawyer's main task is to protect his client's interests.

In this regard, there is a crucial difference between the work of a scholar (or academic) and a practitioner. The former researches a subject so as to summarise it in a readable form and to throw light on any obscure point. In other words, the aim is to get a precise overview of a given topic. This is done by writing an article or a book.

In contrast, the practitioner's objective is to further his client's cause. By way of illustration, take a sale and transfer of property. The lawyer's objective is not restricted to drafting a document that gives effect to the parties' intention but also to dealing with ways and means aimed at minimising the taxes and levies to be paid. Similarly, once a matter has become the subject of a dispute, his object is to centre on and substantiate his client's argument. By way of illustration, take a traffic accident. The driver's counsel is under an obligation to raise the best defences of his client's acts, for instance, to satisfy the court that a road sign was not clearly displayed. His prognosis of a case is usually expressed in an opinion. In it, the chances of success are weighed.

The distinction between the roles of an academic and a practitioner dawned on me clearly when I was asked to review the standard terms of a bank. As expected, the existing forms included a 'verification clause'. Under it, a customer was precluded from disputing any errors in a bank statement not brought by him to the bank's attention within three days.

As an academic, I was opposed to clauses of this type. In my experience, customers did not peruse their statements within three days. The real objective of such clauses is to place on the customer an obligation which is not met in practice. I was of the view that the clauses ought to be struck down as being oppressive.

As a practitioner, my approach had to differ. I knew that three days constituted an inadequate period. The clause could therefore be struck down on the basis of its being unreasonable. I ended up by extending the period given to the customer for raising objections to ten days. It was the best I could do for my client — the bank — although as an academic I continued to have misgivings about all clauses of this type.

In my first year at Rajah & Tann, I came to realise that modern bankers were not customer friendly. Their objective was to protect themselves against actions based on their employees' sharp practices by the insertion of exemption clauses in their standard Terms and Conditions. Some banks went so far as to give their customers misleading advice on investments. As long as they were shielded against their 'lighthearted sales talk' by decrying liability, they were satisfied. Undoubtedly, many tarnished their reputation; but the profit shown in their balance sheets satisfied their conscience. Employees who distinguished themselves by the volume of the transactions initiated by them were promoted as a matter of course.

I recall one particularly disturbing case respecting such a clause. An officer of a bank, which did not usually use our firm, made an appointment to discuss a clause proposed by its in-house counsel. Under that clause, any bank employee who advised a customer would be deemed to be the customer's agent. I had dealt with clauses of this type in books and articles and was satisfied that they would be struck down by a court. At the same time, I wondered why the matter was referred to me by the bank in question. The officer explained that a well-known firm thought the clause would be upheld. Still, their in-house counsel read an article of mine and entertained doubts.

"Do you want to refer the matter to me for an opinion?"

"Can't this be done informally? We may revise our list of panel law firms."

"Sorry. Your bank does not retain our firm presently. And I must cover my back."

A few days later, I received a letter of instructions and rendered a detailed opinion within a week. In an attempt to assist, I included the draft of a comparable clause which was likely to be upheld. To my utter surprise, I received a telephone call from another officer of the bank, who introduced herself as a vice-president and asserted that the clause proposed by me did not 'cut ice' with her.

"Are you then also in the ice cutting business?" I asked, failing to control my temper.

"I meant: I don't like your clause! I am not in any ice cutting business!"

"So, you better cut potatoes," I replied.

My fee was promptly paid although, as expected, our firm was not included in the bank's revised panel, that is, law firms to be engaged by it. Months later, I discovered that my draft clause was, nonetheless, incorporated in the bank's revised general Terms and Conditions. It occurred to me that, in reality, the bank could have saved itself my fee by relying on the analysis in my publication. Still, the bank had plenty of dough.

It was pleasant to note that not all bankers became 'sales talk counsel'. Some adhered to the old standards, which I had come to know during my days as a student. Whilst traditional bankers were, of course, aware that the bank was not a philanthropist, they continued to pay heed to the customer's interests and special problems. By way of illustration, they would take exception to 'representations' aiming to induce aged retirees to invest funds in risky products.

One such conscientious banker was my friend Michael Blum. He was the Head of the Bad Debts Collection Office of his bank. I was pleased to note that even when he set out to collect such debts, he did his best to accommodate hapless investors. In his attempt to recover amounts due to his bank, he was careful not to push borrowers to desperation. Another such banker was Jane Kuok, the head of the legal department of a substantial bank. It did not take me long to glean that she was opposed to the unfair practices of the banking community. On two occasions, she opposed the insertion of clauses in standard Terms and Conditions because she considered them customer unfriendly.

In an attempt to counter the effect of damaging clauses, the courts — influenced by British authorities — drew a distinction between 'sophisticated' and 'unsophisticated' customers. I am convinced that the intention of the courts was praiseworthy but fear that they were not realistic. A person can be singularly sophisticated in some regards but gullible in others.

By way of illustration, take my late friend Lim Teck Hwee. Being a Justice of the Peace and a qualified attorney, he would undoubtedly be regarded 'sophisticated'. All the same, he fell prey to smooth sales talk and was induced to engage in margin trading. Effectively, this type of business involves the borrowing from a bank of a sum of money to be used in trading. As might be expected, the bank usually gets an iron clad security of the loan extended by it. In Teck Hwee's case, the bank's lending officer obtained a mortgage over my friend's dwelling. When the investments went sour, leading to my friend's default, the bank foreclosed. A member of Teck Hwee's family stepped in to aid but, to my dismay, Teck Hwee died of a broken heart. Well, was he sophisticated? He seems to have been unable to see through the sales talk pressed on him.

I, too, was subjected to 'sales talks'. One bank wanted me to invest money in a 'high yield bonds fund', without disclosing that the bulk was junk. On another occasion, a different bank wanted me to invest the bulk of my savings in a discretionary fund. Fortunately, I tracked the fund's record. It was unimpressive. Moreover, I recalled vividly that in some cases, banks were caught with their pants down. The expertise of their select officers did not enable them to foresee the imminent danger.

My misgivings about serving unworthy causes were allayed by the benefit accrued through my satisfactory income. My collection of European porcelain kept growing and, in addition, I started to acquire prints and paintings. Before long, my office in the law firm resembled an art gallery. So did my office in the university.

My personal life during the period was largely pleasant. The main problem was the deterioration in Pat's eyesight. Our ophthalmologist reiterated that Pat's vision could not be restored. This did not stop us from taking a few pleasant trips; but I realised that it would be wrong to ignore the clouds on the horizon.

By the end of my second year with Rajah & Tann, my close friend Cathy Zuzak decided to return to Canada. Our dean would have been happy to extend her contract, but she resolved to join the International Civil Aviation Organisation ("ICAO") — a highly regarded United Nations body — where she went from strength to strength. Before her departure from Singapore, she had introduced a new course entitled Aviation Law. It is still being offered.

Cathy's departure meant that the only person to whom I could talk openly about my problems was no longer in situ. True, Cathy came over to Singapore whenever she had a break. In effect, she spent all her vacations on her visits to me. Moreover, we communicated regularly by phone and continued to shop jointly for porcelain and art works. Thus, I am proud to say that the geographic distance did not affect our closeness. All the same, I kept missing her. Today, when I write my memoirs, I realise that the father-daughter relationship that developed whilst she was in Singapore filled the void left in my life due to my childless and barren marriage.

Cathy's departure had a strange side effect. During my last two years at Monash (in Melbourne), I started to write short stories. I continued to pursue this interest and, over the years, completed a number of tomes. Shortly after Cathy's departure, I investigated the possibly of publishing my work. I ended up by preparing a book on the life of my late friend Lalith, who had been assassinated during an election rally. I found out that the self-publishing process was within my means. At present — in 2022 — my books grace a shelf in my cabinet. One of them — a satire published in 2016 — deals with problems of bible critique. Two of my orthodox friends told me they were not prepared to read it. This lowered my opinion of their fair-mindedness rather than of my self-esteem.

About two years after Cathy's departure, I received a call from the faculty's then dean. He wondered whether I might wish to return to the faculty as a full-time professorial fellow and continue in town on a part-time basis. I jumped at the offer. I knew that my real place was in the ivory tower. Undoubtedly, it was essential to keep a presence in town. The law was a practical discipline and pure academic speculation might detach a scholar from the real world. A healthy mixture of the two was, in all probability, the best solution.

Initially, I moved back to my old office in Kent Ridge. Shortly thereafter, the faculty moved back to its old campus in Bukit Timah. For me, this was a return to my old habitat plus a bonus. Once again, I was an academic lawyer but with a stronghold in town. I recall conducting a number of seminars for bankers and practitioners and also an involvement in some interesting cases. I became, once again, a consultant rather than a practising lawyer meeting with clients.

My life in the refurbished faculty was pleasant. Naturally, technology kept advancing. In the old days, students would take notes of my lectures. During these new times, many came equipped with computers and simply recorded my words or typed throughout. I, too, found modern techniques useful. When I conducted lectures in the old days, I spoke into an amplifier but often turned my head, so my words became muddled or too soft. To my delight, a new loudspeaker had an amplifier attached to a frame which I wore. In consequence, my voice kept carrying even when I turned my head. It was a considerable improvement.

Naturally, I was ageing. But although I started to use a walking stick, I was still able to pace through the benches and could see what was going on in my lecture hall. I recall one amusing occasion, where my curiosity was roused by the interest displayed by some male students who were absorbed in the computer screen of a self-assured young lady. When I had a peep at the screen, my mouth fell open. What was shown on the computer had more to do with certain kinds of bedroom activities than with the dry analysis of legal concepts. I returned to my lecturer's desk without saying a word. The young lady in question, who had taken in my startled glance, radiated amusement when she left the hall. I concluded she had lost the ability to blush. It further dawned on me that ancient mariners like me could learn a thing or two from the younger generation.

During the period involved — that is, after I became a full-time professorial fellow and a legal consultant — my professional life was enhanced by an effective communications system I had developed. Both my secretary at the university, Shamsia, and Zalina at Rajah & Tann were able to contact me on my cell phone whenever a matter of emergency arose. I doubt if, without their constant help and support, I would have been able to remain in control of my affairs. Due to their devotion, I managed to keep the required regard both in the firm and in the university.

My description of my Indian summer at the university would be incomplete without a reference of my involvement with the Centre for Banking & Finance Law established by James (Jim) Byrne. Like many Americans, Jim could occasionally be brusque. However, I enjoyed the seminars he conducted in Singapore, Shanghai and Amsterdam. Jim used to complain that I absented myself from many sessions. As I had to pay for my own trips, I ignored his complaint. I recall how I spent a day in the Rijksmuseum in Amsterdam, with its excellent Meissen collection. I recall ringing Cathy whilst I walked through the museum and described to her the splendour of the 18th century pieces I was privileged to view. On another day, still in Amsterdam, I spent a day in the Van Gogh Museum, which had an instructive exhibit of van Gogh's and Gauguin's paintings. At Jim's suggestion, I also attended a conference of the United Nations Institute of Trade Law ("UNCITRAL"), held in Vienna, on current issues of international trade financing.

Whilst my courses at the university might have been growing stale, I had the fortune to have three outstanding postgraduate students. One of them, a former local police inspector, did his masters by thesis. There could be no doubt about his ability and drive. After completing his LL.M., he started a Ph.D., which would have been a much needed and original contribution to the law of tracing — a complex branch of property law. The pull of the business world, though, was too strong. Mark became a full-time banker and, later on, the CEO of an international business firm. We have remained in close touch.

A Nigerian student read for both an LL.M. and Ph.D. in banking law. He has been successful in his career although his short fuse and occasional outbursts were not endearing. In my assessment, he was a hardworking and enterprising scholar but his tendency to see the trees rather than the wood tended to undermine the quality of his work. At the same time, I was pleased when his doctoral thesis was passed by the examiners and when he obtained a fine academic position in an English university.

The third former student, Sandra Booysen, struck me as the best scholar I have come across. Initially, she enrolled in my LL.M. courses. It did not take me long to realise she was an original thinker and an accomplished researcher. She topped her class and then read for a Ph.D. — the best I have supervised.

When, eventually, it was time for me to retire, Sandra took over my courses in Banking Law and Credit and Security. I am convinced she breathed fresh air into them, and I can see her going from strength to strength. We lunch together regularly, and she has enabled me to keep a foot in the university. In 2018, Sandra took me to a local exhibition of Impressionist paintings. Although I had to use a wheelchair, I enjoyed every moment of it.

The last memorable episode of this period was a one-week trip to Vienna. I had to complete some work and was delighted to discover that Cathy went, at about the same time, for an ICAO function in Frankfurt. We spent a lovely week in Vienna. I took Cathy for an orientation trip of Vienna itself. We went twice to the state opera, once to the popular opera and, on another day, attended a fine chamber music concert. We also went to the Museum of Art and to the neighbouring Museum of Science.

Going to these places with Cathy was a refreshing experience. I knew that Pat had accompanied me to the museums mainly out of a sense of duty. Cathy really wanted to see them. I recall with delight a morning spent in the Belvedere. Although autumn had set in, we walked through the grounds from the Upper Belvedere, with its Klimt paintings, to the Lower Belvedere, with its Medieval Art gallery. Another source of joy was our visits to Vienna's pleasant and wholesome restaurants. We had two meals in the famed Sacher Hotel and one in the Café Mozart. One afternoon, Cathy took me to the cinema. We watched *The Da Vinci Code* and *The Third Man*.

I felt the need to visit my parents' grave. Cathy went to a fitness centre whilst I took the streetcar from the Schwarzenbergplatz to the central cemetery. I recall standing by my parents' grave, in the Jewish section of the graveyard, and thinking that sheer chance — or a guiding hand — had mapped out my route. Did this hand also determine that my parents would marry? Did it select the sperm that fertilised the ovum? Further, did it predetermine which genes would be transmitted to me and determine my make up?

I was unable to answer these questions. They kept intriguing me. Perhaps they had baffled humanity from times immemorial. All I could do was to thank my late parents for all they had done for me. They had escaped from Europe in time to save all of us from the horrors of the Holocaust. They had enabled me to grow up comfortably in Tel Aviv. Father had seen me through Oxford and had visited me in Singapore. I owed my very existence to them. Perhaps they were rewarded in some way by my successful career. But had I been a dutiful son?

That evening, Cathy and I went to a restaurant recommended by one of her colleagues. It was a quiet evening. I felt tired and emotionally worn out. Did Cathy read my thoughts?

Two days later, I returned to Singapore. The following years will be the subject of my next letter. They end with Pat's death and its effect on me.

In the meantime, I wish all of you a pleasant sojourn.

Yours as ever,
Peter

2 September 2018
Singapore

Dear Friends,

Letter 28: Pat's Ordeal

On the surface, all was well. Life at the university continued smoothly. I came to terms with the fact that I had spent all my working life in the law, a subject I did not admire, and that my marriage left much to be desired.

There were developments in my professional life, but I took them in my stride. To start with, Michael Blum was transferred to his bank's office in South America. We remained in close touch, but his successors in the bank terminated my retainer. They came to me occasionally but they ceased to be choice clients.

Another development, much later, was VK's elevation to the Bench. I got on well with his successors but none of them became a close friend. As time went by, I felt it was too difficult for me to hold two jobs. Further, my billings were becoming smaller than before. Fearing I might become redundant, I withdrew from the firm. Once again, I became a full-time academic lawyer. Whilst I missed the excitement of practice, I enjoyed the peace and calm that returned to my life.

Then, I had to deal with a bombshell. Pat and I went to Paragon — a shopping centre both of us liked — and had a quiet meal. It was the

Christmas season so, in an attempt to please Pat, I suggested we buy a Christmas tree. On the way to the display, Pat asked me to proceed on my own and buy any decoration I liked.

"What's the matter, Susu?"

"After you buy the tree, you better take me home."

Alarmed by Pat's words and by her pallor, I took her to the taxi stand. As soon as we reached our flat, I called the doctor. Initially, he thought it was just a touch of the flu. When she remained listless over the weekend, he asked me to take her to the nearest A&E. A full blood count revealed she had become anaemic. A further test, done by a specialist at the National University Hospital ("NUH"), led to an alarming diagnosis. Pat's bone marrow had stopped producing an adequate level of haemoglobin.

Anaemia was not new to me. In my case, it had been a side effect of the treatment I took for the Hep C. Fortunately, a course of injections and a supplement called folic acid got me over it. In Pat's case, this treatment did not work.

Our specialist, who was a fine physician, tried different medicines. None of them helped. Pat needed regular blood transfusions and had to be hospitalised several times. Whenever possible, I took her to NUH, although on some occasions I had to rush her to Changi Hospital, which became the nearest clinic after our move to Mandarin Gardens. In many ways, Pat was unlucky. On two occasions, a cold, transmitted to her by a nurse, developed into pneumonia. Water had to be removed from Pat's lungs.

Pandan Valley became inaccessible. Pat could no longer manage the stairs. The flat in Mandarin Gardens now became our home. The move, however, led to problems. Mandarin Gardens was on the East Coast and, thus, close to the dwellings of Pat's siblings. They and members of Pat's church came over for frequent visits, which deprived Pat of the chance to have a good rest. The flat was also far from the university. It took me well over one hour to drive to work and back.

Eventually, our physician told me that Pat could no longer be left on her own. We had to employ two maids. She also needed assistance of a caretaker, a role I undertook. Further, her behaviour became erratic and unpredictable. During one of her spells in hospital, one of Pat's siblings helped me to engage a contractor who installed protective grills on windows and balconies in our unit at Mandarin Gardens. This, in the very least, prevented any outward accident.

Pat's deteriorating health caused yet another problem. She had always been suspicious but, at this sad stage, developed old age paranoia. On two occasions, she accused some of her siblings of trying to get money from me. On another, she accused me of having another household.

At the suggestion of one of Pat's siblings, I moved back to Pandan Valley, coming over to Mandarin Gardens only during weekends and on Wednesdays. Regrettably, Pat's insurance was not adequate for her medical expenses. As hospital and medical bills accumulated, I had no option but to sell our Pandan Valley flat. To avoid spending all my time in Mandarin Gardens, I rented a flat near the university. If I had stayed put in Mandarin Gardens, I would have lost my sanity.

In point of fact, notwithstanding the move, my life during that period became unbearable. In the morning, I had to rush to work. Later in the day, I often had to take Pat to our doctor for injections. Regrettably, Pat did not trust my skill in this regard, although, as a diabetic then depending on insulin, I was as skilful as a nurse. In addition, whenever Pat needed to be hospitalised I had to rush to Changi Hospital or NUH after work.

Unsurprisingly, the effort took its toll on my health. On one occasion, I blacked out at the university and had to be hospitalised in NUH's Emergency Ward. Although some members of the family came over to visit Pat in hospital, none of them came to see me.

Pat had to be hospitalised several times. After her final spell in Changi Hospital, the doctors concluded she was beyond help and discharged her. As a last resort, a specialist tried chemotherapy. It did not work and, within a matter of days, Pat died.

The entire period has remained fresh in my mind, especially one strange experience I had prior to my sale of the Pandan Valley flat. After cooking my breakfast, I felt I was going to black out. I knew the cause was probably an excess of insulin or a sudden drop in blood pressure. As I was alone in the large flat, I could not call for help. Accordingly, the sensible thing would have been to prostrate myself on the floor and wait for the spell to pass. The floor, though, was hard and so I yearned to get back to my bed. I knew that running would exacerbate the problem. Accordingly, I walked slowly to the bedroom. Suddenly, an inner voice — my subconscious — screamed (in Hebrew): "Help me to my bed." I believe I heard a reply — again in my mind — saying, soothingly (in Hebrew): "All right." I managed to reach my bed, lay down and fell asleep instantly. I woke up refreshed and calm.

When I related my experience to Uncle Henry, he thought I had a hallucination. However, the experience was so real that to date I continue to have my doubts. A firm denial of the supernatural is just as dogmatic as its affirmation. I shall come back to this episode later on. At that time, it was just an unexplainable occurrence. My main task was coping with Pat's condition.

Another development during this difficult period was my decision to return to the Jewish community. I had neglected the synagogue during the years following my return to Singapore. I also feared that my scepticism militated against an act of faith. In the event, Michael Blum, a staunch believer, encouraged me to take that step. My God-Daughter encouraged me to go ahead. I am glad to say that the community received me with open arms.

Michael was by no means the only friend who did his best to stand by me. Cathy volunteered to talk to me twice a day; Jane Kuok went out with me for lunch once or twice a week and, generally, many friends were ready to step in if needed. I am familiar with the saying that blood is thicker than water. In my opinion, the truth is different. Good friends are the lifeblood of our earthly existence.

Pat had requested a Christian burial. I felt bound by her wishes and unwillingly followed the Chinese custom of organising a 'wake', so that Pat's deceased body was displayed for two days in the coffin.

The funeral took place two days later. A colleague drove me to the funeral parlour. Seated in his car, which headed the procession, we proceeded to the cemetery. After the burial, people came and expressed their condolences and shook my hand. To my dismay, the two sisters walked past me and did not speak to me. When another member of their community hesitated to raise his hand as he approached me, I dropped mine. He then raised his hand. Thereupon, I raised mine and shook his.

Pat's sisters came to collect her belongings. The items packed by them were collected by another sibling. As a symbolic act, he dropped a set of spare keys — held by the family — in my letter box. The family had made a tacit decision to ostracise me. Only one of them remained in touch with me: the brother who had settled in London, Robert Goh.

By sheer coincidence, the landlord of my rented flat terminated the lease shortly after Pat's funeral. Within a fortnight, I moved to Mandarin Gardens, retaining but one maid.

Pat's passing brought to a close a sad chapter of my life. We had been man and wife for 43 years but our marriage had lacked harmony. Today, as I write and re-edit these memoirs, I realise that in a way I had been unfair to Pat. Initially, I had been drawn to her because she was beautiful and I was certain she would be a good housewife. Later in life, I became estranged from her because she was unable to share my professional life and my interest in art and in biblical studies. In reality, though, I could not have expected these from her. Similarly, I believe Pat married me because she felt the need for security and a comfortable and peaceful life. Her dream was shattered because I was uncomfortable in her environment, and she was unable to adjust to mine. It is possible that children would have been good glue during their youth. They would have given us a common purpose. Regrettably, the rot was bound to set in upon their leaving home. J.'s summary (before I left Melbourne) had been neat and telling. Pat and I had been unsuitable for one another right from the start.

Pat died in 2011. For a few months I concentrated on my teaching but felt that my courses were getting stale. For a while, the supervision of theses kept me going. All in all, though, I felt the need to retire. At this stage, Cathy came once again to my assistance. Accompanied by her, I flew to Sydney and visited the Montefiore retirement homes. Cathy made all the arrangements and the main retirement home, with its excellent facilities, would have been happy to accept me. For a few months, I hesitated. The facilities were fine and acceptable. Somehow, though, I wanted to remain independent and self-sufficient. This was not possible in a professionally run retirement home.

I believe Cathy enjoyed the trip to Sydney. I knew it was strenuous. All in all though, I managed to show her Sydney (which I had come to know well). We also spent a morning in the neighbouring Blue Mountains. One delightful evening, we went out with my family. In effect, it was a reunion. In most of my trips to Sydney, I failed to call on them. In a sense, I distanced myself. Cathy put an end to that by arranging that we meet. I am grateful to her for uniting me with my own next of kin.

Later in the year, Jane went with her daughter and me to Pangkor Laut, a fine Malaysian holiday resort, stretching over an island located off the west coast of Perak. It was far removed from the everyday hustle and bustle. I enjoyed myself although I soon realised that I was unable to participate in the hikes and exercises. Age was catching up with me. The eager young man, who had been keen to see and explore the world, had metamorphosed into an ancient mariner, who needed his comforts. I recall one evening in which the telephone lines were out of order. I was alone in my unit and panicked. I was relieved when connection was resumed. By then, I was bathed in cold sweat.

An important development during the months following Pat's demise was my regular attendance of prayer meetings in the synagogue. My eerie experience in Pandan Valley motivated me. I knew that, rationally, Uncle Henry made sense. To me, though, the event remained an imponderable. I grappled with it but, just for once, realised that many phenomena — perhaps even the nature of life itself — did not yield themselves to rational examination. Suffice it to say that I felt committed to a faith which in truth I had no rational grounds to accept. All the same, the prayer sessions soothed me.

My feeling for the community has remained deep gratitude. I did at the same time continue with my bible critique. Somehow — in an utterly inconsistent and contradictory manner — I became an observant believer during my spells in the synagogue and remained a sceptic when back at home.

During the entire difficult period, I ceased to pay much attention to the world affairs. It is also possible that old age indifference had set in. Whilst I watched the news — mainly on Channel NewsAsia and BBC — not much registered. In reality, a new publication on bible critique or on archaeological work in Israel or in Egypt became more meaningful than elections in one country or another. I paid particular attention to reports about excavations in the Temple Mount and in choice sites in Egypt. They helped to bring the past and the present era together. Daily politics struck me as transient.

The only event that has remained fresh in my mind is the assassination of Rabin in November 1995. After years in the political wilderness, Rabin won the 1992 elections in Israel. His goal was to bring peace to the region or, in other words, to resolve the Arab–Israeli conflict once and for all. His first significant step in this direction was the signing of the Oslo Accords (of 1993), which created the Palestinian National Authority and granted to it partial control over the Gaza Strip and the West Bank. A year later, he oversaw the signing of the Israel–Jordan Peace Treaty of 1994.

For the first time in modern history, there was realistic hope for a peaceful resolution of the main conflict in the region. Regrettably, and as mentioned before, Rabin was murdered by an ultra-orthodox fanatic. The majority of the Israeli population was aghast. The ruthless elimination of political rivals was irreconcilable with the tenets of Judaism. Sadly, none of Rabin's successors supported the peace initiative. It now seems clear that any solution of the regional conflict would be either by arms or by attrition.

I shall tell you more about my years as an ageing retiree in my remaining letters.

In the meantime, I wish all of you all the very best.

Yours as ever,
Peter

Part V

RETIREMENT

30 April 2018, 7 August 2022
Singapore

Dear Friends,

Letter 29: An Ageing Widower

Pat's demise brought one chapter to its end. Life, though, had to continue. As already mentioned, I was aware that my lectures were becoming stale and, generally, was tired of teaching. To my relief, I realised that Sandra was now able to take over my courses.

When I offered my resignation to the then dean, he asked me to stay for another year. Reluctantly, I agreed. By the end of the next year, Sandra was constituted an assistant professor. My presence was no longer needed. Further, I wanted to leave before I lost my ability to contribute. I had seen how some scholars' attempted to hold on desperately to a discipline that was leaving them behind. In my opinion, such an attitude was undignified.

By the end of 2012, I submitted my formal resignation. My valedictory lecture was delivered in April 2013. It was well attended and, I believe, was favourably received. Shortly thereafter, I vacated my office at the university and donated many of my artworks to the faculty. This, then, was the end of my fifty years as a law teacher.

I now had to decide where to retire. Three cities I loved, namely London, Hamburg and Vienna, had a vile climate and, accordingly, were unsuitable. In any event, Germany and the United Kingdom may not have granted me permanent residence. As I was a born Austrian, I had the right to return to Vienna but, whilst I liked the city, I was not over-fond of its frequently condescending people. Furthermore, the cultural attractions of these three cities could not be visited by an ageing man, who was no longer mobile. Another site, namely Wellington in New Zealand, was too windy for comfort and, in any event, I recalled the maxim advising against the return to a place in which one had been happy.

In reality, I had only three viable options: Israel, Australia and Singapore. Friends in the synagogue urged me to return to Israel. I decided against it because I disliked the party in power as well as Israeli politics. I knew that back there, I should have to take a stand on matters of principle but felt that it was too late for that. I was an old man. As an Australian citizen, Melbourne and Sydney were realistic possibilities. I had close friends in Melbourne but, by and large, had never warmed to the city. Although its Art Centre was outstanding, I knew it would have been difficult for me to visit it.

In contrast, I knew that good protected living facilities — which abounded in New South Wales — would enable me to live near my family. I liked the prospect and admired Sydney. It was a place that, even when confined to a wheelchair, could be enjoyable. So were the adjacent Blue Mountains I had come to know well.

All the same, I decided to retire in Singapore. To start with, Singapore was the place where I found my vocation. Back in Israel, I was one of the many legal practitioners. In all probability, I would have spent my life as an in-house counsel at a bank. In Oxford, I enjoyed the status of a postgraduate student but continued to need my father's support.

My career as a dedicated law teacher began in Singapore. Later in life, I even practised law in my Lion City.

Further, my flat in Mandarin Gardens was a comfortable home. I loved to relax in my sitting room in the evening and watch airplanes descending majestically to Changi Airport. And I was fond of the population. I mixed well with people of all ethnicities and backgrounds.

Another major consideration was my having a fine circle of friends, who saw to it that I would feel active and who came regularly to visit me. In addition, I was pleased with the law and order that governed the city-state. Being a hardliner, the strict legal system of Singapore suited me.

Yet another consideration for staying put was that, in reality, I could obtain all the materials on my major interests, bible critique and culture, by using my computer and iPad. I knew the basics and had reliable computer expert friends, who were always ready to help me in my searches.

I pause to add that a calculation I made in April 2022 established that I had spent more years in Singapore than anywhere else. I saw Singapore's growth and enjoyed watching how it developed from a Crown Colony to a sovereign state that mastered all obstacles faced by it.

Initially, I found retirement irritating and boring. The routine which I used to follow had captivated me. Life without it appeared dull and empty. To break the monotony, I set myself new tasks. I tried to adopt new deadlines although, in reality, there was no need to adhere to them.

The first project I attempted was the writing of a history of our law school. The dean sanctioned the employment of research assistants and, by and large, we were making good progress. In particular, I had clear memories of the early years of our institution. Undoubtedly, the field had been well covered but my objective was to come up with a comprehensive treatment. It then dawned on me that I was no longer the right man for the job. To write an authoritative tome, there was a need for field research or, in other words, of conducting interviews with persons who could shed light on obscure points. During my years in Oxford, I loved to carry out this type of work. At the ripe age of 80, I was no longer up to the task. I had to rely on interviews conducted by younger members of the team. I also had to leave to them the retrieval of old materials. Once again, I sensed that my participation was not necessary. I withdrew from the project and handed it over to a colleague who had the required drive and energy. He completed the work effectively and published an excellent monograph. I read it with pleasure. It was officially launched on the law school's 60th anniversary.

Another new occupation I adopted was the teaching of Hebrew. Quite a number of Singapore's orthodox believers, who were keen to read the Old Testament in the original, thought I was in a position to help. I recall in particular the lessons given to one of my former colleagues and a small group of adherents. My friend was exceptional. His high IQ enabled him to come to grips with rules of Hebrew grammar, which were not easy to explain and even harder to rationalise. Whilst other students had difficulty with the connotations of adjectives and adverbs, my friend excelled in both. I was satisfied that he could acquire a sound basic speaking and reading knowledge within six months. Unfortunately, other activities kept him occupied so, quite often, sessions had to be postponed and became sporadic. In consequence, the topics covered in a class were forgotten when we held the next. After a few months, I couldn't continue and terminated the course.

Another fine student was a medical GP. He had learnt a great deal on his own so he was really getting ready to read the Old Testament in the original. We covered *Jonah*, *Esther*, and parts of *Jeremiah* and of *Job*. Regrettably, my bible critique philosophy militated against his orthodoxy. In addition, quite a number of classes had to be deferred when he had to attend medical and religious functions. After a while, it was best to give up.

During the entire period following Pat's demise, I frequented our synagogue. Still, I did not like the need of waiting for a taxi after prayer hours, although the staff often assisted me. Even so, I was exceedingly nervous during evening services and, after a while, confined myself to attending Saturday morning sessions.

For a few years, I attended the Passover Feast (Seder, סדר) in the house of a leading member of the community. His Seder, though, was lengthy. On one occasion he went on until 3.00 a.m. In subsequent years, I left at 11.00 p.m., which meant I was in for a tiring but highly satisfying experience. I became particularly fond of the 'punitive/symbolic' exercise — which involves beating each other with a vegetable branch. Usually, one of the guests took the brunt of the 'assault'. As it was considered 'unbecoming' to strike anybody whose own branch broke, we made sure to supply the victim with a new branch whenever his own snapped. Regrettably, I have ceased to leave home after dark and so was unable to continue attending; but I do miss the feasts.

My regular telephone conversations with Cathy became an essential and integral part of my existence. Without them, I should have sunk. She managed to soothe me when it turned out that, in consequence of exertions during Pat's struggle, the Hep C virus — which had been dormant for two years — had reactivated itself. A new medicine got me out of the abyss. I remained under treatment for another three years. By then, a new antiviral medicine came onto the market, and I was cured. I recall Cathy's delight when I was in a position to tell her the outcome.

Cathy was not the only friend who came to my aid. Before long, I was leading an active social life, attending luncheons, dinners and functions. Jane Kuok and her young daughter went out with me regularly; like me, Jane was a gourmand and knew all restaurants worth visiting. Peng Koon and his wife Lean (pronounced LeeAnn) often invited me over to their pleasant home and, in addition, took me to theatres, concerts and exhibitions. Sandra (my successor in the field of banking) and I met regularly for lunch. All in all, I became a social animal — an attribute that had been hidden for years.

I do feel grateful to friends who stood by me during these years. Tan Chuan Thye, S.C, whom I knew well from my days as a consultant and whose parents were my students, became a close friend on whom I could always count. Others who treated me extremely well included Chan Sek Keong, whom I first met after my arrival in Singapore in 1961 and who served some time as Singapore's Chief Justice; T.P.B Menon, (a one-time President of the Law Society) whom I knew from the sixties and who welcomed my late wife and me when we returned to Singapore; and VK Rajah, who (as already mentioned) was my students in 1982 and later on my boss in Rajah & Tann prior to his elevation to the Bench, then to the Court of Appeal and eventually to the post of Attorney General. Without the help of all my friends life would have been dire.

For a short while, I remained a member of our law school's Centre for Banking & Finance Law but, after a few months, withdrew. My main occupation became my non-legal writings. By 2017, I had self-published six books. One of them — *The Counter Bible* — drew on my bible critique studies. Another tome — *Ephemeral Stories* — appeared in 2017. Then, in 2018, I self-published the forerunner of this work and followed it with *Bright Lion* (2020), and with *The Nose Puncher* (2022). In view of their very personal nature, all these works were gifted only to a few friends (whose discretion could be trusted). They were not published commercially.

About two years after Pat's demise, Michael Blum, who had left his bank and returned to Germany, invited me to spend two weeks at his estate near Frankfurt. It was a splendid break. During the first week, we visited Bamberg and Coburg. I was impressed by the Bamberg Dome, especially by the crane left over to demonstrate how huge blocks of stone had been lifted into their place in the fortified wall. The inside, too, was exciting. One relief of a well-fed and good-looking woman represented the notion of a committed Christian. On the other side of the aisle, the relief depicted an undernourished and poorly groomed maiden. This, Michael explained, was the conceptual representation of infidels. I also discovered some antique stores. I would have liked to climb a peak known as Stachelberg (not to be confused with its Czech namesake). Regrettably, such a feat was out of the question.

We spent the second week in Vienna. Michael drove us to Nürenberg, from where we proceeded by train to Vienna. For the next few days, we toured the town. Michael discovered an excellent restaurant. It was located next to the Simpel (a satirical variété) and Café Prückel, where I used to play bridge when I visited Father during my Oxford days. In more than one way, I was walking down memory lane.

We spent two days in the Museum of Art and History. Michael was fascinated by the antiquities department. I knew he was going to come back to it. To my surprise, he was not keen on the paintings gallery. Like me, he admired the remote past.

Towards the end of the visit, we went to the cemetery. I recall that as we left the hotel, the porter, who took in my limp and walking stick, offered to call us a taxi. "Highly sporting," he muttered when I decided to walk.

As I stood by my parents' grave, I realised that from their point of view, my professional success was also theirs. Michael retired as I said my prayers. I was aware that my parents' souls — if indeed mankind has such a thing — did not rest in the burial site. But the memories were tagged to it. Before I left, I commissioned the chemical cleaning of the abandoned grave. It was all I could do; and I knew I was unlikely to be able to visit them again.

The trip back from Austria to Germany was an anticlimax. A few days later, I flew back to Singapore. When I arrived at my flat, I was delighted to find that an extensive renovation, which I had commissioned before my flight to Europe and which had been supervised by Lean, was ready. I now had a refurbished flat, which suited my needs. I had installed cabinets suitable for the display of my large porcelain collection and shelves for my books. I was, once again, at home and at some peace with myself.

During the next few months, I amassed additions to my porcelain collection. It dawned on me that the 20th century had seen great master-modelers, who made use of the advanced technology. The pieces are lovely, and I am proud of them. Currently, they grace my sitting room. I am aware that, at present, these newer pieces' worth is lower than the 18th and 19th century artifacts. In the future, though, their artistic value is bound to impress judicious collectors.

By the end of the year, I took another trip. This time, my objective was to spend some two weeks in a retirement home in Sydney. In a sense, it was my last attempt to decide whether to retire in Singapore or in an Australian protected living home. I admired the facilities but realised, once again, that the extra care you were able to get in such an environment entailed restrictions of your freedom of action. Further, the inhabitants had formed factions and, in general, had negative things to say about each other. In particular, I found it objectionable to come to meals at prearranged times, occupy one and the same seat on all occasions and listen to the ensuing (and to me meaningless) gossip. By the time I was making ready to return to Singapore, I was convinced that a regimented living system did not suit me. I was a loner by nature and communal life was alien to me. In a sense, my final conclusion was in tandem with my original reflections.

My maid, Sri, was glad to see me back. She had known from the beginning that I was unlikely to leave Singapore. In the course of the next few months, she helped me to develop a routine. So did Sri's successor, her sister Ati, who came to work for me when Sri returned to her hometown and got married.

During the entire period following Pat's demise, I intensified my bible critique studies. Although I was not an accomplished philologist by training, I could not help noting the significant variations of styles in biblical books. Further, although I had come to grips with Hebrew grammar, it had struck me as irrational. I noticed substantial departure from its rules in biblical texts and in the *Dead Sea Scrolls*.

Shortly after my return from Sydney, I made up my mind to study Mid-Egyptian. I knew that most Orientalists had a smattering of this ancient tongue but tended to concentrate on Semitic languages, like Assyrian and Akkadian. The Fertile Crescent — that is, the Via Maris (the cities along the Mediterranean coast) and the rest of Palestine — came in touch with the country of the Pharaohs from times immemorial. Further, the Old Testament relates how the Israelites had been enslaved in Egypt. Auxiliary sources and archaeological findings established the peaceful migration of Semites to the delta. Was it then possible that the tongues remained unaffected by the mass migration?

A friend in Oxford enabled me to get in touch with the head of the relevant department. For the ensuing two years, I studied the revived language, the 'pearl of antiquity', under the guidance of a doctoral student. Whilst I did not attain the proficiency expected of an Oxford B.A. in Oriental Studies, I acquired a reading knowledge of Mid-Egyptian and of hieroglyphs adequate for my objective. Before long, I realised how the convoluted Hebrew grammar, as well as some biblical texts, including Psalm 104, displayed the influence of Juda's southern neighbour.

Originally, the Pharaoh's script used pictorial images to express words. By way of illustration, each animal known in Egypt had a pictorial representation, such as the hieroglyph for a crocodile. In due course, though, the script resorted to the 'Rebus Principle', under which the sound, or oral expression, of given words can be agglutinated so as to express an abstract metaphor. A well-known example is the use of the combination of the pictorial representation of a 'bee' and of a 'leaf' to convey the idea of 'belief'.

It is true that Mid-Egyptian did not take the next step, that is, the development of an alphabet. The complicated hieroglyphs could, however, be read by the scribes of both Upper and Lower Egypt, each of which developed dialects of its own.

The writing of hieroglyphs required a certain skill and training. Some modern Egyptologists, who acquired a good reading command of the language, were unable to write hieroglyphs. In a sense, the intricacy of the script made it the domain of those trained in its use from childhood.

The study of Mid-Egyptian helped me to understand obscure passages in books of the Old Testament. From my point of view, Mid-Egyptian provided a pigment not available to traditional scholars. My appreciation of the debt owed by the composers of the Old Testament to the culture of the Nile intensified as I studied the Mid-Egyptian wisdom literature. Its influence on *Proverbs* and on *Ecclesiastes* is clear beyond any doubt.

My studies of the culture and history of Egypt clarified yet a further aspect. It is now generally accepted that the historical annals of Egypt and of the Levant in general are irreconcilable with the account of human history put forward in the Old Testament. A rational examination of the two convinced me that the Old Testament was not a reliable historical source of periods predating the reign of the House of Omri (and Ahab). This realisation did not affect my deeply ingrained love for the Old Testament. I continue to revere it as the brilliant literary contribution of Judaism to humanity. In consequence, I can readily accept the tenets of evolution and the scientific analysis of the universe without feeling any need to discard or denounce the Bible.

My course of studies of Mid-Egyptian opened my eyes to yet a further, quite separate, aspect of progress. My tutor — a native of Switzerland — traveled regularly between Lugano, Oxford and European cities with oriental collections. However, our course was not interrupted by his nomadic existence. By means of Skype and some other programmes, we had video calls from wherever he resided. Hieroglyphs which he wrote on a whiteboard located in his room were displayed on my computer screen. I had no doubt that these developments were bound to revolutionise studies. A teacher could conduct an entire course from overseas.

By sheer coincidence, my tutor had to proceed to a location without a network connection. He suggested that we proceed by means of emails. I was inclined to agree but, on further thought, realised that I had accomplished my objective. My basic reading knowledge of Mid-

Egyptian and my ability to peruse source materials enabled me to pursue my established interest of bible critique. Whilst it would have been pleasant to gain a better knowledge of Mid-Egyptian, the effort involved was too burdensome. Accordingly, it seemed best to bring my course of studies to an end.

Shortly after I reached my decision, Peng Koon and Lean suggested that we take a cruise to the Indonesian Islands. Cathy flew over (all around the world) and joined us. The cruise was enjoyable, except for the chatter of one of our fellow travellers, who dominated the conversation incessantly.

Separating ourselves from our fellow travellers, Cathy and I went on a few excursions. We spent a pleasant day in Bali. We next left the ship at the Komodo Island. I enjoyed the hike, which led to a waterhole, where doped and sleepy dragons hardly noticed us. Two days later, the ship anchored in Makassar (Ujung Padang) in Sulawesi (Celebes). Here, Peng Koon and Lean joined us on a tour. To my disappointment, this pleasant island did not look like a huge crab in the manner it is displayed on the world map. What we saw was a pleasant stretch of land. All of us enjoyed the scenery, the waterfalls and the museum of butterflies.

To my surprise, the organisers made provision for the Shabbat prayers. A small group of fellow Jews attended. I recall with amusement how I managed to beat a quick retreat when a member of the congregation handed out canned gefilte fish, which had no appeal for me. I hope that those who stayed behind enjoyed the traditional European Jewish delicacy, coming out of a tin.

Back in Singapore, life reverted to its usual pace. However, the peace in my personal life had one undesired side effect. I overlooked the importance of a number of major developments in the world. The first was the re-emergence of Russia as a superpower. Having lost a substantial part of its sphere of influence after the collapse of the Soviet Union, the tendency was to regard the United States as the major player and the People's Republic of China as the second.

In reality, Russia was simply biding its time. Its new president, one Vladimir Putin, concentrated on the extraction of gas and oil found in Siberia. In due course, many countries in Western Europe became dependent on energy provided by the use of Russian supplies. Indeed, a pipe was planned for pumping gas directly to Germany. Unsurprisingly, the West did not take a firm stand when Putin's Russia used force to annex the Crimean Peninsula, which was a Ukrainian territory. This annexation included Sevastopol, which became, once again, a base for Russia's fleet in the Black Sea.

The second major development was the continuing rise of the PRC. I was aware that many heartland Chinese in Singapore were avid admirers of what they regarded a cradle of civilisation. Frequently, I tired when Peng Koon sang the PRC's praise. Today, in 2022, I often wish I had listened more carefully.

The third development was the decline of the United States. The rot set in when Trump became President. He had no political experience or acumen and, alas, no integrity. His reign weakened NATO, led to havoc in the Western World and exacerbated the disunity prevailing in the United States. The harm caused by him could not be repaired. By the end of 2020, I had to agree with Peng Koon that the PRC had overtaken the United States.

I shall tell you more about the recent years in my next letters. In the meantime, I wish all of you all the very best.

Yours ever,
Peter

13 August 2022
Singapore

Dear Friends,

Letter 30: The Pandemic and After Events

Back in 2018, I hoped that my remaining years would pass peacefully and without upheavals. Today — in August 2022 — I have to admit that I could not have been any more wrong. The last four years were turbulent and currently it seems to me that we are in the middle of a reorganisation of world order.

The first blow struck in February 2019, when the Covid-19 virus made its appearance. It is true that this was not the first outbreak of a virus of this type in our time. Whilst the Spanish flu of 1918 was long forgotten, there was a SARS (severe acute respiratory syndrome) outbreak in the 1990s. It lasted for some six months and then disappeared. Initially, we hoped that Covid-19 would take the same course. Indeed, I recall how I fixed a lunch appointment with a colleague. When the malady broke out, we agreed to postpone our engagement until 'things went back to normal'. Well, in due course, Covid-19 was declared a pandemic. Our lunch was, effectively, postponed sine die.

Initially, there were no vaccines or effective remedies. Then, two American firms and a British one came up with inoculations. So did the PRC, although its product was not accepted in many countries and the evidence suggested it was inferior. Further, the Covid-19 virus kept mutating. By now, it is accepted that some variants defy all the vaccines and, further, that an individual can succumb to it more than once.

Most countries tried to fight the virus' spread by imposing lockdowns. Singapore was no exception. For about two years, tourism ceased altogether. Some industries, such as aviation, became dormant.

Generally, most people were confined to their homes. My regular two daily telephone conversations with Cathy saved me from getting too lonely. On the few occasions I had to go by taxi to medical appointments, I was sad to note on my way the number of establishments that had closed down. Here, I am pleased to be in a position to commend the steps taken by the government in Singapore. In effect, the Republic dug into its financial reserves and kept the economy floating. Further, home delivery services flourished so that many restaurants were able to brave the storm. Similarly, limited travel was sanctioned but travellers had to spend up to fourteen days in quarantine. They were sent to designated hotels and, in this way, many establishments survived.

One particular disturbing effect was the need to avoid going to the Saturday service in the synagogue. Praying whilst wearing a mask appeared unnatural. Further, one of the pleasures of attending on Saturday morning was the ability to mix with members of the community and to attend communal luncheons. This involved eating in the company of others. As some members shuttled between Israel and Singapore, joining them might have exposed me to the risk of infection.

I had to curb my social activities. This gave me ample time for reflections. One of them — perhaps the major one — concerned my stand on religion. I often recalled my blackout in Pandan Valley. Whilst Uncle Henry and others considered it a hallucination, I had my doubts. This event and my attendance of religious functions pushed me in the direction of faith. It led me to the rereading of a translation of the New Testament. I admired St. Paul's epistles, particularly his masterful *Letter to the Romans*.

Then, shortly before the outbreak of the pandemic, a well meaning, ardently Christian, orthodox friend invited me to have lunch with her and with an acquaintance, a Messianic Jew. I kept an open mind until he asked me why I was not convinced by the last few chapters of *Job*. I knew from my biblical studies that these chapters were late additions. His ignorant arrogance rekindled all my initial doubts and scepticism. Further, I was perturbed by the very notion of Messianic Judaism. One of the main tenets of the Christian religion is the belief that the Messiah — in the person of Jesus Christ — has come. In contrast, Judaism postulates the Messiah is yet to come. I knew that both beliefs were tenable. But in my eyes, they were irreconcilable. This realisation, and the preaching I was subjected to, pushed me in the opposite direction: to disbelief. Being a guest, I thought it best not to argue. However, by the time I was free to leave and return home, my mind was made up.

Ethnically, I was and would always remain a Jew. When attending a service or when visiting the synagogue, I would feel as one with the crowd. At the same time, in everyday life, I became once again an ardent agnostic. I concluded that the experience at Pandan Valley had been a mirage. I pause to add that, occasionally, misguided proselytizing backfires. I suspect that, in matters of faith, it is best to leave a person to his or her own devices. In particular, it is unwise to preach to a person a dogma which, to the preacher's own knowledge, has been rejected by the listener. I appreciate that, in some cases of this sort, the preacher feels that he (or she) is performing a 'duty'. Regrettably, the listener frequently finds the preacher's exercise of such a duty irritating.

The experience did not affect the regard and admiration I had always felt for my hostess. She had welcomed Pat and me whenever we visited Singapore during my years in New Zealand and in Australia. She came over to comfort Pat when my late wife had her last and final ordeal. I also knew that my hostess' attempt to convert me was motivated by her concern. Still, I was driven in the opposite direction.

The agnostic orientation I had reached just before the Covid outbreak was reinforced by studies I undertook during the lockdown. I managed to acquire materials needed for a seminal essay on the *Book of Job*. In the course of three years, I even got books that were out of print. These, to my surprise, were obtainable from antiquarian bookshops in Germany.

Another, totally unrelated, subject that occupied me was the universe. I watched many programmes on cosmology and astronomy. I was aware that my grasp of mathematics and physics was negligible. However, the programmes posted on YouTube were meant for the layman. I followed them and comprehended their messages. It dawned on me that the universe was vast. Initially, I took in many of the programmes based on the discoveries and findings of the Hubble Telescope. They fascinated me. The very thought that the observable universe was just a fraction of its unknown, and perhaps unknowable, immensity impressed me deeply.

I followed up my interest by rushing to read and observe findings based on the Infrared Cameras of the James Webb Space Telescope. Nowadays, I appreciate that the size of our planet in relation to the universe's resembles the ratio of the size of a pebble of sand to the mass of our own planet.

I was fascinated by the speed of light. A beam that originated from our planet would show our state during the period of the dinosaurs when it reached a spot that was 65 million light years away. If this beam were received by an intelligent race, would its observers appreciate that a highly developed society — mankind — would emerge in due course?

The Big Bang theory and Hubble's law respecting the ever-expanding universe presented further issues. I read that the Big Bang took place about 13.8 billion years ago and saw representations of the cosmic microwave background ("CMB"), which reflected an early stage of the universe, about 400 million years after it commenced. This too was mind-blowing. Light which reached us after billions of years might have been produced by an object that was no longer in existence.

It dawned on me that mankind had a short history. Its origin was still hotly debated but no scientist claimed that it emerged earlier than 3.5 million years ago. In comparison with the universe's age, this was a minute span of time.

I knew that the Big Bang theory was subject to heated debates but was not in a position to take part in the argument. I was out of my depth. In the circumstances, I felt compelled to adhere to the theory which was widely accepted.

The findings of science, and the Big Bang theory in particular, had an effect on my religious orientation. I knew that two major issues were unsolved by the scientists. The first concerned the creation of something from nothing. In plain language, what caused the Big Bang? The second was the appearance of life. Whilst it was agreed that primitive forms of life were triggered off by the mutation of amino acids, all attempts to 'create' life in the laboratory have failed.

I was aware that religions — not only the three monotheistic ones — thought to provide an answer by interjecting God. According to them, He created the universe and life. However, this argument led to the next paradox: who created God? It seemed to me that whilst the existence of a prime mover could not be dismissed offhand, there was, alas, no means of proving it empirically. Further, mankind constituted a minute facet of a vast, probably infinite, universe. I was accordingly perturbed by the postulation of a 'personal God'. It struck me as presumptuous to argue that a supernatural power, that created a vast universe, would be concerned about the activities of mankind or of any individual. In the event, my scientific explorations fortified my agnosticism.

Yet another effect of the lockdowns was my being driven to classical music. Shortly after Pat's demise, I experienced black moods, growing anxiety and a feeling of isolation. Initially, a medical man prescribed tranquillisers. I was aware of the danger of dependence and, accordingly, with my doctor's help, managed to cut down on the use thereof. Then, during the first rigid lockdown, I discovered that listening to music alleviated my anxiety and uplifted my spirits. Although I did not have any background in music, and did not play a single instrument, I found that some compositions helped me to relax. I have to concede that my taste remained haphazard. I simply liked or disliked given pieces. Before long, I realised that listening to violin and piano compositions enabled me to attain inner peace. This helped me to further reduce my dependence on prescription drugs.

A particularly sad event was Paul Zollman's suicide, which took place just before the onset of the pandemic. Paul's wife had passed away peacefully of old age. For a while, Paul remained in their town near Ottawa. He then went to stay near his sons, who resided in British Columbia. He conceded that the food and the company in the protected environment he lived in were good. One day, though, he rang and told me:

"I have had enough, Bushi. I'm really fed up."

"What do you mean, Paul?" I asked with trepidation. I knew that Paul was a member of Exit, an organisation that advocated the legalising of assisted suicide. I was also aware that Paul considered suicide a viable option.

"You know what I mean, Bushi," he told me bluntly.

"What is the hurry, Pauli?" I reverted to German. "You have close friends. They will miss you if you go ahead!"

"I know; but they will get used to it. Look here, Bushi, I am really fed up and have no wish to carry on."

I realised that arguing was futile. Paul told me that he had already fixed the day. One of his two sons was going to accompany him to the hospital, which had agreed to administer the fatal injection (a procedure legalised in certain places). He promised to contact me from the 'other side' if this was possible. Paul's life was terminated a few days later. I have not heard from him from the other side and am not in contact with his sons. In my heart of hearts, I understood him.

After some two years of the pandemic, most countries started to revert to life 'as normal'. International travel resumed, and restaurants opened up to vaccinated patrons. Even bars and nightclubs started to function once again. For a while, patrons had to prove their vaccinated status but eventually even this control ceased. Still, some major countries have continued to impose lockdowns. One of them is the PRC.

Personally, I remained cautious. To my relief, Singapore continued to enforce (and later, to recommend) the use of masks. This means that, even on the grounds of my condominium, people don face masks.

The next major event in 2022, which affected me just as it impinged on the rest of the world, was the invasion of Ukraine by Russia. It is ongoing as I write. This development should not have come as a surprise. Generally, though, matters become clear with hindsight. I am not certain about the objective of Putin's breach of international law and order. By and large, I opine that he wishes to gain absolute control of the Black Sea and, for this purpose, wants to annex Ukraine's port city of Odessa. Others believe that Putin's objective is to restore Russia to its Soviet Union grandeur.

Be this as it may, Ukraine is fighting valiantly, has been armed by the West in general and by the United States in particular and has proved itself on the battle ground. Further, Western European states have decided to decrease their dependence on energy procured from Russia. I hope it is not too late!

The war continues to rage, and the outcome is not predictable at this stage. The loss of life and the sufferings of innocent civilians are appalling. In my opinion, this is one of the worst episodes since the defeat of Nazi Germany in 1945. Regrettably — and I feel I have to express my opinion — the world, including its politicians, does not learn from mistakes of the past. Murder, war and mayhem are part and parcel of the human condition.

An inescapable result of the pandemic and of the tribulations caused by war is the current high inflation. The cost of petrol would increase dramatically. This, in turn, would lead to the escalation of the price of goods and services. Whilst central banks have taken measures to combat inflation, it is too early to gauge the outcome.

The impact on my own way of life has been moderate. My weekly expenditure on food and drink has escalated. So has the price of taxi rides and my electricity bill. Fortunately, I leave my home infrequently and use my air condition judiciously. Thus, I am less affected than most people. The impact on large families is devastating. In many parts of the world, governments had to step in and assist them. Singapore is but one of them.

A separate, discouraging development is climate change. Many countries all over the world have experienced devastating storms, fires, floods and unbearable heat waves. These, in turn, have led to droughts.

I was surprised to note that even the United Kingdom — known for its wet climate — had to introduce water rationing.

It is not clear whether climate change is a natural phenomenon or triggered by human activities. Conventional wisdom puts the blame on the use of fossil energy, which has led to pollution and to global warming. I am not in a position to express firm views on the subject but, by and large, am satisfied that human activity is one of the causes of this unfortunate occurrence.

The tragic development in the Dead Sea region of Israel is an example in point. I recall that in 1982, Pat and I made a stop at Ein Gedi (on the Dead Sea shore). I swam in the warm mineral-rich waters and enjoyed myself.

At present, the Dead Sea is dying. The shallow waters in which I swam are now a bare stretch of exposed land plagued by sinkholes. The whole area is cordoned off because falling into such a hole, or experiencing its sudden emergence, endangers life and limb. A once thriving industry had vanished altogether.

The disaster is not confined to the Dead Sea. This very morning, I read the news about the Rhine's depletion. If this were to continue, Europe would lose one of its main commercial arteries. If a similar event overtook the Danube, both Western and Eastern Europe would be seriously affected. Further, the pleasant river trip from Passau to Vienna and Budapest may have to be discontinued.

Another sad development is the ever-increasing social disunity prevailing in the United States. The country has experienced hurricanes, floods, droughts and raging fires. On top of this, the two major political parties, viz. the Democrats and the Republicans, are at each other's throats. The current Federal Reserve Bank attempts to solve all problems by printing money. I fear that the Pax Americana, which commenced in 1945, is drawing to its close. It is known that at present, oil and gas exports from Russia have to be settled in rubles. Does this mean that the mighty United States Dollar may lose its hegemony?

I shall sum up my odyssey and my predictions about our future in my next (last) letter. Until then, all the best to all of you.

As ever,
Peter

P.S. A number of developments have taken place since I completed this letter (in August 2022).

First, although the pandemic is still in effect, life is returning to normal. Lockdowns have largely ceased. Even in the PRC, free travel has resumed. Further, most countries, including Singapore, have confined the mask mandate to places such as hospitals and, in some countries, to public transport.

Secondly, Europe and North America experienced a singularly harsh winter. Shortage of fuel has exacerbated the situation. A related issue is climate change. Torrential rains have led to floods and landslides, which plague many countries. Even the Northern Island of New Zealand succumbed. Other acts of God have shattered mankind. A catastrophic earthquake in Turkey is the latest.

Third, inflation continues to affect all of us. The problem is becoming serious. It is felt even in first world countries like Singapore.

Finally, the war of Russia against the Ukraine continues relentlessly. The outcome is unpredictable. Hopefully, it will not trigger off the use of nuclear devices.

Peter
15 February 2023

15 October 2022
Singapore

Dear Friends,

Letter 31: Ithaca

In my previous letter, I finished the narration of my odyssey. It is time to sum up. On 25 April 2018 — my 85th birthday — Cathy flew over from Canada to celebrate the occasion with me. She invited some friends and me for lunch in the French restaurant of St. Regis. It was a fine occasion.

I suppose that in my own way, I have arrived in Ithaca. Although its location was shrouded in doubt most of my life, I opted for Singapore. In this regard, my route differed from Odysseus' trip back home. Although the hero's voyage was protracted and full of setbacks, there had been no question about his destination. The stormy seas, as well as his encounters with the Sirens and the Cyclopes, were adventures or, perhaps, obstacles. The target, though, remained clear from the beginning. In a similar manner, Leopold Bloom's one-day odyssey, as described by James Joyce, commenced and ended in a single place, namely Dublin. My own odyssey, which was also full of obstacles and mishaps, differs in one crucial manner: My final destination remained undecided whilst my ship was at sea.

There is yet a further distinction between my protracted voyage and the journeys of Odysseus and that of Leopold Bloom. Both of them returned to, or remained in, their origin. Neither Ithaca nor Dublin underwent a change during the respective hero's trip. Equally, Peer Gynt returned to a Norway he knew and to the home that Solveig had tended for him. Yet another case in point relates to Josef Schwejk, whose antics as an Austrian soldier and as a Russian prisoner of war are the subject of a German television series dealing with him. Schwejk's voyage commences in his pub in Prague to which he returns at the end of WWI.

In contrast, my lengthy journey took me through a changing world. When Peter'le saw light in the Moll Clinic in Vienna, Britannia still ruled the waves and the world map was full of pink dots and spaces, defining the boundaries of the British Empire. Indeed, I grew up in Palestine, which was one of Her spheres of influence.

Then, after the tribulations of WWII, I witnessed the foundation of Israel and the phenomenal growth of the United States. When the Bretton Woods Agreements were signed in 1945, the American dollar became the effective reserve currency of the world. The pound sterling took a back seat.

During my youth and early adulthood, I observed the Cold War between the mighty Soviet Union and the Western World, headed by the United States. The most populated country in the world, China, was a sleeping giant, firmly in control of its own realm but not seeking to be a factor in world politics.

The next phase was the growth of Europe, especially after Britain joined the European Economic Community ("EEC") in 1973. The European bloc became an important player in the political arena.

The collapse of the Soviet Union and the entry of China into world politics led to yet a further change. Free trade and the mass migration of populations continued to affect the environment. Within a matter of two decades, China saw phenomenal growth, to which I have already referred. Further, Russia — which remained intact notwithstanding the collapse of the Soviet Union — is currently becoming a leading force in its own right.

Today, in 2022 — when I shall soon be 90 years old — I suspect that the era of mass migration and of free trade is likely to end within a few years. What we are likely to encounter is an entirely new and unprecedented era of trade and currency wars. It is my ardent hope that these will not trigger off another world war. The signs are ominous.

Early in the 20th century, Oswald Spengler made his predictions in *The Decline of the West*. His prophecy has come true. Will this 'decline' now engulf the United States as well? I suspect it already has.

Actually, my own life flows smoothly. I continue with my bible critique studies and am playing bridge regularly on my computer. I speak with Cathy twice a day. Recently, she visited me after conducting an aviation course in Nepal. I have also remained in touch with many of my friends. For instance, I ring Tony Guest, who is now in full retirement in London, at least once a month.

Still, the account of my odyssey from birth to old age (ca. 90) is complete. Future developments affecting the world will be the start of a new journey. In all probability, I shall not be a part of it.

I do hope you will sympathise with me as you browse through this volume.

As ever,
Your friend
Peter

www.ingramcontent.com/pod-product-compliance
Ingram Content Group UK Ltd.
Pitfield, Milton Keynes, MK11 3LW, UK
UKHW022109170926
8624IPUK00024B/297

9 789811 271021